3-D Hand Loom Weaving

Weaving SCULPTURAL TOOLS AND TECHNIQUES

3-D Hand Loom Weaving
SCULPTURAL TOOLS AND TECHNIQUES

SALLY EYRING

Foreword by Stacey Harvey-Brown

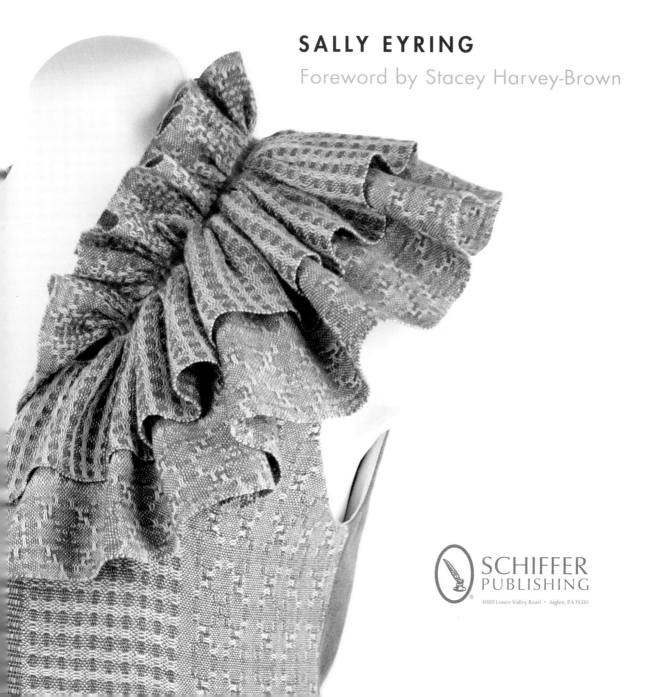

SCHIFFER
PUBLISHING
4880 Lower Valley Road • Atglen, PA 19310

Library of Congress Control Number: 2020930545

Cover design by Brenda McCallum
Type set in Usherwood/Times New Roman

ISBN: 978-0-7643-5990-3
Printed in China

Published by Schiffer Publishing, Ltd.
4880 Lower Valley Road
Atglen, PA 19310
Phone: (610) 593-1777; Fax: (610) 593-2002
E-mail: Info@schifferbooks.com
Web: www.schifferbooks.com

For our complete selection of fine books on this
and related subjects, please visit our website at www
.schifferbooks.com. You may also write for a free catalog.

Schiffer Publishing's titles are available at special
discounts for bulk purchases for sales promotions or
premiums. Special editions, including personalized
covers, corporate imprints, and excerpts, can be
created in large quantities for special needs. For more
information, contact the publisher.

Other Schiffer Books on Related Subjects:

Ondulé Textiles: Weaving Contours with a Fan Reed, Norma Smayda with Gretchen White,
ISBN 978-0-7643-5358-1

Weaving Innovations from the Bateman Collection, Robyn Spady, Nancy A. Tracy & Marjorie
Fiddler, Foreword by Madelyn van der Hoogt, ISBN 978-0-7643-4991-1

In their book *Ideas in Weaving*, Ann Sutton and Diane Sheehan muse on a tension device developed by Janice Lessman-Moss. The device, they say, "broke one of the cardinal rules of even tension maintenance," and they note that "More work like this would bring the handweaving loom (which suffers from innovation deprivation) out of rustic technology and into the twentieth century."

This book hopes to, in some small way, remedy the "innovation deprivation" of the hand loom, albeit in the twenty-first century.

CONTENTS

Foreword

Stacey Harvey-Brown

This is an exciting time to be part of the handweaving world, not just for the innovations in yarns, e-textiles, and computer technology, but for ingenuity of weavers' minds.

Many weavers are curious about materials, structure, and techniques. That is how most of us learn and push our knowledge. We ask "What if I do/try/use this?" We learn from each other in classes, online tutorials, and social media conversations, and through books and conferences.

However, comparatively few handweavers take their curiosity to the next level—to that of altering and adapting their looms to fulfill their creative imperative. And yet the loom is a tool that has been adapted many times over the centuries, especially during the Industrial Revolution, to control tension, to speed up the physical production of cloth, and to have greater patterning potential with the addition of more shafts.

One twentieth-century innovator that springs to mind is Peter Collingwood. His main adaptation in loom control, known as shaft-switching, not only enabled him to extend the possibility of his hardware (the loom), but because he made the information and the design available to the Harrisville loom makers, he also bequeathed this development to the rug-weaving world. Sally Eyring is another such hardware innovator.

The marriage of mind and materials, together with an insatiable curiosity, is what you find in this book. Sally shares her innovations and techniques that take weaving from the rectangular to shaping on the loom, for garments, or for other three-dimensional results. If you have an interest in weaving for garments, you will find her approach to shaping thought provoking. If you have an interest in materials, you will find her tools, tips, and techniques in weaving with metals as well as more-common yarns invaluable. If you have an interest in engineering, and how looms work, you will find her loom adaptations intriguing but totally logical.

This is a book that may lead weavers on many different paths and interpretations. The tools and ideas here will, I have no doubt, inspire new and exciting cloth from other curious weavers for years to come.

Stacey Harvey-Brown is an experienced weaver, teacher, and the author of *Honeycomb Hybrids: Honeycomb for All Tastes*. She explores plain weave derivative structures to create surface texture and three-dimensional woven art. In 2017 she moved to the southwest of France to set up The Loom Room France for teaching, workshops, writing books on three-dimensional weaving techniques, and developing her art further.

Preface

As a child, I was a member of a 4-H club. We learned all sorts of practical skills, and one of them was sewing. But I was also very nearsighted. So, when I needed to closely investigate a seam or do hand stitching, I took off my glasses to see more detail. One day, while looking at a piece of fabric without my glasses, I noticed for the first time that it was made up of very small threads that ran left to right and up to down. I had discovered weaving!

Fascinated by these fine little threads that worked together to create the fabric, I was determined to understand how cloth was made. But since this was the early 1960s, I couldn't just look it up on the internet.

One day, I found an advertisement for a small plastic potholder loom. I saved my allowance until I had the required five dollars, sent it off, and soon received my first weaving loom in the mail. Of course, I could make only little square or rectangular pieces and had to sew them together at the edges to make anything larger.

Many years later, I bought my first real four-shaft floor loom. I was shocked to learn that I had to pull each individual thread through a heddle and then through a reed! Doing a warp of several hundred threads seemed like a daunting prospect. I've long since gotten over that and think nothing of working with warps from several hundred to well over a thousand threads. I mention this only to remind the experienced weaver of an important point: you were not always experienced. As you learn the new techniques we'll explore, you'll find it useful to take on the attitude of a beginner.

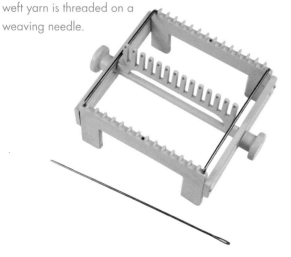

My first loom, the Wonder Weave Hand Loom, built by the Karbercraft Company of New York. I think I paid about $5 for the loom sometime in the early 1960s. Instead of a shuttle, the weft yarn is threaded on a weaving needle.

I took lessons, gained experience, and learned to weave by following the rules of weaving. Eventually I started experimenting with these rules and determined that if I broke the rules, I could weave cloth that was much different and, to me, more exciting. My experimentation was inspired by a weaving teacher who did not mean to set me off in a totally unexpected direction. She simply made a statement of fact, that "when you weave, you always get a rectangle."

The problem was that I was going to art school after a thirty-year career in the tech industry, and I was a 3-D major. I was interested in working with dimensional shapes and didn't want to create just flat rectangles. Although I loved weaving, it's primarily a two-dimensional art form. The way I saw it, I had two choices; I could change my major, or I could figure out how to weave cloth in three dimensions. And so began the journey toward the techniques described in this book.

At first, I wove with copper wire and fine wool, making sculptural pieces. Eventually I started working with cottons, linens, and silks, and I started making nonrectangular pieces that I incorporated into clothing. But the human body is not a rectangle, so when I turned my attention to clothing I wanted to weave the shapes found on the human body rather than cut the cloth to fit it.

Over the years, this journey has required me to invent tools, terminology, and various techniques. I've become a master at controlling tension on a warp. I've developed several ways to do each part of the process, and I've learned how to work with a variety of materials. Throughout, I made my own tools, and I'll show you how to reproduce these tools for your own use.

Although this book is about techniques, it's also about a way of thinking. It is about recognizing the rules of weaving in order to break them, much as a musician must first learn chords and scales in order to improvise jazz tunes.

Come with me as I explain these new and innovative processes. I can promise you that the journey will be both fun and satisfying, and that it will open up your mind to exciting new possibilities. You will never think of your weaving in the same way again, and you will make much more interesting cloth—cloth that isn't just a rectangle.

Acknowledgments

I am thankful for the help and support I received from my dear friend Sara Ann Gephart, who greatly improved my writing and helped edit the book. I thank Stacey Harvey Brown, who buoyed me up with her enthusiasm for the topic and wrote the foreword. My editor at Schiffer Publishing, Sandra Korinchak, provided me with practical and timely advice and patiently answered my questions.

My husband, Daniel, not only helped with the editing but took on a greater share of the household duties during the process, shoveling sidewalks, doing dishes, shopping, and not complaining about the inconsistent dinner schedule. Finally, my thanks to my little pups, Inky and Peanut, who made sure that my lap was never cold as I sat and wrote, day after day.

Introduction

There are many techniques that are called 3-D, or *three-dimensional*. In an industrial context, 3-D weaving is truly dimensional, with threads traveling on X, Y, and Z axes. These fabrics require specialized looms and create fabrics that have considerable depth as well as width and length. They are used for a variety of applications such as construction, ruggedized fabric, forms for injection molds, airplane wings, and the like.

Industrial weaving is well beyond the scope of this book; we are interested in weaving on a hand loom. Because there is no well-accepted definition of 3-D hand loom weaving, I can only give you my thoughts on the subject. I call my technique 3-D because in one variation it causes the weft threads to pile up on top of each other, creating some depth and a nonrectangular shape. In another variation, it causes the finished fabric to rise up out of the plane of the surrounding cloth. In yet another variant, it is possible to weave gently curved clothing shapes that do not require darts to pull in at the waist or flare out for a skirt. All my techniques can be used with any weave structure, with any material, and don't depend on special finishing processes. You can still weave rectangles if you wish, but you are no longer limited to weaving only rectangles, and your weaving doesn't need to be flat.

Weaving is an ancient technology, and weavers have had a long time to develop their craft and invent new ways of weaving. Double weaves, with their multiple layers of warp threads, can be used to create dimensionality in the form of layers, tubes, or pleats. Pile weaves create a depth of fabric by using small lengths of yarn that are added and knotted as the weaving progresses, or by using a double warp to weave in the pile threads. There are many different weaving structures that create surface embellishments, such as Danish medallion and leno. Interesting surfaces can be created by combining fibers with different amounts of stretch or shrinkage, or by weaving with groups of differently tensioned threads. Weavers can use tapestry techniques and incorporate various nontraditional materials and threads of different weights to create dimensionality in cloth. But the end result of using any of these techniques on a hand loom is still a rectangular piece of fabric.

Although I incorporate many of these weaving techniques into my own work, they are not the focus of this book and are not described here. In this book I hope to open your mind and expand your weaving horizons in new directions. I will show you how to break the rules of weaving and manipulate them in creative ways to weave flowing curves and organic forms. I will show you how to weave sculptural shapes and how to weave fabric for sewing that is not just a rectangle, but shaped to your body.

You can do all these things and more with a hand loom. And while you learn to challenge the rules, you will learn to think about your weaving in new and creative ways, and you will learn techniques that you can use while weaving both three-dimensional and two-dimensional pieces.

This new approach to 3-D weaving on a hand loom requires some new terminology and a few new pieces of equipment. All the techniques I describe in this book have evolved over time and are the result of trial and error. All the projects presented are ones that I have woven myself. I built all of the special weaving devices myself, and you can build them for yourself with the help of a few common tools from the hardware store. In one case, I had a piece of inexpensive equipment designed for my 3-D process, and it's now available on the internet for anyone to purchase.

In order to really understand the techniques, you must first understand the terminology and the approaches. Chapter 1 discusses and defines the weaving terminology that I had to invent to explain how to weave in this new way.

Chapter 2 gives a brief overview of the weaving rules that are broken to do sculptural weaving. A summary of the different 3-D handweaving processes is included with a comparison of their advantages and disadvantages.

Chapter 3 describes the specialized tools and devices that are required, and briefly explains how they are used. If the tool or device can be created with only very simple tools, such as scissors, a ruler, and a piece of cord, its construction method is included. For the weaving tools that are more complex or require additional hardware store tools, you'll find the construction methods in appendix 1.

Chapters 4 through 6 describe, respectively, the three 3-D weaving techniques: weaving an expanded area, weaving a dense area, and weaving an area with infinite tension control. In almost each case, several alternatives are available to control the tension on the warp and the cloth, depending on the purpose of the weaving and the shape being woven. In some cases, the same tools can be used, but in other cases the tools are specific to the technique.

To use these tools and techniques to weave a 3-D shape, and to create that shape by using your own favorite weaving structure, requires some special considerations. The arithmetic behind creating a desired shape, as well as the required threading and treadling considerations, is discussed in chapter 7.

Chapter 8 suggests several easy beginning projects that have been tested in a workshop with other weavers. All these projects use leapfrogging rods, which work on any loom and require fewer and simpler tools than the cloth trap technique. For that reason, I suggest that weavers start with leapfrogging rods.

The special considerations of weaving a sculptural piece with nontraditional materials, such as copper wire, can be found in chapter 9, along with the use of one additional tool that makes weaving with copper wefts more efficient.

Chapter 10 illustrates a selection of 3-D weaving projects that I've done in the past, with the hope that these examples will inspire you to devise your own projects.

Appendix 1 describes, in detail, construction of the more complex tools and sources for parts. When loom modifications are required in order to use the tools, these are described as well. Appendix 2 offers sewing and finishing tips.

I assume that the reader is experienced enough to be able to plan and execute a weaving project on their own. Nevertheless, to an experienced weaver, the processes that I describe will at first seem a bit bizarre. But if you understand the processes and work with patience to overcome the challenges, you will have techniques at your disposal that you can use to create your own fantastic shapes and forms. You will be rewarded with cloth that is both beautiful and far different than anything you have woven to this point, and you will become a master at controlling tension on a warp.

Weaving software: The drafts in this book aim to show the reader which shafts and which areas of the warp are being woven for any given pick. Weaving software assumes that the entire warp width is woven on every pick. This assumption is incorrect for many of my techniques, and as a result you will not be able to use weaving software to create drafts that look like those shown in this book.

That doesn't mean that you can't use your weaving software or a dobby loom with these techniques. It just means that the software will show long floats where none exist.

Weaving-pattern drafts in this book are written with the threading at the top left and treadling on the right side. The tie-up is not shown because it is a direct tie-up. On looms that have a limited number of treadles, it may be necessary for you to use both of your feet to do the treadling. The weaving structures shown in the examples, aside from the tabby used to weave the dense areas, are just suggestions or are the structures that I actually used for the piece shown. Feel free to use any structure you want, as long as you have the extra shafts, or sets of shafts, to accomplish the 3-D weaving technique itself.

All of my first sculptural pieces were headdresses inspired by the immigrant experience. These pieces used fine wool and wire and were woven on a table loom that required me to manually lift the shafts for each pick by pushing down various levers. Although it did slow down the weaving process a little, it also gave me complete treadling freedom since I could lift any number or combination of shafts for each pick. If you have such a table loom, I encourage you to use it when first trying these techniques.

I hope you find this new 3-D weaving approach interesting and useful. But more than that, I hope you are inspired to break some of the rules from time to time!

Terms and Definitions

Wherever possible I use commonly understood weaving terms, but in order to describe the techniques for weaving 3-D shapes, it was necessary to invent several new terms. This isn't surprising because, to my knowledge, these techniques aren't used by anyone else with the exception of the students I've taught. These terms are used throughout the book, so without an understanding of them, the technique discussions won't make much sense.

Since there are only a few new terms, they are listed in the order in which they are best understood, rather than in alphabetical order. I have also included a few standard weaving terms that may not be known to beginning weavers.

Normal Area

A normal area of weaving is just that—weaving done in the normal way. Normal areas of weaving produce rectangles,

just as weaving on a hand loom has always done. However, a normal area will be deformed by a dense area of weaving that is right beside it. This term is necessary in our 3-D weaving vocabulary to differentiate it from the weaving done in order to produce shapes. Normal weaving can use any structure that you like, such as tabby or twill, and with any sett that is appropriate for the yarn being used. A floating selvage can be used or not, depending on the weaving structure you are using.

Dense Area

A dense area of weaving is weaving in which (1) the warp threads use a different set of shafts than the normal area, (2) the warp threads have a sett twice that of the normal areas of weaving, assuming the same size of yarn is used, (3) the structure used is always tabby, (4) the dense-area warp threads are tensioned separately from the normal area

Close-up of a dense area, woven in the center of a warp. This is how a dense area appears before it's pulled in or gathered.

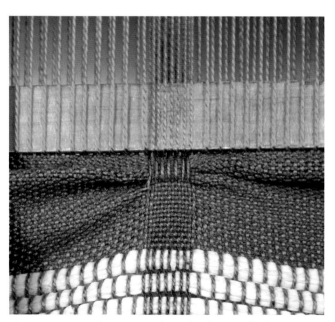

The same woven dense area after it has been pulled in. Note the gathers that are created on the right and the left of the dense area.

of weaving, and (5) a floating selvage is always used if the dense area is placed at a selvage.

After a dense area is woven, it contains very long floats, which are pulled in to cause gathers in the adjacent normal area or areas. As a result, weaving a dense area at a selvage results in a much-shortened selvage. For example, 50 weft picks through a dense area can result in a selvage length of only a quarter of an inch, or a little over half a centimeter.

A dense area can be woven at either or both selvages, or in the middle of a warp. Several dense areas can be spaced out over the width of a warp.

Floating Selvage

A floating selvage is simply a warp thread, usually at the selvage, that does not go through any of the heddles. When the shed is open, this thread should float in the middle of the two layers of warp threads as they are viewed from the side. While you are weaving, the tip of the shuttle goes over the floating selvage at the beginning of the pick. The shuttle passes under the floating selvage at the end of the pick, assuming that you have a floating selvage at both sides. In this way each weft pick will be captured by the floating selvage at the edge of the cloth. Certain kinds of weaving structures (twills, for example) produce an uneven selvage with different lengths of weft threads if floating selvages are not used.

While the floating selvages are usually at the selvage, as the name suggests, there can be exceptions. If a double weave is being woven and one of the layers is not the entire width of the warp, it may be necessary to have floating selvages in the middle of the warp. To explain it another way, the floating selvages are at the selvages of the cloth layers, but the layers are sometimes in the middle of the warp. This can become inconvenient as the different layers of the double weave are woven, because the floating selvage in the middle of the warp can easily get caught in the wrong layer and prevent the different layers from developing properly.

If your floating selvage is not in the middle of your shed and it's floating too low, you may have to raise it by putting a string around it and attaching that string to the castle of your loom. If it's floating too high, you may have to weigh it down by adding a weight, inside the back beam at the back of the loom.

Because floating selvages don't have the same amount of take-up as normal threads, it's often necessary to tension

A floating selvage can be raised with a hanger or lowered with weights. If a weight is necessary, I place it behind the last shaft, near the back beam. If a floating selvage must be lifted, I use a paper clip attached to a piece of Texsolv to grab the thread either behind the last shaft at the back or between the reed and the first shaft at the front of the loom. Putting it at the front is especially convenient for floating selvages that are in the middle of the warp, as when weaving a double-weave cloth, because the height can be easily adjusted as needed.

Placed properly, a floating selvage should rest in the middle of an open shed.

them apart from the normal- or dense-area warp by hanging a weight on them. The appropriate amount of weight to use for a floating selvage is about 2 ounces or 50 to 60 grams. Each dense area at a selvage will require a floating selvage, and although it's easier to wind the floating selvage when you wind the warp for your dense area, it's sometimes easier to tension the dense area and floating selvage independently for 3-D weaving.

Pick

These are the terms that weavers use to describe the weft thread that is laid down in the warp by a single throw of the shuttle. A pick may or may not be the entire width of the warp. For example, when weaving an expanded area, the picks are considerably shorter than the normal-area picks because the entire warp width is not being woven

Fell

The fell is the place where the unwoven warp meets the woven cloth. It's where the reed strikes the woven fabric as a pick is beaten in. The fell should be parallel to the breast beam and the beater.

Expanded Area

An expanded area is weaving in which (1) the warp threads use a different set of shafts than the normal area, (2) the warp threads use the same sett as the normal areas of weaving, assuming the same size of yarn is used, (3) the structure used, like the normal area, can be anything you like, (4) the expanded-area warp threads are tensioned separately from the normal area of weaving, and (5) if the expanded area is placed at a selvage, a floating selvage can be used or not, depending on the weaving structure being used.

Weaving an expanded area results in an area of weaving that produces more cloth length than that produced by a normal area. For example, an area of 30 weft picks in a normal area of weaving might have 60 to 120 or more picks in the expanded area of weaving. Weaving expanded sections of warp alternately with normal areas will result in *bubbles* on the surface of the cloth.

An expanded area can be woven at either or both selvages, or in the middle of a warp. Several expanded areas can be spaced out over the width of a warp.

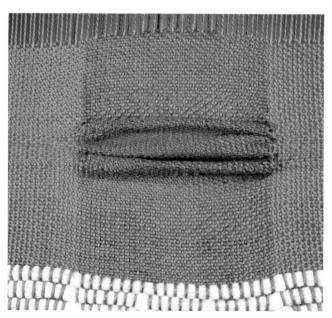

A woven expanded area that has been clasped at each side

Clasped Weft

A clasped weft requires two weft threads that come toward each other from opposite selvages. Where the threads meet, they wrap around each other and proceed back to the selvage. These threads can meet anywhere along the warp width, inside the shed or outside the shed above the warp. When they meet inside the shed, the result is two weft threads in that shed. In this book, all the clasped weft threads that are discussed travel around each other above the warp, the shed is changed, and the threads travel back to their respective selvages inside the new shed. In this way there is only one weft thread in each shed. This requires that both shuttles pass only partway along the warp width and exit the warp before being clasped.

Tension Rods, or Leapfrogging Tension Rods

Because the cloth beam is useless when a shaped fabric is being woven, it was necessary to devise other tools and techniques. Leapfrogging tension rods are the fastest and easiest way to control the tension of the cloth being woven.

A tension rod is a length of metal rod used to hold the tension on the woven cloth. One rod is inserted into the shed, tensioned with bungee cords, and weaving continues.

After the required number of picks is woven, a second tension rod is inserted into the current shed. Tension is transferred from the first rod to the second one, and the first rod is pulled out. In this way the rods leapfrog past each other as weaving continues.

When an expanded area is being woven, the tension rods don't necessarily need to be as long as the entire warp width. In this limited case, shorter rods may be used to tension only the expanded area and not the entire warp width, while the rest of the cloth continues to be tensioned by the cloth beam.

Leapfrogging tension rods can be used to control the cloth while you are weaving a dense area, an expanded area, or an infinitely tensioned area, which is explained later.

Leapfrog! This is a game played by children. One child squats on the ground with his head down. A second child places his hands on the first child's back, jumps over him in the direction that the kneeling child is facing, and then squats. The first child jumps over the second child in the same way. This continues with each child taking turns jumping over the other.

This is a cloth trap, without the cinches. The bottom of the trap curves up and has padding on the surface under the woven cloth. The top of the cloth trap curves down and has tacks, which are not visible here, that penetrate the woven cloth and the padded surface under the cloth. When the top and bottom are cinched together, the cloth is trapped. Appendix 1 has information about how to construct a cloth trap.

Cloth Trap

The cloth trap is the second of two techniques that can be used to control the tension of the cloth being woven. Experienced weavers are familiar with the use of a temple to prevent the excessive pull-in that causes a reduction in the cloth width while they are weaving. A cloth trap works in much the same way as a temple, except that it operates on the entire cloth width, as well as in both the direction of the warp and the weft. A temple operates at the selvages and provides tension only in the direction of the weft.

The cloth trap does what the name suggests—it traps the cloth at the fell so that tension can be maintained, regardless of the shape of the cloth being woven. This requires a bit more equipment and is a little slower to use, but it allows the creation of a cloth that does not expose the technique that was being used to weave it. A more detailed discussion of the advantages and disadvantages of the two tensioning devices, leapfrogging rods and the cloth trap, can be found in chapter 2.

Tension Bar

The weaving process requires that tension be maintained on the warp at all times. But periodically, the cloth trap must be opened and repositioned in order to advance the warp. While that is happening, tension on the warp cannot be maintained by the cloth trap. A tension bar is a flat metal bar that is used to temporarily hold the tension on woven cloth, while the cloth trap is advanced to capture the most recently woven fabric. The tension bar is made of aluminum since it's inexpensive and readily available.

Rod Beam

A rod beam allows you to provide different tension control and to advance the warp at different rates on different sections of the warp. In this way a rod beam is similar to having a second warp beam on your loom. The rod beam differs from a second warp beam in that it is capable of providing separate and independent tension and warp advance control to any number or width of warp sections. It is not limited to providing warp advance control to just one or two different sections of a warp.

A rod beam can control different warp sections at the back of the loom, but it can also be installed at the front of the loom and be used to control different sections of woven cloth. Consider weaving an apron with apron ties and a gathered skirt. The apron ties, the waistband, and the gathered skirt of the apron can all be woven at once on the same

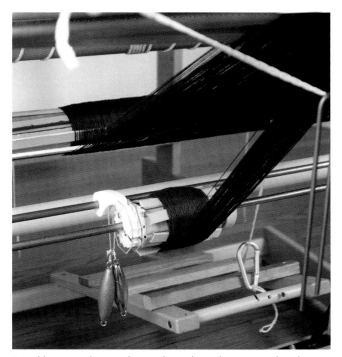

A rod beam with a ratchet and pawl can be mounted at the back or front of your loom.

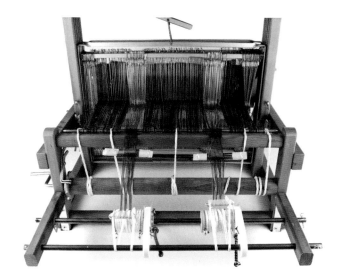

A table loom with a rod beam holding two sets of ratchets and pawls. Several more ratchet-and-pawl sets could be added, limited only by the width of the loom. The result, whether on a floor loom or a table loom, can be like having as many warp beams as you wish!

warp. One apron tie is woven first and tensioned by a rod beam at the front of the loom. Weaving then proceeds to the waistband and apron of the skirt. Finally, the second apron tie is woven, still tensioned by the rod beam at the front of the loom.

The rod beam works by using a series of ratchets and pawls, placed on metal rods at either the back of the loom to control the warp, or at the front of the loom to control the cloth. Information for the construction of a rod beam can be found in appendix 1.

Multiratchet and Pawl Sets

A ratchet-and-pawl set is a mechanical system of warp tensioning that will be familiar to most hand loom weavers. The ratchet is a gear with angled teeth that is prevented from turning by a pawl that catches in those teeth. Typically, a single ratchet and pawl is used on a warp beam or cloth beam. The rod beam uses multiple sets of ratchets and pawls in order to provide simultaneous tensioning for multiple sections of the warp or cloth. These multiratchet-and-pawl sets are placed beside each other on the two rods that make up a rod beam, at the front or back of the loom. The rod beam together with multiple sets of ratchets and pawls is

one way to tension the warp or, in some cases, the cloth. You can purchase these ratchet-and-pawl sets from the source listed in appendix 1.

Warp Weights and Lingos

A common nonmechanical way to tension sections of the warp is to use weights. If you don't wish to use a rod beam, a heavy object such as a jug of water can be hung on each section of warp that needs its own tensioning device.

Floating selvages are often tensioned by using individual weights. Weaving a dense area requires that several warp threads on either side of the dense area be individually weighted, because their take-up will be different than the rest of the threads in the normal area of the warp. This typically applies to the six threads adjacent to a dense area, but that number will be higher for finer yarns.

Most weavers are familiar with using pill bottles containing pennies, or other small weights, to tension the repair for a broken warp thread. But having many of these little bottles right next to each other can result in tangled threads. A better idea is to borrow a solution from the draw loom world and use lingos.

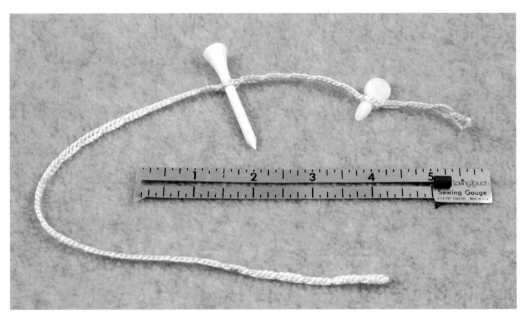

Standard-size Texsolv has about 11 holes every 5 inches (12.7 centimeters). A piece of Texsolv is shown with a golf tee and an arrow peg inserted into two of the holes.

A lingo is a piece of metal rod that has been folded in half. Once folded, it has a length of about 12 or 13 inches (30 centimeters) and a weight of about 2 ounces (57 grams). Because of their shape and the fact that they can be hung directly on the warp threads, lingos don't get tangled around each other as easily as other kinds of weights.

You can make your own lingos very inexpensively by using the instructions provided in appendix 1. I recommend that you do make some lingos because you will need many of them to weave dense areas, and they work better than any other small weights.

Infinite Tensioning

The ability to weave shapes is dependent on the ability to weave using differently tensioned sections of warp, with different amounts of take-up. But the ultimate in versatility and ability to weave shapes is the ability to tension each individual warp thread independently. The infinite-tension device borrows ideas both from velvet looms and draw looms, but the weaving technique is different. The use of infinite tensioning can also be used to weave expanded areas at will, without the requirement of separate sets of shafts for each expanded area in the warp.

Texsolv Loom Cord

Texsolv is the trademarked name of a truly marvelous material! It's a specialized type of strong nylon that is constructed out of two cords in such a way as to create a series of holes. Along with two different types of pegs that fit into these holes, it's commonly used on Scandinavian-type countermarche looms to hang shafts, tie shafts to lams, and tie lams to treadles. Weavers who are familiar with only American-type jack looms may not be familiar with Texsolv, although it's being used more and more in the weaving community.

This versatile material can be purchased in two sizes and different lengths from most weaving-supply companies. I use it in several different ways in my 3-D hand loom weaving processes, and you will see it mentioned throughout the book.

Bout

A bout is a group of warp threads. Sometimes it refers to the warp thread groups as they are tied on to the loom at either the front or the back. At other times it refers to a group of warp threads as they are wound, in preparation for warping.

Now that you have an understanding of the new terms used in this book, and some of the standard weaving terms that you might not have known, you are ready to learn about the 3-D hand loom weaving process. Let's break some rules!

2 | The Process Overview

Breaking the Rules

Now that you understand the new terms and have reviewed some of the old ones, we are ready to talk about the weaving conventions that we need to challenge. The ability to break these rules, and the tools and techniques used to break them, is what makes it possible to weave 3-D shapes on a hand loom. You have probably broken some of these rules already if you have woven double-weave pleats or combined thick and thin threads in the same warp.

Let's look at these rules, or conventions, in more depth.

RULE

THE SAME TENSION IS USED ACROSS A GIVEN WARP.

You may have broken this rule when weaving double-weave pleats, but in that case, you had two warps on top of each other, and each was wound onto and tensioned on its own warp beam. The 3-D handweaving techniques described in this book require different sections of the warp to be threaded on different shafts and to be placed side by side, although they can also be placed on top of each other. However, the threads on each different set of shafts are also tensioned independently from all of the rest. Further, you are not limited to just two warp beams, should you be lucky enough to have two.

If you are weaving a dense or expanded area, this allows the selvages on each side of the warp to be of dramatically different lengths. If you are weaving expanded areas, different sections of the warp can have very different numbers of picks, and where there are more picks than in the normal area, the fabric will bulge out.

Another example of breaking this rule is the infinite-tensioning technique, where each warp thread is tensioned independently but some warp threads may be tensioned in groups. This method requires both a different weaving technique and a different warp-tensioning technique, as explained in chapter 6.

RULE

THE SAME TAKE-UP IS USED FROM SIDE TO SIDE ACROSS A GIVEN WARP.

This rule is broken by all of the techniques here and is at the core of how 3-D hand loom weaving is accomplished. There wouldn't be much point in threading different areas of the warp on different sets of shafts and tensioning them separately, just to have the take-up be the same!

RULE

ALL THE WARP THREADS ARE THE SAME LENGTH.

All the warp threads could be the same length, but in many cases that would just be a waste of your yarn. For example, when dense areas are woven, they require a lot less yarn, since 30 to 50 picks requires about the same amount of warp as weaving approximately six picks in the normal way. The normal area of warp might be 3 to 6 yards, but the dense area itself will seldom need more than 2 yards, and most of that length will be used to tie the warp onto the front and back and for loss on the loom.

The opposite is true when weaving expanded areas. In that case, a longer warp is required since expanded areas raise out of the face of the normally woven cloth. The details and the amount of the length reduction or elongation for certain sections of the warp will depend on the project and the shape that you are trying to achieve. If the dense areas or expanded areas are woven only for a short length (such as, for example, to add interest to the front fabric of a jacket), then the differences in the warp lengths will not be very large.

THE LOOM GETS THREADED AND SLEYED ONCE PER WARP.

Whether or not you break this rule will depend on the fabric you are planning to weave. Because dense areas and expanded areas are threaded on separate shafts and tensioned separately, they can also be moved to a different location in the warp in the middle of your weaving project. Or, the dense area, which has a sett that is twice that of the normal area, could be resleyed and woven normally once you are done weaving the required dense areas.

The key is to plan ahead and remember to leave empty heddles in place if necessary, so that you can minimize the amount of rethreading or resleying work that you do.

It's also important to remember to plan for the best use of the number of shafts that you have available. I am lucky to have a 24-shaft dobby loom for my 3-D projects. For my huck lace ruffled vest (see chapter 10), I'd originally planned to use all 24 shafts and designed three different eight-shaft huck weave patterns for the ruffles. I finally realized that I also needed two shafts for the dense area. One of the huck layers was redesigned as a six-shaft huck weave pattern, so that the extra two shafts could be used for the dense area.

ALL FIBERS USED IN THE WARP OR THE WEFT SHOULD HAVE APPROXIMATELY THE SAME AMOUNT OF STRETCH.

This rule is frequently broken when weavers want to create surface interest by using elastic threads, threads that have been spun differently, or threads that have different shrinkages. You may not consider this an actual rule, but breaking it can cause problems if your goal is a simple flat fabric.

When this rule is broken in the extreme, interesting sculptural shapes can be woven. The headdresses that I have woven consist of fine stretchy wool combined with copper wire in the warp and a copper weft. These projects are discussed in chapters 7 and 10.

WEAVE THE WHOLE WARP WIDTH WITH EACH PICK.

Tapestry weavers break this rule frequently, as do weavers who use the wedge-weaving technique. This rule can also be broken to weave expanded areas or to simultaneously weave different-width layers of fabric.

Three huck lace ruffles. The left two ruffles were woven as double weave, and all three ruffles were woven simultaneously.

THE SAME SETT IS USED ACROSS THE WHOLE WARP.

As you already know, the sett used for dense areas is twice that of the normal areas. This rule must be broken to weave a good-looking dense area. However, you can still weave a dense area with a sett that is the same as the normal area of weaving; it just won't look as good.

WHEN MULTIPLE WARPS ARE USED, THE WARPS ARE LAYERED ON TOP OF EACH OTHER, NOT BESIDE EACH OTHER.

The common double-weave technique is woven with the warp layers on top of each other, and the layers are usually the same width. Neither of these norms is required for the 3-D handweaving techniques. In fact, these techniques often call for multiple warps of different widths that are positioned side by side. The project you are weaving will determine whether the different warp sections should be put on top of each other, side by side, or both, and whether they stay in the same position during the entire project.

This dense area was woven with a sett twice that of the normal area.

This dense area was woven with a sett equal to that of the normal area. I like the look of the denser sett.

Overview of the Techniques, or, How Does This Work?

To understand how the 3-D shapes are accomplished on a hand loom, it's important to first understand the distinction between the weaving techniques and the tension control devices.

Weaving an expanded area is a weaving technique, as is weaving a dense area or weaving a shape by using an infinite-tension-control device. Leapfrogging rods and cloth traps are cloth-tension-control devices that work with all of the weaving techniques.

The warp tension is typically controlled in one of two ways: by using weights or mechanically with a ratchet and pawl or a friction brake.

The infinite-tension-control device works by using a small weight on each warp thread. You can use this mechanism to control the warp tension while weaving expanded areas, but I would not recommend using it for weaving dense areas. That is because the amount of tension required to weave dense areas cannot easily be provided by weighting individual threads, and the required thread density is in conflict with the space needed to tension each warp thread individually.

Dense areas are usually fairly narrow, and all the warp threads are handled in the same way and have the same take-up, so there is no need for infinite tensioning to weave a dense area. Since all the warp-tensioning devices can be combined in a single project, it's possible to weave dense areas incorporated into an infinitely tensioned warp, by also using the warp-tensioning mechanism appropriate for dense areas.

The various combinations of the techniques and the control devices can be summarized like this:

	Shafts Needed	Weaving Structure	Sett	Warp tension		Cloth tension		Floating Selvage?
				Type to Use	Infinite Tensioning?	Leapfrogging Rods	Cloth Trap	
Normal Area Weaving	Needs its own set of shafts	Any	Determined by yarn and structure	Warp beam, typically	Yes	Yes	Yes	As needed
Dense Area Weaving	Needs its own set of shafts	Tabby	Double the normal area	Weights or rod beam	No (Needs its own warp beam and shafts)	Yes	Yes	Required at the selvage
Expanded Area Weaving	Needs its own set of shafts	Any	Determined by yarn and structure	Weights (preferred) or rod beam	Yes	Yes	Yes	As needed
Infinite Tensioning	Depends on the shape planned	Any	Determined by yarn and structure	Infinite tensioning alone, or combined with any or all other methods		Yes	Yes	As needed

The combinations of techniques and control devices

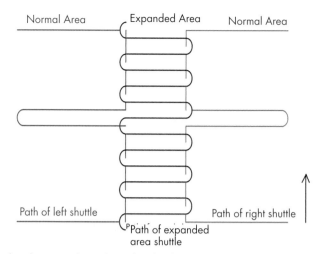

Normal Area   Expanded Area   Normal Area

Path of left shuttle   Path of right shuttle

Path of expanded
area shuttle

This diagram shows how the shuttles are managed when an expanded area is woven in the middle of a warp. Only the weft is shown.

WEAVING EXPANDED AREAS: AN OVERVIEW

In order to weave an area of cloth that expands, it must have more picks than the areas of normal weaving that surround it. The process is slightly different depending on whether the expanded area is placed somewhere in the middle of the warp or at the selvage. An expanded area placed at the selvage will require two shuttles, while one placed in the middle of the warp will require three. If you have two expanded areas within one section of the warp, you will need five shuttles: two for the two expanded areas and three for the normal areas of weaving (one on the left, one between the expanded areas, and one on the right).

Consider the example of one expanded area in the middle of the warp, requiring three shuttles. Although only one shuttle is required to weave normally, a second shuttle must be added just prior to the start of the expanded area.

When the expanded area is about to be woven, the normal-area shuttles both start from their respective selvages and proceed toward the expanded area. Each shuttle rises out of the warp at the nearest edge of the expanded area. A third shuttle is used to weave the expanded section of the warp, but each time the third shuttle reaches the outside edge of the expanded area, the weft thread is clasped with the weft thread on the shuttle resting there.

Because the expanded area has been threaded on a different set of shafts from the normal area, only those shafts are used while the expanded area is being woven. The normal areas of weaving, on the left and right of the expanded area, can be threaded onto the same set of shafts. Even if the normal areas are not always planned to be woven together, the fact that they are separated by the expanded area makes it easy for them to be woven separately if you wish.

The number of picks that are woven this way is dependent on the effect that you want. If you use too few picks, the area won't expand enough. If you use too many picks, a small hole will be created by the large number of clasped threads. The solution is to weave four to eight picks in the expanded area and then weave two picks in the normal areas at each side of the expanded area, sending the shuttles to the selvage and back to the edge of the expanded area. If you are unsure about how many picks you want in the expanded area as compared to the normal area, leave some extra warp at the beginning of your weaving to try out different ratios. In other words, sample until you find the look you want.

If you are having trouble imagining how to weave an expanded area, this diagram should help. It shows six expanded-area picks for every two normal-area picks.

Note that you will be using more warp length to weave the expanded area than the normal area, so it will be necessary to advance that warp more often. And eventually it will be difficult to keep tension in control over the entire warp. When this happens, either insert a tension rod into the next shed of the expanded area and tension it, or insert a tension bar into the next shed of the entire warp and use the cloth trap to tension the full warp width. In the first option, small leapfrogging rods are used, but only on the expanded area of the warp.

If you use small tension rods on only the expanded area, the cloth tension and the location of the fell on the expanded area and the normal areas must be adjusted to match.

A third option is to insert a tension rod in the next shed of the entire warp width and use the leapfrogging-rods method to tension the cloth.

A fourth option is to tension the entire warp with a tension bar, fold the expanded area over itself, and pin the layers together with T pins or quilting pins. For small sections of expanded areas, this is the fastest and easiest technique.

WEAVING DENSE AREAS: AN OVERVIEW

Weaving a dense area is almost the opposite of weaving an expanded area. Instead of weaving just a small area of the warp to create an area of cloth that expands out of the normal weaving, the entire warp width is woven on each pick. Expanded areas and dense areas change the length of the selvages in different ways. A dense area placed at a selvage will reduce the length of that selvage, while an expanded area placed at the selvage will cause it to expand.

When weaving a dense area, a shed is created by using the appropriate shafts in the normal area of weaving and one of the tabby shafts in the dense area. Many picks are woven, changing the shed in the normal area between each pick, without changing the shed in the dense area. If the dense area is placed at a selvage, the weft threads will travel around a floating selvage to prevent them from disappearing into the dense area.

Once the required number of picks is woven, the shed is changed in both the normal area and the dense area. A tension bar or rod holds the warp tension while the warp is advanced in the normal area in such a way as to pull forward on the cloth. This causes the weft threads to bunch together, creating a bundle of weft threads inside the dense-area warp threads. Releasing the tension on the normal area allows the cloth to advance as much as is required while creating gathers next to the dense area.

Once the first dense area is woven, you can no longer use your cloth beam to tension the woven fabric. From here on, the cloth tension must be controlled by using either leapfrogging rods or a cloth trap.

The dense-area weaving technique is explained in chapter 5, including detailed photographs of the entire process.

WEAVING WITH INFINITE TENSIONING: AN OVERVIEW

An infinitely tensioned warp is one where each warp thread has its own tensioning device, in the form of lingos hung on each thread. This allows you to place weft picks that start and stop anywhere along the warp width. The only restriction is that the weft must change direction fairly close to where it stopped on the previous pick to avoid long floats, unless multiple shuttles are used.

When weaving with infinite tension, unlike expanded areas or dense areas, there is no need to put sections of the warp on different shafts or different tensioning devices, since each warp thread already has its own tension. The other techniques that have been described require much preplanning to determine which shafts and tension devices to use. Weaving with an infinite-tension mechanism is more free-form and can be done with as few as two shafts, although more shafts allow for more interesting weave structures and you can decide how to shape the cloth as it's being woven. The shapes woven in this way can be gently curving, since

the shape is entirely determined by the width, number, and placement of the weft picks rather than the start and stop of an expanded area or dense area. Note that it's not necessary to use infinite tensioning on the entire warp if it's not needed.

As with the other techniques, infinite-tension weaving can use leapfrogging rods or a cloth trap to tension the cloth once it's woven.

There are also some trade-offs. Dense areas require more tension than can be reasonably accomplished with lingos. Dense areas can still be woven with an infinitely tensioned warp, but their location must be planned ahead of time, they require a separate set of shafts, and they must use either a mechanical tension device of their own or the dense-area section of the warp must be very heavily weighted.

Weaving structures or yarns that require a heavy beating are not appropriate for use with an infinitely tensioned warp. Since each warp thread is weighted with just one lingo, a heavy beat will cause the lingos to bounce up and down, preventing the cloth from being beaten heavily.

Advancing an infinitely tensioned warp can be a slower process than advancing other warps. Because each warp thread has a lingo hung on it at the back of the loom, releasing the tension on the warp beam simply allows each lingo to drop a little bit but does not release the warp tension. As a result, the lingos must be placed on a lifting device in addition to being hung on the warp threads. To advance the warp, the lifting device must be raised up enough to carry the weight of the lingos while the warp is being advanced. The lifting device must be lowered again before weaving can continue.

The expanded-area and dense-area techniques can require a large number of shafts, depending on the weave structure being used and the shape being woven. An infinitely tensioned warp requires only the number of shafts needed by the weave structure, assuming no dense areas are planned. The technique does require some loom modifications in order to accommodate the lingos and to allow for their appropriate spacing, and as a way to carry their weight while the warp is being advanced. And because there must be someplace for the lingos to hang, you can't use this technique on a table loom.

See chapter 6 for a full explanation of the entire process for weaving with infinite tensioning. The required loom modifications are described in appendix 1.

A Comparison of the Techniques

The leapfrogging-rods technique was developed first, and I used it on my sculptural headdresses, which were made of fine wool with an elastic quality and a slippery copper weft. Whenever cloth is woven, both the warp and weft threads bend, or deflect, a little bit in order to pass over and under each other.

But because fine wool can be deflected so much more easily than a piece of copper wire, almost all the deflection occurs in the wool yarn and very little occurs in the wire, even if you are using fine-gauge copper wire. When weaving with fine wool and copper wire, the extra space in the cloth that is created by weaving with a tension rod in place is almost eliminated. Once the rod is removed, the natural elasticity of the wool and the ability of the wire to slide fill the space created by the rod, because wire is deflected so little by the weaving process.

When I decided to weave shapes for clothing by using cotton, linen, silk, and rayon, and without copper, it was obvious that I needed another technique to tension the woven cloth. I needed to eliminate the marks left by the tension rods. The cloth trap was the solution that I devised.

Each of these different tensioning techniques has advantages and disadvantages. The leapfrogging rods are the easiest to use; however, the results are less satisfying because you can often see where the rods were placed during the weaving. You can decide to consider them a design element and obscure them with a ribbon or thick weft thread, but that may not be the look you wanted. The cloth trap produces better results but is a bit slower and requires that you build a cloth trap. It also requires a loom with side pieces so there is someplace to rest the trap while it's being set up and used. This can be overcome if your loom does not have the required side pieces, but that is additional work.

The advantages and disadvantages of the techniques are explained on the opposite page.

Instructions for building a cloth trap can be found in appendix 1. There you will also find information about how to use a cloth trap on a loom without sides, such as, for example, a Macomber loom or any loom with an X-shaped frame.

By now you should have a good idea how the 3-D handweaving process works. But to actually start weaving you will need to assemble the required tools. The next chapter explains all the tools and how to construct the simpler ones. Construction of the more complex tools and any required loom modifications are explained in appendix 1.

	Warp Tension				Cloth Tension	
	Regular Loom Warp Beam	Rod Beam	Weights	Infinite Tensioning	Cloth Trap	Leapfrogging Rods
Your time	The easiest to use.	Easy to wind on and advance the warp.	More time required to advance the warp.	Weights must be raised to advance the warp.	More time consuming to advance the warp.	Less time consuming to advance the warp.
Loom	Always available but limited to one or two beams, typically	Any number of warps can be managed	Any number of warps can be managed.	Each warp thread is tensioned individually.	Easier on a loom with side pieces on which to rest the bottom of the cloth trap.	Can be done on any loom with no modifications.
Tools Needed	No extra tools required.	A rod beam must be constructed and installed on the loom.	The tools can be quite simple—milk jugs, lingos, pill bottles	An infinite tensioning warp beam must be constructed. One lingo is needed for each warp thread	You must build the cloth trap and need a way to support it	You have to cut rods to the length of the shaft width
Woven Result	N/A; the result is more dependent on the technique and cloth tension device used.	N/A; the result is more dependent on the technique and cloth tension device used.	N/A; the result is more dependent on the technique and cloth tension device used.	More complex and free-flowing shapes can be woven.	Resulting cloth doesn't leave a mark because the tension bar is removed prior to weaving.	Tension rod leaves a mark in the cloth. The mark can be hidden with the addition of a thick weft or ribbon weft.
Notes	Best used for the widest part of the warp.	Works well for warp sections that are advanced at different rates.	The warp tension must be equalized across the warp.	Can be done with as few as two shafts.	Works best for clothing.	The rod marks are less visible when weaving an elastic type fiber warp and wire weft.

3

Tools and Devices

Before you can start weaving 3-D shapes on your hand loom, you will need to decide what you want to weave, and plan your project. And you will need to gather or make a few new tools and understand how to use them. All the tools you will need are described in this chapter. If the tool can be made easily with simple materials and tools commonly found in a weaving studio or a basic household tool box, then its construction is described here. However, if you need woodworking tools such as a saw or drill press, or if the construction is a bit more involved, then it's described in appendix 1.

Warp-Tensioning Tools

No matter what you are weaving, you will need to tension different sections of the warp in different ways and will need tools to do that. Since most looms have only one warp beam, you will need additional ways to tension sections of the warp and individual warp threads. If your loom has two warp beams, by all means use them both! As you become more experienced with these techniques, you will eventually need to tension more than just two different sections of your warp, and this chapter will give you options for tensioning as many sections as you need, all at the same time.

WARP WEIGHTS

Empty half-gallon plastic juice or milk jugs with a loop handle make excellent warp weights. After the warp has been threaded, sleyed, and tied on at the front of the loom, these jugs can be hung off the back beam of your loom to create the tension usually provided by a warp beam. A section of warp can be attached to the jug in various ways. Make sure that your jugs have tops that screw on, to avoid spills when you eventually drop them.

The easiest way to hang the jug from a section of warp

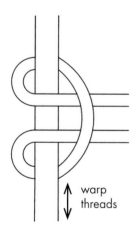

A lark's-head knot with a warp bundle running through it. The weight of the water in a jug will cause the knot to tighten and prevent it from slipping.

A jug hanging on a section of warp. In this case I used Texsolv and an arrow peg for the cord loop.

is to use a piece of strong cord about 18 inches (46 centimeters) long and loop it through the jug handle and tie a knot. I like to use a piece of Texsolv and an arrow peg instead of cord. Using the other end of the loop, make a lark's-head knot and pull the entire warp bundle through the lark's-head loop. The height of the jug can be adjusted by picking up the jug to release the tension on the warp, loosening the lark's-head knot, and sliding it down the warp bundle. Once that is done, let the jug hang from the warp bundle. The lark's-head knot will tighten, and won't slide any further. Chain and secure the extra warp length with a bobbin to keep it from tangling and let out the chain as needed. You need to make sure only that the jug is not resting on the floor and is hanging from the warp bundle, which is hung over the back beam.

If you are using a table loom, you can use the same technique; however, the piece of strong chord must be long enough to allow the jug to hang over the backside of the table that your loom is sitting on. The table you use should be either large enough or heavy enough that the weights hanging off the back of the loom don't upend the table.

Another method of hanging a jug from a warp is to chain the warp from the end, pull a loop of the chain through the handle of the jug, and then put a weaving bobbin into the loop to prevent it from slipping through the jug handle. If this seems a little too insecure for you, you can pull a second loop around the jug handle and through the first loop. Place an ordinary weaving bobbin through the second loop to keep it secure. The height of the jug must be adjusted so that it hangs without touching the floor. The same technique can be used with a table loom, but you may have to switch to using a cord near the end of your warp.

These instructions assume that you are warping back to front, but they work just the same if you are warping front to back. In both cases, don't add the weights until the warp is threaded, sleyed, and tied on at the front.

Once the entire warp is on the loom and tensioned, adjust the tension of the weighted sections by adding or removing water from the jugs. You want the entire warp to be at approximately the same tension before you start weaving.

Chaining a warp: A chained warp is just a length of warp that has been treated like a single thread by making a loop, pulling a loop through that loop, pulling another through that, and so on. It's basically a giant crochet stitch, but made with an entire section of warp. A warp can be chained in this way to keep it from getting tangled with itself.

A jug hanging on a section of warp with a weaving bobbin through one loop of the chain

THREAD WEIGHTS

Individual threads, such as floating selvage threads or the approximately six threads on either side of a dense area, can be tensioned by hanging a small weight on each of them. Each weight should be about 2 ounces (57 grams) and can be made from pill bottles filled with pennies or other weights.

The easiest and most tangle-free weights to use are lingos, borrowed from the draw loom world. Lingos are simple metal rods that are folded in half and so don't require strings to hang them. And because they are metal, they slide easily along the threads as the warp is advanced. Lingos are easy and inexpensive to make, with a few basic tools. The process for making lingos is explained in appendix 1.

Depending on how your loom is constructed, the lingos hung on individual warp threads will slide toward the warp beam. You can prevent this by tying a chord or hanging a stick from one side of the loom to the other. If you leave the lease sticks in the warp and suspend them from the back beam, they can prevent the lingos from sliding toward the warp beam.

If the threads being tensioned are not on a warp beam but instead are part of a section of warp that is being weighted,

you can still hang a lingo on them. In this case each lingo will have to be removed and rehung every time you advance the warp.

A more convenient option that is less work when you are advancing the warp is to put different small warp sections on their own small warp beam, using a rod beam and a ratchet and pawl. We will discuss that next.

THE ROD BEAM AND MULTIRATCHET AND PAWL SETS

It would be a shame to learn how to weave 3-D shapes on a hand loom and be limited to using only weights to tension different sections of your warp. If you are using a smaller lightweight loom, a lot of weights hanging from the back beam might even threaten to upend the loom. Advancing hanging weights periodically and adding and removing water from jugs to adjust the tension can become tedious, especially if you have a lot of differently tensioned sections on your warp. The rod beam together with a ratchet-and-pawl set solves all these problems.

The back of my loom is a busy place! You can see a piece of Texsolv stretched from one side to the other, to prevent the lingos from sliding toward the warp beam. You can also hang your lease sticks from the back beam and use them to keep the lingos from sliding.

Appendix 1 explains how to build a rod beam with multiratchet-and-pawl sets. The equipment requires the following pieces:

Two steel rods, ⅜ inch (1 centimeter) in diameter: The rods are mounted parallel to the floor at the back of the loom and reach from one side of the loom to the other.

Mounts for the rods: The rods are mounted at the same height and spaced apart so that one rod can be used to hold multiple ratchets and the other can hold the matching pawls. The mounting material can consist of pieces of wood or eye screws that are large enough to hold the rods.

Ratchet-and-pawl set: I had my ratchets and pawls designed for me. They are 3-D printed on demand from a strong nylon material; a set can be purchased from the Shapeways company. See appendix 1 for details.

Something on which to wind the section of warp: Each ratchet has three small holes that are used to screw it onto a small piece of wood that acts as a limited-width warp beam. The wood can be an old thread spool or a dowel of any length with a ⅜-inch hole drilled through lengthwise. The wood does not need to be round, but if it isn't, the edges should be smoothed so that they don't damage your warp threads.

Ratchet stops: The pawl is prevented from sliding off the ratchet by placing a stop on either side of it. I use small pieces of transparent plastic for this, but cardboard would work just as well.

Keeping the ratchet and pawl engaged: The pawl has three small holes in the side. These holes are for the purpose of holding a piece of string and a weight, or as a place to attach a bungee cord. The weight or bungee cord keeps the pawl engaged with the ratchet by pushing the ratchet into the pawl. I use fishing weights, but any small weight of about 6 ounces (170 grams) will work.

A cord to prevent the rods from bending: Even steel rods can bend a little due to the force of a narrow section of tensioned warp. If they bend too much, the pawl will fall out of contact with the ratchet. To prevent this from happening, the rods must be held together at the correct distance. The easiest way to do this is to put a piece of Texsolv around both rods, pull one end of the Texsolv through a hole in the other end, and secure it with an arrow peg. If this loop of Texsolv is situated close to the ratchet and pawl, it will prevent the rods from bending and will keep the pawl in place.

The rod beam along with its mounting. The beam consists of two rods positioned to be able to hold the ratchet-and-pawl set. A fishing weight keeps the pawl engaged with the ratchet, and pieces of clear plastic at each side of the ratchet keep it from sliding off in one direction or the

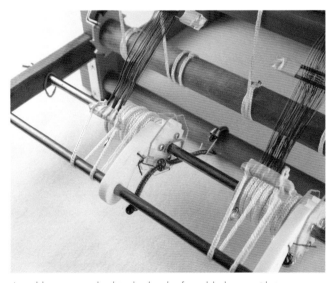

A rod beam attached to the back of a table loom with two ratchet-and-pawl sets holding narrow copper warps. Note that the pawl must be held against the ratchet with bungee cords or a rubber band because there is no room to hang a fishing weight.

You can also mount a rod beam on a table loom. The only difference is that you will need to hold the ratchet against the pawl with a bungee cord or a rubber band since there is not enough space to hang a weight.

The rod beam together with sets of ratchets and pawls has the advantage of being customizable. The piece of wood that is attached to the ratchet and that acts as a warp beam can be of any length. It will typically be just a little bit longer than the width of the section of warp being tensioned. This allows many small, independently controlled sections of warp to be placed beside each other, located wherever they are needed along the warp. I use finishing nails or small sticks as lease sticks for these narrow warps, with a bit of masking tape to keep them together as a set.

See appendix 1 for sourcing information for the ratchet and pawl, detailed information on how to build a rod beam and the necessary loom mounts, and where to place the loom mounts.

INFINITE TENSIONING

Infinite tensioning is the ability to individually tension each thread in the warp. The warp is wound onto a warp beam in the normal way, and a lingo is hung on each of the warp threads at the back of the loom. As a result, infinite tensioning works only on floor looms, since the space required to hang lingos isn't available on table looms.

But this is not as simple as it sounds. The first issue is the width of the lingos. Seven lingos hanging together on individual warp threads take up an inch (2.54 centimeters) of width on the warp. This isn't a problem if only a few lingos are hung, but it can cause problems if your warp is set at 24 threads per inch. A warp 12 inches (30.5 centimeters) wide needs 288 lingos, requiring just over 41 inches (105 centimeters) in width to hang all the lingos. This means that your warp, which is just 12 inches wide in the reed, will expand to 41 inches in width at the back of the loom. This change in the width also means that the warp threads cannot travel in a straight line from the warp beam, through the heddles, to the cloth beam.

Lingos are borrowed from the draw loom world, where we find the solution to this problem. The answer is to stagger the lingos by hanging them at slightly different places along the warp so that they are not all hung beside each other. The use of spacing bars gives the lingos the room they need without affecting the warp width. Hanging 24 lingos an inch requires that the lingos be hung in at least three rows. The warp will still spread out just a little, but not excessively. Three rows of lingos require four spacing bars.

The second issue is finding a place to hang the rows of lingos, so that they don't interfere with the warp as it travels from the warp beam and over the back beam. The solution is to relocate the warp beam to behind the back beam. This way, the path from the warp beam to the reed is parallel to the floor. This requires an extension at the back of the loom to give you someplace to install spacing bars for the lingos, and to get the warp beam out of the way of the hanging lingos.

The third issue involves advancing the warp. If you release tension on the warp beam, the weight of the lingos causes each warp thread to fall a little bit, while remaining under tension. And because of the collective weight of the lingos, you risk the warp beam suddenly letting out much more length than you had planned. All the lingos can end up in a pile on the floor! To advance the warp there must be some way to release tension on the warp threads despite the fact that each warp thread is tensioned with a lingo hanging from it.

The solution is to remove the weight of the lingos without removing the lingos themselves. This is done by hanging an aluminum bar between the spacing bars. As each lingo is hung over a warp thread, it is also hung over the suspended aluminum bar. This bar has a hole at each end with a piece of Texsolv looped around the spacing bars and through the hole. Before advancing the warp, the bar is raised enough at each end to allow the lingos to rest on the bar, thus relieving the tension on the warp threads. Once the warp is advanced as much as needed, the bar is lowered so that the lingos again hang free and provide tension to the warp.

Appendix 1 explains how to build infinite tensioning onto your loom. The equipment requires the following pieces:

An extension on the back of the loom that is attached to the sides of the loom: The far end of the extension holds a warp beam with a ratchet and pawl, and a rod attached to the warp beam with cords so that the warp can be advanced as much as possible.

Support legs: Optionally, you may need support legs for your back beam extension. The weight of many lingos hanging from an extension to the back of your loom may make it unstable and cause it to tip over. If you have any concern that this will happen, add a leg at each side of the extension to prevent accidents.

Several lingo-spacing bars or sticks: These must each be a little longer than your loom frame width so that they can be attached to the loom extension. The number needed will depend on the sett of the fabric you wish to weave, as explained above.

Lingos: One lingo is needed for each warp thread for which you want to provide infinite tensioning. Note that you may not need infinite tensioning for the entire warp, depending on the shape of the cloth that you are planning to weave. Chapter 8 explains the design considerations that will determine how many lingos you will need.

Aluminum bars, Texsolv, and arrow pegs, to allow you to raise and lower the lingos: One bar with holes drilled at each end, two pieces of Texsolv, and two arrow pegs will be required for each row of lingos. The length of the bars should be a little less than the width of the back beam extension.

Note that some of the aluminum spacing bars can be mounted inside the loom's back beam. That allows the rod on the infinite-tension warp beam to get closer to the back of the shafts at the end of the warp. But it also prevents you from using the loom's warp beam where the lingos are hanging. See chapter 6 and appendix 1 for more details.

The back of my loom is set up to weave with infinite tension. An extension is added to the back of the loom, and four pieces of C-channel aluminum are mounted to allow four rows of lingos to be hung, using the back beam as one of the spacers. Aluminum bars are hung from the spacing bars to carry the weight of the lingos while the warp is being advanced. Simple legs are added to carry the weight of the lingos and prevent the loom from toppling over. The two black warp threads that hang on fishing weights are for demonstration purposes only, to show the path of the warp.

Cloth-Tensioning Tools

The goal of all the 3-D hand loom weaving techniques is to produce nonrectangular cloth. The described warp-tensioning methods are ones that weavers have used for centuries, although they have been modified here to be a little more versatile.

The cloth-tensioning methods, however, require much more inventive solutions. Once you have started weaving a shape, you can no longer use your cloth beam to tension the woven fabric. In addition, it's necessary to tension the cloth in a way that allows the fell to be kept in a straight line and parallel to the reed and breast beam.

Chapter 2 describes the two methods that I developed to control the cloth—leapfrogging rods and the cloth trap—and the advantages and disadvantages of each. Now we will look at each of them from the point of view of making the tools.

LEAPFROGGING TENSION RODS

This is the easier and faster of the two cloth-tensioning methods. It can be used with any of the weaving techniques and requires only simple tools. For these reasons, I suggest that you first try these techniques with the leapfrogging rods. They are my preferred tools for weaving sculptural headdresses, but I prefer the cloth trap for fabric that will be sewn into clothes.

Because one of the rods is in place while you are weaving, it leaves a mark or gap in the woven fabric where the rod was. If you would like to use leapfrogging rods to weave a piece for clothing, you can disguise that mark by turning the gap into a feature with a heavy piece of yarn or a piece of ribbon, placed in the shed at the same time as the rod. This is a good way to learn the 3-D hand loom weaving techniques without having to invest time building more-complicated tools.

The leapfrogging tension rods technique requires the following pieces:

Two steel rods, ⅛ inch (0.32 centimeters) in diameter, and a few inches longer than your weaving width: Although a smaller-diameter rod would create a less noticeable gap in the weaving, it won't be stiff enough to create a straight fell.

A length of strong cord or a metal rod long enough to create an anchored line under your loom: If you use a strong cord, you will attach it or tie it to either side under the loom, creating a tight line. If you use a rod, it should be long enough to reach from one side to the other. A piece of the same ⅜-inch-/1-centimeter-diameter rod used to build a rod beam works well. It can be held in place at the front of the loom in the same way as the rod beam, or with eye screws of the appropriate size, mounted facing forward on the frame of the loom.

Two mini bungee cords of the type with hooks at each end: These come in packages of eight or ten and are about 10 inches (25 centimeters) long. One hook on each bungee cord will need to be unbent a small amount. If the bungee cords are a little too long, such as, for example, if you are using a table loom, they can be shortened by pushing the hook toward the center and tying a knot somewhere along the elastic.

Two pieces of Texsolv: The length will depend on your loom. The Texsolv must be able to reach between one end of the bungee cord and the anchor line or rod under your loom.

Attach each piece of Texsolv to the anchor line by passing it around the rod or cord, and pull one end of the Texsolv through a loop near the other end of the same piece of Texsolv. This allows the Texsolv cords to be moved to the left or right along the anchor line as needed.

If you install a rod beam on the front of your loom, you will have everything you need for an anchor line. See appendix 1 for information about where and how to install a rod beam on the front or the back of your loom.

Using the leapfrogging rods is easy. After weaving the first bit of shaped cloth to the point where the fell is no longer straight or parallel to the breast beam, insert a rod into the shed. If you are using a thick warp thread or a piece of ribbon to disguise the space created by the rod, insert it at the same time. Somewhere near the selvage on each side of the warp, insert the slightly unbent hook of the bungee cord into the warp to capture the rod. The fact that the hook is unbent a small amount will make it easier to remove later.

Attach the other end of each bungee cord to one of the Texsolv cords under the loom by passing it over the breast beam and putting the hook into a hole on the cord. Using the elastic of the bungee cord and the different loops of the Texsolv, tension the warp so that the tension rod is parallel to the breast beam, and the tension is appropriate for weaving.

Continue weaving. Once the fell is again no longer straight or parallel to the breast beam, open the shed and insert the second leapfrogging tension rod. Move the bungee cords from the first tension rod to the second and remove the first rod. Adjust the warp tension as needed by either moving the hooks on the bungee cords under the loom, or by advancing warp sections at the back of the loom.

As a practical matter, you should plan how often to leapfrog the tension rods and weave the same number of picks before leapfrogging the rods. That number will be dependent on the shape you are weaving. If your warp is wide, the tension rod may bend in the middle as you pull the tension tight. To solve this, you can either reposition the bungee cord hooks more to the center of the warp, or you can use more than two bungee and Texsolv cord sets. The

anchor rod or cord under the loom will allow any number to be used.

The entire weaving process using leapfrogging rods is explained in more detail in chapter 4.

THE CLOTH TRAP

The cloth trap is a little more complex than the leapfrogging rods, but it's used to prevent the gap left in the cloth from the rod. Since metal rods can bend when under tension, it can be difficult to get a straight fell when using leapfrogging rods. The cloth trap uses a metal bar instead of a rod to provide tension at the fell, since a flat metal bar will not bend under tension, and the metal bar is not left in place during weaving.

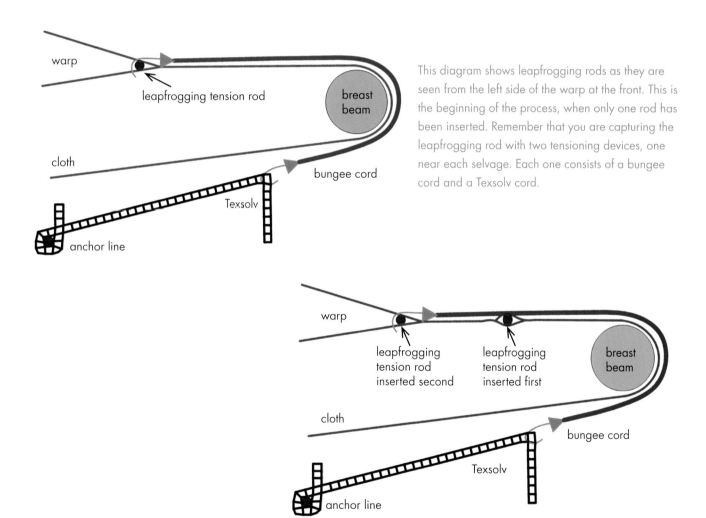

This diagram shows leapfrogging rods as they are seen from the left side of the warp at the front. This is the beginning of the process, when only one rod has been inserted. Remember that you are capturing the leapfrogging rod with two tensioning devices, one near each selvage. Each one consists of a bungee cord and a Texsolv cord.

In this diagram, a second rod has been inserted into the warp. Once this second rod is tensioned, the first rod is pulled out.

A cloth trap consists of the following pieces:

The cloth trap itself: The cloth trap consists of two metal bars. One has a convex bottom with a padded surface facing up. The other is a concave top with a series of tacks facing down. The tacks are attached as described in appendix 1. Woven cloth is placed between the bottom and the top, and when the trap is closed, the cloth is trapped.

Cinches: Four loops of Texsolv, four golf tees, and a bit of masking tape are used to create four tension loops, or cinches. Each tension loop is set up in such a way as to allow it to be pulled tight and held with the golf tee. Two of the cinches are used to close the cloth trap, and two are used to hold the cloth trap in position in relation to the breast beam.

A tension bar: This is an aluminum bar that is ¾ inch (about 2 centimeters) wide, ⅛ inch (⅓ centimeter) thick, and the length of your loom's weaving width. It can be purchased at most hardware stores and cut to length with a hacksaw. The tension bar takes the place of the tension rod used in the leapfrogging-rods technique, but it's tensioned in a slightly different way.

Tension bar tensioning device: The tension bar holds the cloth tension while the cloth trap is being positioned or repositioned, so it must have a tensioning device of its own in order to do that. Two tensioning devices are required: one for each end of the tension bar. Each device consists of a loop of fine but strong nylon cord, a small bungee cord, a piece of Texsolv, and an anchor point under the cloth beam under the loom.

Quilt or T pins: In addition to tensioning the cloth in the lengthwise direction, the cloth trap also provides selvage-to-selvage tension much like a weaving temple. The bottom of the cloth trap is padded, so that the cloth can be pinned to it with quilt pins or T pins, which is done before the top piece of the cloth trap is situated and closed. The ends of the pins are positioned between the cloth trap and the breast beam so that they can be left in place during weaving. If you prefer, you can use a weaving temple between the cloth trap and the breast beam, but you will have to reposition the cloth trap more often, and you won't be able to place the temple at the fell since the cloth trap will be in the way.

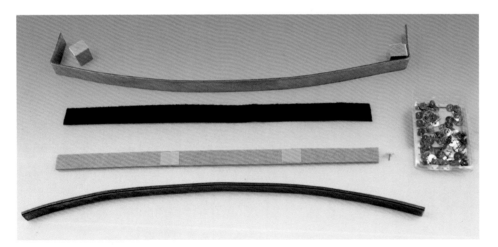

The parts required to construct a cloth trap, without the cinches. Also not shown are the fine nylon cords used to tie the tack strip to the top of the cloth trap. See appendix 1 for detailed parts and construction information.

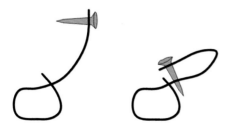

The cloth trap cinches. One pair is used to close the cloth trap, and another pair is used to tension it with respect to the cloth beam. One end of Texsolv is passed through the last hole of the other end to make a loop. The golf tee is inserted as shown and kept in place with a piece of masking tape (not shown). Once the loop is tightened, the golf tee can be inserted into a hole of the Texsolv, creating tension and preventing the loop from opening, as shown on the right.

To tension the cloth, insert the tension bar into an open shed. Loop the fine nylon cord around the tension bar and the bottom of the cloth trap. Attach it to the near end of the bungee cord with a lark's-head knot. It works better to use a lark's-head knot rather than using the hook on the bungee cord because the lark's-head knot won't fall off while you are repositioning the cloth trap.

Attach two pieces of Texsolv to the anchor point under the loom, one on each side of your warp. Adjust the tension at each side of the warp by hooking the far end of each bungee cord into the appropriate hole in the anchored piece of Texsolv.

When you are repositioning the cloth trap and pinning the cloth to the bottom of the trap, you will be pushing down on it, which requires that it be supported by your loom. The way the cloth trap is supported will be different for each loom and will depend on how your loom is constructed. In some cases, you will need to add parts to your loom.

Having to make changes to your loom to support a cloth trap is a little more work at the beginning, but it's quite possible to use a cloth trap on any type of loom. Appendix 1 contains detailed information about constructing a cloth trap and using it with several types of looms, including table looms.

Other Weaving Devices

Here are a few small, simple tools that are easy to construct and make 3-D weaving a little easier.

KNITTING-MACHINE WEIGHTS

Knitting-machine weights are little weights with hooks that are hung onto knitted fabric as it comes off a knitting machine. These weights are inexpensive and come in a variety of widths. Sometimes it's necessary to drill holes in the handles of the weights in order to attach cords to them. The weights themselves are not useful for our purposes here, but the spaced-out bent hooks that hang on the fabric are handy in some limited cases. Another knitting machine tool called a cast on comb is a different, but wider, tool with spaced-out bent hooks. The use of these tools is described in chapter 9.

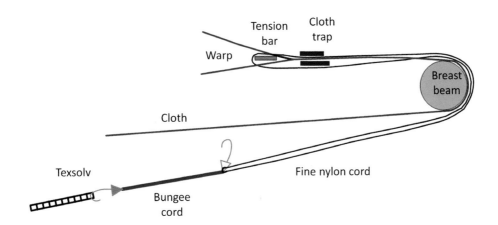

Looking at the warp from the left side, this diagram shows the relative positions of the warp, the tension mechanism, and the cloth trap. It does not show the cinches used to close the cloth trap or tension it with respect to the cloth beam. Note that the fine nylon cord that provides tension for the tension bar also goes around the bottom of the cloth trap.

If you are weaving a dense area at the selvage, you need an additional option to provide tension along the width of your cloth, to prevent pull-in. A weaving temple won't work because the teeth of the temple will damage the dense area. If you are using a cloth trap you could use quilt pins or T pins to help tension the cloth, but they could also deform the dense area. A mitten clip temple with an *S hook* attached is a good solution.

For those who aren't familiar with mitten clips, they are the clips that mothers use to ensure that their children don't lose their mittens in the winter. One clip is attached to the mitten and the other clip is attached to the sleeve of the child's coat.

A mitten clip temple is a pair of devices, one for each selvage of the cloth being woven. Each device requires a water jug for a weight, a mitten clip, a piece of ribbon or braid (15–18 inches or 40–50 centimeters) to attach the mitten clip to the jug, and an S hook. In one end of the ribbon, sew a loop large enough to allow the mitten clip to pass through it. Sew the other end of the ribbon to the mitten clip through the metal loop in the clip. Put one end of the S hook through the metal loop on the mitten clip and tighten it with a pair of pliers so that it cannot come off. Attach the mitten clip to the jug weight by passing the mitten clip and S hook through the sewn loop and the jug handle.

Chapter 5 explains how to weave a dense area. For now, you just need to know that after a dense area is woven at a selvage, there will be a loop that captures all the weft picks that are woven into the dense area. The S hook can catch that loop and provide tension to the cloth to resist pull-in. If a dense area is at the selvage, the S hook is used to provide tension; if there is an area of normal weaving at the selvage, the mitten clip is attached directly to the cloth.

Whether or not you are doing 3-D loom weaving, a mitten clip temple makes a very portable temple that you can take to weaving classes. If you would rather not travel with empty water jugs, you can carry bungee cords instead and use elastic rather than weight to provide the tension. To do this, catch the loop in the ribbon with one end of the bungee cord and attach the other end to an appropriate spot on the loom.

A mitten clip temple, attached to a water jug

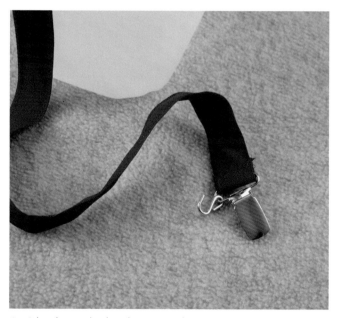

An S hook attached to the mitten clip

THIMBLE FOR WEAVING WITH COPPER WIRE

Chapter 7 discusses weaving with wire. When you weave with wire in the weft, it's necessary to carefully control the cloth width so that it is consistent. This requires that the wire bend sharply at the selvage, before it travels to the other side of the cloth.

The easiest way to do this is to bend the wire around a weaving needle before each pick; however, that requires handling a shuttle and a needle and juggling them between your left and right hands. When I do this, I inevitably drop the needle and waste time under the loom looking for it. I've tried attaching a magnet to the front of my loom so that I can park the needle until it's needed, but I still drop it from time to time.

The solution I finally developed is to attach a short, blunt weaving needle to each index finger. While weaving I hold my index fingers up and out of the way and use the rest of my fingers and my thumbs to do the weaving. To make the needles easy to put on and take off, I use two rubber thimbles. The needles are attached to the thimbles by punching two small holes in each thimble and threading the needle through these holes. The needles are always ready to be used and can be easily put on and taken off.

Caution: if you do this, remember that you are wearing needles and shouldn't scratch your face or adjust your glasses!

TEXSOLV-THREADING TOOL

The great advantage of Texsolv over ordinary cord is its series of holes, each of which can be used as an attachment point. It's very common to use Texsolv by pushing one end of the cord through one of these holes; however, that can be difficult to do. There is a commercial tool available to make it easier. The tool is a sharply bent piece of metal wire attached to a handle. To use it, the metal loop is pushed through one of the loops, an end of Texsolv is threaded through the metal loop, and the Texsolv is pulled through the hole. This tool works just like the needle-threading tools commonly used for hand sewing, but it's larger in scale.

To make your own tool, you need only a piece of wire, something to use as a handle, and some glue or tape to attach the wire to the handle. To make my tool, I drilled a hole lengthwise into a piece of wooden dowel. I folded the wire in half, inserted the ends into the hole, bent the wires back up against the sides of the handle for a short distance, and wrapped electrical tape over the wire ends. Because I kept losing it, I also wrapped red tape around the handle so that it would be easier to find.

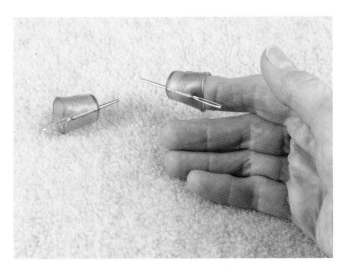

Rubber thimbles with weaving needles used to weave with a wire weft

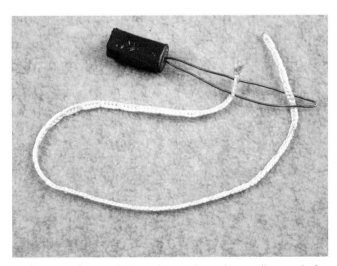

My homemade Texsolv threading tool, ready to pull an end of the cord through one of the holes

MODIFIED CLOTHESPINS

The problem with ordinary clothespins is that they don't grip a single thread easily without sliding off. To correct this, I use the type of foam rubber that is commonly sold in rolls and used for door and window insulation. It has a sticky backing that is exposed when a plastic-covered strip of paper is removed. I insert this foam rubber into the clamp part of the clothespin so that the sticky side is attached to the wood of the clothespin. Depending on the size of the clothespins and the thickness of the rubber foam on hand, I may use one or two pieces of foam on each clothespin.

These simple clothespins are handy for a variety of tasks. I used them as a third hand to hold on to a thread that is threatening to slip through a reed, for example. Or, I use them to mark a broken warp thread until I can walk around the back of the loom to repair it. When I thread the loom or sley the reed, I use them to temporarily hang on to a group of threads until I can tie a slipknot in them.

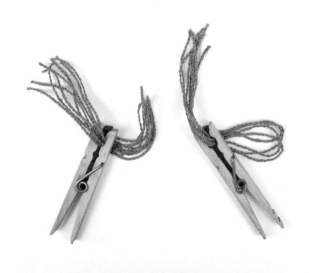

These clothespins have been modified to easily grab a single thread or small groups of threads.

Now that you understand the new terms and the new tools needed to weave 3-D shapes on a hand loom, and have a general understanding of my techniques, we are finally ready to talk about the weaving processes in detail. We will start with the easiest process: weaving expanded areas.

4

Weaving
Expanded Areas

An expanded area is an area of the warp that is woven with many extra weft picks, causing that area to rise out of the surface of the cloth. The expanded area is threaded on its own set of shafts so that the cloth can be advanced at a more rapid rate than the normal areas around it. During weaving, the expanded area can be tensioned with T pins or quilting pins, leapfrogging rods, or a cloth trap. Each of these options is explained in detail.

I prefer to weave small expanded areas in the middle of areas of normal weaving, but you can weave expanded areas of any size, depending on the effect that you are trying to achieve. You will need to decide how your expanded areas will be woven before you wind the warp, so that you can create a section of warp threads that is long enough to accommodate the extra length required. See chapter 8 for a discussion of the design considerations.

The weaving in the following sections shows the creation of sleeves for a jacket. I planned each sleeve to have five expanded areas separated by normal areas of weaving. These expanded areas start on the outer upper arm of the jacket sleeves. For each sleeve, my plan requires weaving several inches of fabric for the sleeve cap, prior to weaving the first expanded area.

Because the expanded and normal areas are on their own sets of shafts, they can be raised independently. It is easy to see where the normal-area shuttles will exit the shed.

Before weaving an expanded area, several inches of normal weaving are completed using one shuttle. A few picks before starting the expanded area, a second shuttle is added so that there is a normal-area shuttle at each side of my planned expanded area. Because this fabric will be used for a sewing project, the selvages are not important and will either be cut off or disappear into a seam. This means that a new shuttle can be started at the selvage, and the weft tails can be left to hang out rather than being woven into the fabric.

On the pick prior to starting an expanded area, each normal-area shuttle should be at a different selvage. For the first pick of the expanded area, raise only the normal-area shafts and weave both shuttles toward the expanded area, letting them exit the warp at the edge of the expanded area.

Add a third shuttle for the expanded area. For the next several picks, only the expanded area is woven. When the expanded-area shuttle is on the left, the weft is clasped with the weft yarn on the left normal-area shuttle. When the expanded-area shuttle is on the right, the weft is clasped with the normal-area shuttle on that side.

The weft picks are clasped when the two yarns are wrapped around each other before weaving continues.

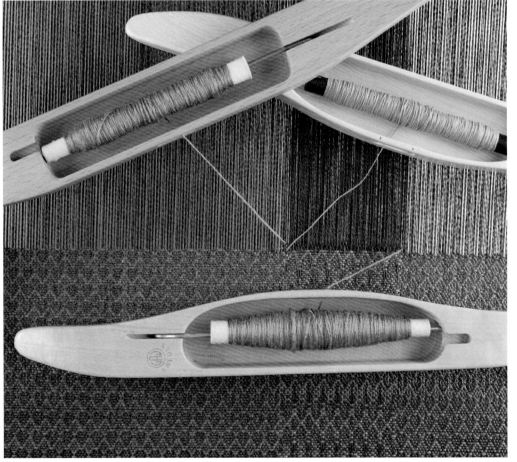

All the shuttles are in place to start weaving an expanded area. The normal-area shuttles contain blue yarn, and the expanded-area shuttle contains pink yarn. The pink yarn will be clasped on each side of the expanded area with the blue yarn.

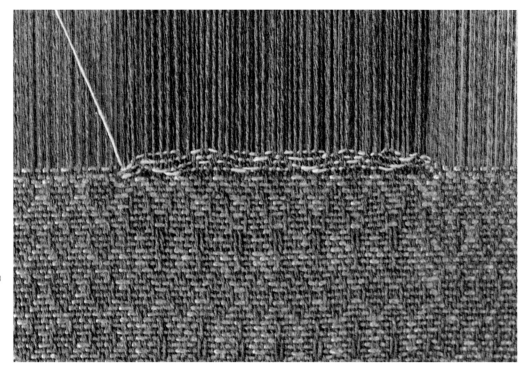

In this example, four expanded-area picks were woven for every two normal-area picks, using both normal-area shuttles. Even after only four picks, you can see the fell starting to bulge out in the expanded area.

The number of expanded-area picks that are woven is a design decision. After weaving four to eight picks in the expanded area, weave two picks in the normal areas on each side of the expanded area. This will return the normal-area shuttles back to the edges of the expanded area.

Eventually it will become difficult to weave the normal area because the expanded area will prevent the normal area from being beaten properly. Or, if the normal area is beaten with enough force, the expanded area will be too tightly beaten. When that point is reached, it's time to retension the warp.

The goal of retensioning the warp is to make the fell into a straight line again. If your weaving consists of just one expanded area somewhere in the middle of the warp, any approach will work. But if you have a series of expanded areas spread across the warp width, the best option is to use a cloth trap. Leapfrogging rods can be used with multiple expanded areas if you don't mind the gaps in your finished weaving that are created by the rods.

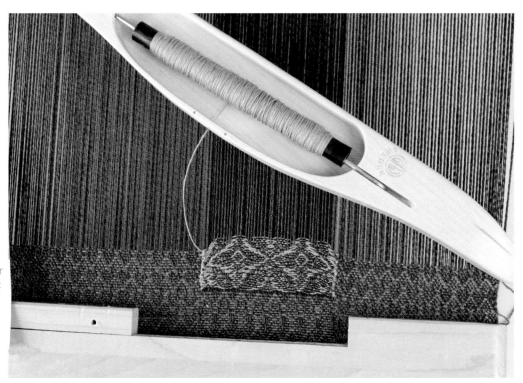

Notice that the fell is no longer a straight line from one side of the warp to the other. At this point, weaving becomes difficult, and it's time to retension the warp.

Cloth-Tensioning Options

RETENSIONING THE CLOTH WITH PINS

Retensioning with T pins or quilting pins is the easiest method to use if there is just one expanded area in the weaving width. It can be used with multiple expanded areas, but it's necessary to pin each area separately, and that can make it tedious to get the tension and the fell to be the same across the entire weaving width.

Release tension on the expanded-area warp, open the shed along the entire warp width, and insert a tension bar. Use a bar because it provides a straight fell, and since we are using pins to take up the excess fabric, the bar can be removed before weaving proceeds.

After the tension bar is inserted, it must be tensioned. Note that the tension bar has a hole drilled through it at each end. Since a cloth trap isn't being used, the hook at one end of a bungee cord can be inserted into this hole. The bungee cord hook is easier to insert into the hole in the tension bar if it has been opened up slightly with a set of pliers.

One end of a piece of Texsolv is attached to an anchor point under the loom. The hook on the end of the bungee cord not attached to the tension bar is inserted into the appropriate hole in the Texsolv. This provides the needed tension for the tension bar. This tensioning mechanism is used on each side of the warp.

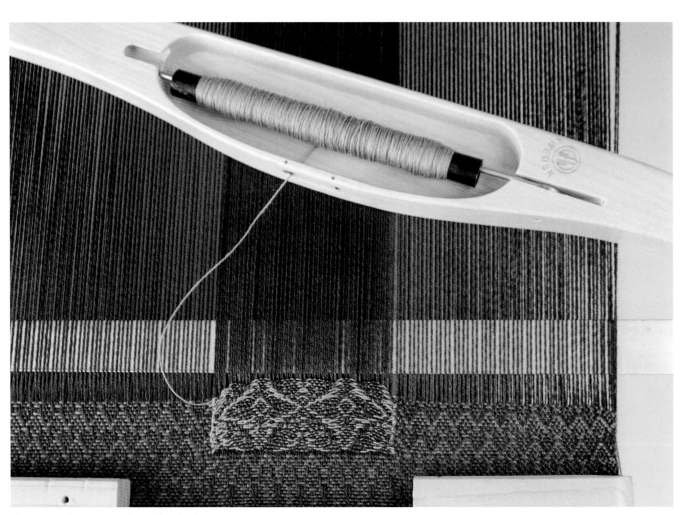

The tension bar, inserted into the shed

One end of a bungee cord is hooked into the hole at the end of the tension bar.

The other end of a bungee cord is attached to a piece of Texsolv under the front of the loom.

The Texsolv is anchored to a rod beam or some other anchor point under the loom.

With the tension bar in place, the bulge in the expanded area can be folded over itself and pinned down. With one hand, reach through the warp in front of the tension bar to the underside of the bulge, while pinning it with the other hand. Adjust the tension across the warp from the back of the loom. The tension on the normal areas and the expanded area should be approximately the same.

Now that the fell is straight once more, the tension bar can be removed from the shed and weaving can continue.

You may have to retension the warp area several times in this way for a single expanded area. Leave the pins in place until you are ready to remove the warp from the loom. Tension will be lessened in the expanded area, making weaving difficult if you remove the pins. Once the expanded area has been wound onto the cloth beam, the tension is held and the tension problems may go away, unless the expanded areas add too much bulk to the cloth beam.

If you would rather not leave the pins in place, you can hand-sew folds into the expanded area with a contrasting color of thread and remove the thread after the warp is off the loom.

The expanded area is pinned down with T pins or quilting pins.

RETENSIONING THE CLOTH WITH LEAPFROGGING RODS

If you are weaving several expanded areas spaced across the warp, it can be tedious to use pins to tension each of them every time the tension needs to be adjusted. A tension rod can be used instead, but the rod must be left in place during weaving, and its placement will be visible in the finished cloth. As previously mentioned, the gap left by the rod can be turned into a feature by weaving a ribbon or other heavy decorative yarn in the shed that contains the rod.

To use tension rods, open the shed for the expanded

area and insert the first rod. The rod should pass through the open shed of the expanded area, or each expanded area, and lie on top of the normal areas of weaving.

Once the rod is in place, insert bungee cord hooks into the expanded area of the warp and use them to capture the rod. At least two bungee cords are used, one near each end of the expanded area of weaving. The hooks that capture the rod should be bent open a little to make their later removal easier. Always hook the rod at places inside the warp to keep the hooks from sliding off the rod.

The placement of the bungee cord hooks along the rod is important and will depend on the overall width of your warp. If your warp is wide and you hook the bungee cords too near the edges of the warp, the rod will bend outward. Move the hooks more to the center of the warp or use a third bungee cord to capture the rod in the middle. You may need to experiment to find a placement that lets the rod lie in a straight line.

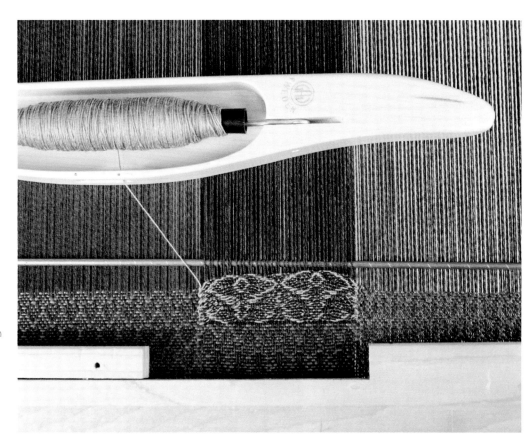

A tension rod used to tension an expanded area. The tension rod is inserted into just the shed of the expanded area, not the shed of the entire warp.

The other end of the bungee cord is hooked onto a piece of Texsolv that is attached to an anchor point under the loom. Weaving can continue once the tension on the expanded and normal areas has been adjusted to be approximately equal. When the expanded area grows to the point of making weaving difficult, a second tension rod is inserted. The bungee cord hooks are moved onto the second rod and tensioned, and the first rod can be removed. Please review the leapfrogging-rods diagrams in chapter 3.

After the last expanded area is woven, the last tension rod must be left in place until the warp is completed. Tension on the rod must be adjusted from time to time as weaving progresses. If there is a great deal of warp left to weave, the rod will eventually become too close to the Texsolv anchor point for it to provide the needed tension. The solution is to wrap a piece of ribbon or braid around the tension rod in at least two places and pin the ribbon to the warp in the direction of the cloth beam. This holds the tension rod in place until it can be captured by the cloth beam. Once the rod is enclosed by cloth on the cloth beam, the tension problems are usually resolved if the bulk of the expanded areas is not too great.

Leapfrogging rods are easy to use but create gaps that can be seen in the woven cloth, as has been discussed. The cloth trap eliminates these problems but is a little slower to use.

Note the placement of the bungee cord hooks on this narrow expanded area. The hooks must be placed in the weaving to capture the rod. If they are placed to the side of the expanded area, they will slide off. The bungee cords pass around the breast beam on top of the woven cloth, and to the anchored piece of Texsolv below.

RETENSIONING THE CLOTH WITH A CLOTH TRAP

Whenever the woven cloth is not a flat rectangle, as when weaving expanded areas or dense areas, the different amounts of bulk on different areas of the cloth beam can cause problems. Even an area of double weave that is not the entire warp width can cause tension problems. That is because the extra bulk in the double-weave area doesn't allow the rest of the warp to wind onto the cloth beam with the same tension.

The warp tension is easy enough to control since warp areas of different lengths can be tensioned with various devices such as a rod beam, a second warp beam, or warp weights. But tension must also be controlled on the cloth in order to weave. The cloth trap is the best solution for controlling cloth tension because it works in all situations and does not create a visible mark on the finished cloth.

The following description of the use of a cloth trap assumes that you understand the pieces of the cloth trap that are described in chapter 3. It also assumes that you have built one for your own use, including the cinches, and that your loom is able to support the cloth trap at each side. See

appendix 1 for detailed information on building the cloth trap or modifying your loom to work with it as necessary.

Once the expanded area has bulged out enough to make weaving difficult, it's time to install the cloth trap. Open the entire shed by using a tabby structure, or as close as you can get to tabby, and insert the tension bar as shown previously. Drop the shed and release tension on the entire warp.

Slide the bottom piece of the cloth trap under the woven cloth and support it at each side of the loom. The bottom piece curves upward along its length, and the soft pad sits under the cloth. You can also place the bottom of the cloth trap under the warp at the beginning of your weaving so you don't have to put it in place later. That is more efficient, but for some reason, I never remember to do it!

Tension the tension bar. At each end of the bar, place a loop of fine nylon cord, wrapping it around the tension bar and then around the bottom of the cloth trap.

These cords don't lie on top of the woven cloth but are near each selvage. Under the loom, each fine nylon loop is attached to one end of a small bungee cord with a lark's-head knot placed on the elastic just behind the hook. The hook at the other end of each bungee cord is inserted into one of the holes on a piece of Texsolv. The Texsolv pieces are anchored to a point under the loom.

For more tension on the warp, move the bungee cord hooks onto loops on the Texsolv that are closer to the anchor points under the loom. It will usually be necessary to release tension on the expanded area so that the tension bar can pull the expanded area into a straight line with the fell.

Move the bottom of the cloth trap to be parallel to the fell. Between ⅛ and ¼ inch (⅓–½ centimeter) of fabric in the normal area of weaving should be between the front edge of the padded metal bar and the fell, as it's now defined by the tension bar. The amount of distance you need will depend on how your reed approaches the fell. If the bottom of the cloth trap is too close, it can prevent your reed from beating directly on the fell.

If you find it necessary to use a mitten clip temple in order to put some tension on your cloth in the direction of the weft, attach the clips to each selvage now, before the next step.

The bulge of the expanded area must be secured to the bottom of the cloth trap before the top of the cloth trap can be placed into position. Use T pins or quilting pins to hold the expanded area flat against the bottom of the cloth trap and to pull the expanded cloth in the direction of the breast beam. While holding the fabric taut, push the pins through your fabric into the padding on the bottom of the cloth trap. Make sure that all the ends of the pins are between the cloth trap and the breast beam, so that they don't get in the way of the reed while you are weaving. These pins are left in place until the next time you need to retension the warp. Notice that the direction in which the pins are placed can help provide tensioning.

The tension bar is now under tension. Note that the fine nylon cord goes around both the tension bar and the bottom of the cloth trap and then passes over the breast beam next to the cloth selvage.

Whether or not you use mitten clip temples, you can also pin the cloth to the bottom of the cloth trap at each selvage if you wish. A weaving temple does not work well with a cloth trap because it would have to be placed between the cloth trap and the breast beam rather than close to the fell, as is normally done. The use of both a weaving temple and a cloth trap together would reduce the amount of weaving area available.

Place the top of the cloth trap on top of the pinned cloth so that the curved portion faces downward. The tacks will pierce the cloth and go into the padding on the bottom part of the cloth trap.

The expanded area has been pinned down to the bottom of the cloth trap before the top of the cloth trap is put into place.

In addition to the mechanism providing tension for the tension bar, there are two sets of cinches needed for the cloth trap. The first set is used to close the cloth trap, and the second set is used to position the cloth trap with respect to the breast beam. All three mechanisms consist of a set of two pieces, with one placed at the right of the woven cloth, and the other placed at the left. Unlike the bungee cords used for leapfrogging rods, none of these cords sit on top of the woven cloth; all are placed to one side or the other.

To close the cloth trap, one set of cinches is placed around the bottom and top of the trap at each end. The Texsolv is pulled tight and the golf tee is inserted into the hole that provides the most tension. It's often necessary to tighten one end, then the other, and then to adjust the first one again. Place the cinches as far away from the cloth as is practical, since this will give you the most leverage to tighten the cloth trap. It doesn't matter which set of cinches is closest to the woven cloth.

The cloth trap is installed close to the fell, but not so close that it interferes with the beater.

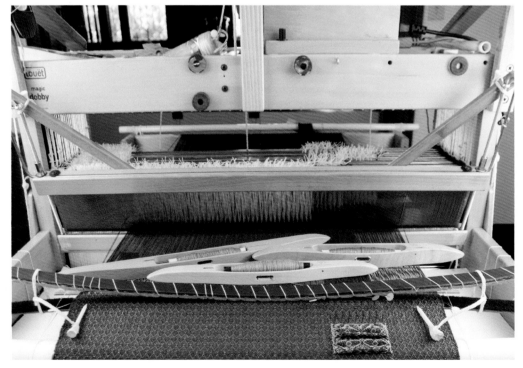

The top of the cloth trap is in position, before being closed.

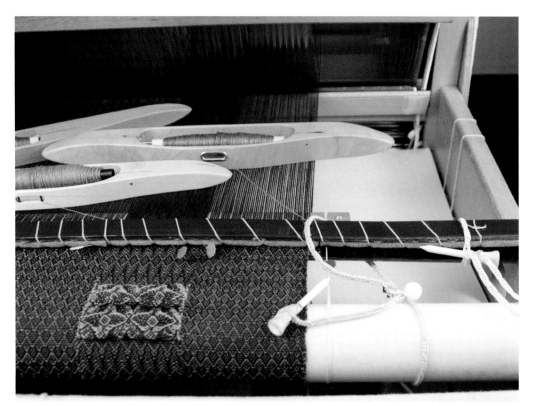

The closed cloth trap, as seen on the right side. The cloth trap is closed when the cinch around the bottom and the top of the trap is tightened and secured.

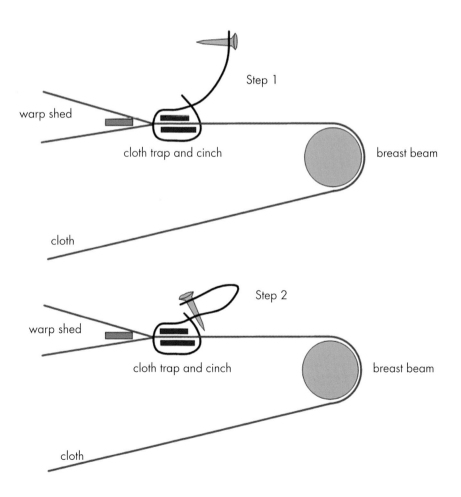

warp shed

Step 1

cloth trap and cinch

breast beam

cloth

warp shed

Step 2

cloth trap and cinch

breast beam

cloth

Looking at the warp from the left side, the cloth trap is closed, cinched and secured with a golf tee.

Next, the cloth trap must be tensioned with respect to the breast beam. Longer pieces of Texsolv should be used for these cinches than were used to close the cloth trap. For each cinch, one end is wrapped tightly around the breast beam, and the other end passes through one of the last holes in the other end of the Texsolv. An arrow peg or a golf tee secures it from loosening. If you use a golf tee, wrap a piece of masking tape around it in such a way as to prevent it from falling out or being removed accidentally.

The other end of the Texsolv passes over the closed cloth trap, around it from top to bottom, and is pulled up through the Texsolv hole closest to the breast beam. A golf tee, not an arrow peg, is passed through the last hole of the Texsolv and taped in place with masking tape. You can pull on this end to bring the cloth trap closer to the breast beam. Adjust one side or the other if the cloth trap is not parallel to the breast beam.

When the cloth trap is in the correct position, the golf tee taped to the end of the Texsolv is inserted into the appropriate hole in the Texsolv, securing the tension.

The tension on the normal and expanded areas should be approximately the same and appropriate for weaving. If not, adjust the tension at the back of the loom.

After the cloth trap has been tensioned with respect to the breast beam, the tension bar can be removed and weaving can proceed.

Pull the tension bar out. Because the tension bar was held in place by a fine nylon cord attached to an elastic bungee cord, the nylon cord will spring back toward the cloth trap to wait for the next time the expanded-area warp must be advanced.

Continue weaving as before. Now that the cloth trap and all the related tension devices are in place, the process is less complicated.

When you need to retension or advance the warp again, open a tabby shed, insert the tension bar, drop the shed, and release the tension from the back of the loom. Using a medium-sized crochet hook, grab the fine nylon tension cords in turn and pull each one around one end of the tension bar on that side. You can use your hands to pull the nylon cord onto the tension bar, but using a crochet hook will be much easier on your fingers. Adjust the tension on the tension bar as before.

Pull out all the golf tees on all four of the cinches: the ones holding the cloth trap closed and the ones holding the cloth trap parallel to the breast beam. The cinches that hold the top of the cloth trap closed can be slid off to the sides, releasing the top of the cloth trap. Carefully lift the top of the cloth trap off the cloth and roll it toward the breast beam. If the cinches that hold the cloth trap parallel to the breast beam are long enough, you will be able to move the top of the cloth trap out of the way without removing the cinches from the cloth trap.

Remove the pins holding the cloth onto the bottom of the cloth trap. Reposition and pin the cloth as before, close the cloth trap, tension everything, remove the tension bar, and continue weaving.

From this point on, the process is the same. Once you have completed weaving the expanded areas that you planned, you will probably need to continue using the cloth trap to tension the cloth until the weaving is completed. The extra bulk of the expanded areas will build up on the cloth beam and prevent correct tensioning in the normal areas of weaving. Once you are weaving just normal areas and are no longer weaving expanded areas, you will not need to retension the cloth as often, and weaving will be faster.

Expanded areas of weaving require a longer warp than do normal areas. The amount of extra length required depends on how many expanded areas you are weaving and the number of picks in an expanded area. Plan your warp accordingly.

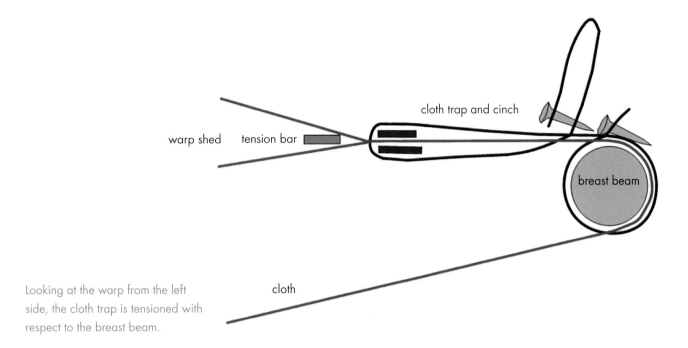

cloth trap and cinch

warp shed   tension bar

breast beam

Looking at the warp from the left side, the cloth trap is tensioned with respect to the breast beam.

cloth

Once the cloth is off the loom, another consideration is apparent. The expanded areas cause bulges, and those bulges can cause the weft threads in the normal areas woven before and after the expanded areas to deflect; that is, to travel in lines that are not straight.

Dealing with Deflected Weft Threads

After the cloth is off the loom, there are several ways to deal with the deflection of weft threads caused by weaving an expanded area. See appendix 2 for more information.

To prevent these deflected weft threads while you are weaving, consider setting up the expanded areas as a double weave. If the top layer is an expanded area and the bottom layer is an area of normal weaving, the bottom layer will prevent the expanded area from deflecting the normal areas woven before and after.

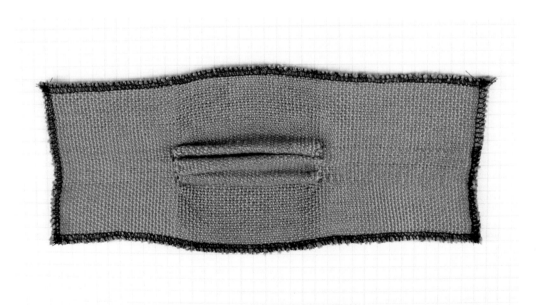

This small sample shows how weft threads can be deflected by an expanded area.

Double weave threading: For those who are less familiar with it, double weave requires that the threads from two or more layers be threaded alternately. Assuming a tabby structure, double weave can be woven on as few as four shafts. Double weave is typically woven across the entire warp width. Using it with an expanded area means that the double-weave portion and the expanded-area portion are the same width, and that there are normal areas of weaving to the right and the left.

The different double-weave warp layers cannot rest directly on top of each other because they are usually advanced at different rates. For that reason, the layers must be separated from each other at the back beam. Appendix 1 explains how to construct a simple device to separate these layers, and how to add a second back beam to your loom.

EXPANDED AREAS WITH DOUBLE WEAVE

Double weave presents other design possibilities if different-colored warp threads are used for the two layers. Double weave allows different-colored warp threads to rise out of the surface of the cloth, be woven as an expanded-area layer, and then drop under the cloth again until the next expanded area.

The expanded areas that we have already discussed are clasped on each side by the weft threads of an adjacent normal area of weaving. But if there is a double layer under the expanded area, there is no reason to clasp the expanded area on both sides. With a bottom layer holding things in place, the expanded area can be clasped on only one side, creating a sort of side-facing pocket. Or it can be clasped on neither side, creating a band that rises out of the surface of the cloth.

Before an expanded area with double weave can be woven, a small section of the expanded area must be woven underneath the rest of the warp. Otherwise, it has nothing to anchor it in place when it rises up through the warp. This is simple if you have enough shafts for at least three sets: the normal areas right and left, the expanded area, and the bottom layer of the double weave under the expanded area.

Threading for Double Weave Area
Sett Will Be Double - Tabby Structure

								4			4			4			4									
									3			3			3			3							
2		2		2		2		2		2		2		2		2		2		2		2		2
	1		1		1		1		1		1		1		1		1		1		1		1

Threading for Double Weave Area
Sett Will Be Double - Twill Structure

							6					6									
					5			5			5			5						
							4						4						
	3			3			3					3			3			3	
2		2		2		2		2		2		2		2		2		2	
		1			1					1				1			1			1

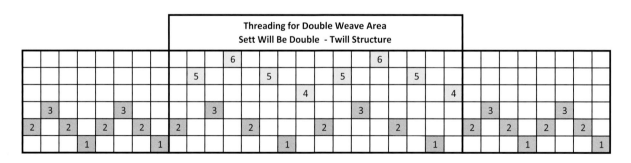

Normal area of weaving
Expanded area of weaving

Double-weave threading: notice how the expanded-area threads in yellow are alternated with the bottom layer of the double weave in blue. The sett for the double-weave area is double that of the normal areas because of the two layers.

It is important to understand how to weave an anchor cloth because it gives you a way to weave expanded areas separated by normal areas. The expanded-area layer and the layer under it can exchange places and can be woven with different structures or different color yarns. Once an expanded area is complete, the bottom layer is moved to the top. The expanded area is woven below it and then raised to the top again when needed for the next expanded layer.

The anchor cloth is woven *using the expanded-area shafts*, but woven as the *bottom double-weave layer*. While the anchor cloth is being woven, none of the normal areas next to it are woven. To weave the anchor cloth, weave the needed number of picks by using the expanded-area shafts. The entire non-expanded-area weave layer must be lifted on every pick to move it out of the way while you weave the anchor cloth. The expanded area will become an independent piece of cloth with its own selvages, underneath the rest of the warp.

Release the tension on the expanded area enough to allow the reed to push the entire bottom anchor cloth, which was just woven, all the way to the fell. Weave the normal area of the warp, including the non-expanded-area layer of the double weave, for the same number of picks.

Be careful! As you weave, be careful not to catch threads from the layer not being woven. While you are weaving the expanded area as an anchor cloth, you are unlikely to catch threads of the layer floating above, since it's under tension and lifted for every pick. But while you are weaving the normal area together with the non-expanded-area layer of the double weave, the expanded-area layer floats under the warp at a very slack tension. This is when problems occur. To prevent the unwoven warp threads from getting caught in the top layer, wrap a cord around the previously woven anchor cloth and attach a small weight.

My process might sound complex, but I find it easier and faster to weave the layers independently. This method makes it easier to avoid catching the wrong threads in a pick, and makes it easier to discover when it does happen. The alternative is to use alternating picks and multiple shuttles to weave the layers. Do it whichever way works best for you.

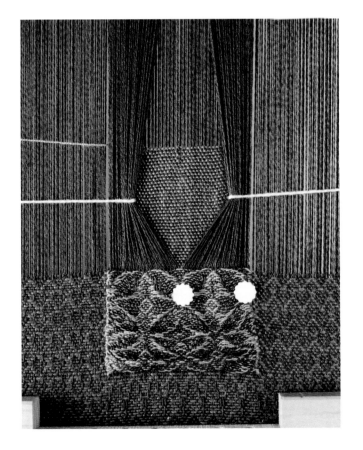

An expanded area was woven and pinned into place. The expanded-area layer and the bottom layer exchanged places so that the expanded-area layer could be woven as *anchor cloth* underneath the rest of the warp (the strings pull the top layer apart so that you can see the layer woven underneath). The next step is to release tension on the anchor cloth enough that the whole warp width can be woven normally for the same distance. After the layers exchange positions again, another expanded area will be woven.

After the normal area of cloth is woven, retension the expanded-area warp so that the fell for the anchor cloth and the fell for the normal area line up.

It's more difficult to weave the expanded-area anchor cloth if you are limited to two sets of shafts. That is because you will have to raise all the normal-area shafts on every pick and reach under the loom to weave the anchor. If your warp is very wide, this will be especially difficult. To make it easier, wrap a length of weft yarn onto a small piece of cardboard and use that for a shuttle until the anchor cloth is woven. This will be easier because you can reach through the warp to pass the small amount of yarn back and forth as you weave. Again, be careful not to catch threads from the layer not being woven.

Once the anchor cloth is woven, you are ready to use the expanded-area warp to weave a raised band, an expanded area clasped on one side, or one clasped on two sides.

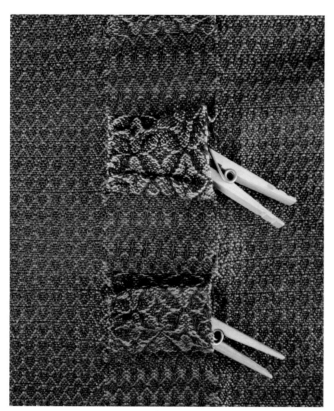

An example of Option 2 (see page 58): Expanded areas clasped on one side to create little side-facing pockets. The clothespins show the scale and the pocket openings.

The diagrams: There are two types of diagrams that I use to help explain how to manage the different shuttles and weave an expanded area with double weave.

The expanded area and the layer under it will each be threaded on different sets of shafts, and each layer will have its own tension control. The same weaving structure does not have to be used on both layers, but the repeats should be multiples of each other.

Planning the warp: The first diagram is a table that explains how to plan how the sets of shafts are managed and which shaft sets are woven during each pick. A set of shafts is an area of threading that can be tabby or some other structure such as twill. The number of shafts in a set will depend on how many shafts you have available on your loom and the weaving structure that you use.

The expanded area is threaded as a layer over an area of normal weaving, but the layers are shown beside each other because that is how it will be shown in the *treadling* area of your weaving draft.

For simplicity, these diagrams show only four expanded-area picks for every two picks in the rest of the warp. The number you use will depend on the effect you are trying to achieve.

The weft pick diagram: The second diagram is a weft pick diagram that helps you understand how to weave with the multiple shuttles that are required. All pick diagrams start at the bottom because that more closely matches what you are doing while weaving. Each pick of a single woven *cycle* is numbered from bottom to top, and colors are used to indicate which shuttle is being used. A cycle is complete when a given shuttle starts from one selvage and returns to it. A cycle is two picks if you are weaving normally and using one shuttle, but it is eight picks if you are weaving a double-weave expanded layer that is clasped at both sides, requiring three shuttles. This assumes that twice as many expanded-area picks are woven as normal-area picks.

These diagrams don't represent the only way to weave double-weave layers, or the only order in which to pass the shuttles. If you find a way that is more convenient for you, by all means use it!

DOUBLE-WEAVE OPTION 1: WEAVING A RAISED BAND

A band that rises out of the surface of the cloth and is not clasped on either side is the easiest option to weave. This requires two shuttles, that the double-weave layers are on different sets of shafts, and that each layer of the double weave is tensioned on its own mechanism. The normal areas to the right and left of the expanded area can be on the same or different sets of shafts, while the expanded-area layer and the bottom layer of double weave are each on their own set of shafts.

If only a limited number of shafts are available, the right normal area, the bottom layer of the double weave, and the left normal area can all be on the same set of shafts.

Weaving an expanded area that is not clasped on either side requires two shuttles. One shuttle weaves the normal areas and the bottom layer of the double weave. The other shuttle is used to weave the expanded area. At the end of the second pick, the normal-area shuttle comes to rest at one selvage, and the desired number of raised-band picks can be woven.

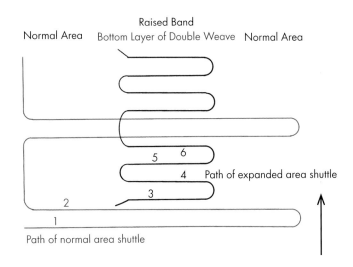

Weaving a raised band: the weft pick diagram

Raised Band and Double Weave			
Normal Area - Left	**Expanded Area**	**Double Weave Bottom Layer**	**Normal Area - Right**
Shaft group 1	**Shaft group 2**	**Shaft group 3**	**Shaft group 1 or 4**
Pick:			
6		<-------------------Weave		
5		Weave------------------>		
4		<-------------------Weave		
3		Weave------------------>		
2	<-------------------Weave	Raise All Shafts	<-------------------Weave	<-------------------Weave
1	Weave------------------>	Raise All Shafts	Weave------------------>	Weave------------------>

(Clasped picks)

Weaving a raised band: The plan for which sections of warp belong on which shafts, and which shafts are raised for each pick. There are no clasped weft threads when a raised band is woven.

DOUBLE-WEAVE OPTION 2: WEAVING AN EXPANDED AREA CLASPED ON ONE SIDE

Weaving an expanded area with double weave and clasped on only one side results in little side-facing pockets. In this case I had all the pockets open in the same direction, but it would be just as easy to alternate them.

Weaving an expanded area that is clasped on one side requires two shuttles. One shuttle weaves the normal areas and the bottom layer of the double weave. The other shuttle is used to weave the expanded area. At the end of the second pick, the normal-area shuttle comes to rest at the edge of the expanded area. This is where the normal-area weft thread is to be clasped with the weft thread from the expanded-area shuttle.

Once the normal-area shuttle is positioned at the correct edge of the expanded area, any even number of expanded-area picks can be woven. The last expanded-area pick should end at the same side on which it started. The normal-area shuttle weaves one final pick to end at the selvage where it started, to complete the cycle.

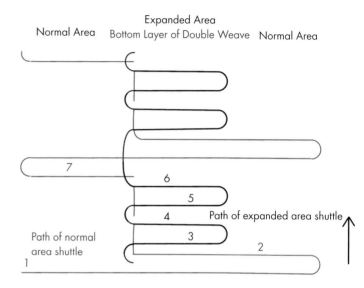

Weaving an expanded area clasped on one side: the weft pick diagram

	Expanded Area and Double Weave Clasped at One Side			
	Normal Area - Left	**Expanded Area**	**Double Weave Bottom Layer**	**Normal Area - Right**
	Shaft group 1	**Shaft group 2**	**Shaft group 3**	**Shaft group 1 or 4**
Pick:				
7	<-------------------Weave			
6		<-------------------Weave		
5		Weave------------------->		
4		<-------------------Weave		
3		Weave------------------->		
2		Raise all Shafts	<-------------------Weave	<-------------------Weave
1	Weave------------------->	Raise all Shafts	Weave------------------->	Weave------------------->

(Clasped picks)

Weaving an expanded area clasped on one side: the plan for which sections of warp belong on which shafts, and which shafts are raised for each pick

DOUBLE-WEAVE OPTION 3: WEAVING AN EXPANDED AREA CLASPED ON TWO SIDES

Weaving an expanded area that is clasped on both sides requires three shuttles. One shuttle weaves the normal area on the left and the bottom layer of the double weave. A second shuttle weaves the normal area on the right. The third shuttle weaves the expanded area.

During the first pick, the right shuttle weaves the right normal area, coming to rest at the right edge of the expanded area. At the end of the second pick, the left shuttle comes to rest at the right side of the expanded area, where it's clasped with the thread from the first shuttle. At the end of the third pick, the left normal-area shuttle comes to rest at the left edge of the expanded area. The expanded area can now be woven and clasped at both sides because there is a normal-area shuttle positioned both at the right and left of the expanded area.

Once the desired number of expanded-area picks has been woven and clasped, both normal-area shuttles travel back to where they started at their respective selvages. It's not necessary to weave an even number of expanded-area picks, since the picks are clasped on both sides. The number of picks required in a cycle will vary if you use a different ratio of expanded-area and normal-area picks.

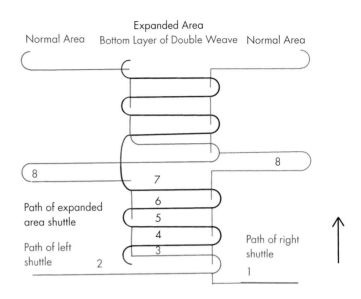

Weaving an expanded area clasped on both sides: the weft pick diagram

Expanded Area and Double Weave Clasped on Both Sides				
	Normal Area - Left	**Expanded Area**	**Double Weave Bottom Layer**	**Normal Area - Right**
	Shaft group 1	**Shaft group 2**	**Shaft group 3**	**Shaft group 1 or 4**
Pick:				
8 & 8	<------------------Weave			Weave------------------>
7		<------------------Weave		
6		Weave------------------>		
5		<------------------Weave		
4		Weave------------------>		
3		Raise All Shafts	<------------------Weave	
2	Weave------------------>	Raise All Shafts	Weave------------------>	
1				<------------------Weave

(Clasped picks)

Weaving an expanded area clasped on both sides: the plan for which sections of warp belong on which shafts, and which shafts are raised for each pick

Once the expanded area has been woven, the double-weave layers change positions. The expanded-area layer drops under the warp, and the bottom layer rises up to be woven with the adjacent normal areas. The expanded area must again be anchored using the process previously explained. If additional expanded areas are planned, that section of the warp must be woven under the rest of the warp until it's ready again to rise to the surface.

The cloth-tensioning options that were explained at the beginning of this chapter are the same techniques that are used when weaving expanded areas with double weave.

Because the different sections of the warp are each on their own sets of shafts and tensioned independently, it's possible to weave different sets of shafts in turn. After a section of weaving is complete on one set of shafts, tension on it is released so that a different set of shafts can be woven. In this way, different sections of a warp can be woven in a leapfrog manner. This ability is useful for double weave only when the normal and expanded areas of weaving do not share selvages, as is the case when weaving an anchor cloth under the normal warp.

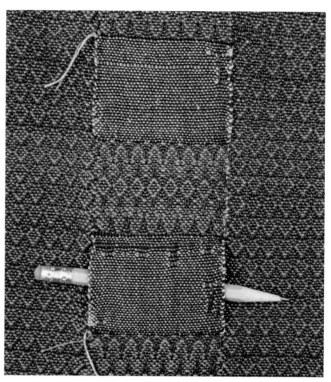

The underside: This is what the underside looks like after a series of expanded areas are woven. Because the underside of the fabric isn't going to be seen, I used tabby. Notice that the underside consists of a series of anchor cloth bands that are not attached on either side.

The top: This is an expanded area clasped at both sides and woven as double weave. Notice how much the expanded area rises up out of the surface of the cloth after being woven with just four picks for every two in the normal area.

Now that you understand how to weave expanded
areas, let's turn our attention to weaving dense areas.

The finished expanded-area jacket. The expanded areas on the
sleeves are clasped on both sides. The expanded areas that run
down the front of the jacket are open,
facing the buttons.

5 Weaving Dense Areas

A dense area is an area of the warp that is woven without changing the shed. Since the shed is not changed for as many as 20 to 60 picks, the dense-area warp threads can be pulled together tightly around the weft threads. The result is an area of warp that is densely packed, causing gathers to form in the adjacent normal areas of weaving.

As with weaving expanded areas, it's important to weave a header of normal weaving before weaving a dense area. Without a header, the dense-area warp threads cannot be pulled together to create a dense-area warp bundle. The size of this beginning header will depend on what you want to do with the finished cloth. If it is for a piece of clothing, you will need enough fabric to create a hem or to sew it onto another piece of cloth. If you are weaving a wall hanging, you may want less of a header. The minimum width of the header should be about an inch (2–3 centimeters), depending on how slippery a yarn you are using. Silk will require more picks than cotton, for example.

There is considerably more tension and stress on the warp when you are weaving a dense area than when you are weaving an expanded area. For that reason, you need to make sure that the warp yarn you use in the dense area is very strong. If you break a warp thread while pulling in a dense area, it will be difficult to repair, and the repair is likely to be visible on the finished cloth.

An example of a dense area woven at one selvage with gathers on only one side

For this sample, a single massive dense area was woven in the middle of the warp. Each selvage is one half of the circumference of the circle.

A warp can contain just one or several dense areas, but they must all follow the same five rules:

Rule 1: *The dense-area warp threads must be on a different set of shafts than the normal areas of warp.* Having the dense-area warp threads on different shafts allows for weaving the normal areas without changing the shed in the dense area. When there are multiple dense areas in a warp, they can all be threaded on the same set of shafts or on different sets of shafts. Threading them on different sets of shafts enables the different dense areas to be woven at different times, and for different numbers of picks. When all the dense areas are threaded on the same shafts, they must all be woven in the same way.

Rule 2: *The dense area has a sett twice that of the normal area, assuming that the same size of yarn is used in both.* If the sett is not dense enough, the underlying weft yarns will show through the dense areas. You may want to use a normal sett if the dense area is woven only for a short time and then reverts back to being an area of normal weaving. In this case the weft yarn will not show as much if the dense-area warp uses the same color of yarn as the weft. I prefer that the dense-area wefts not be visible through the dense-area warp, but that is a design preference.

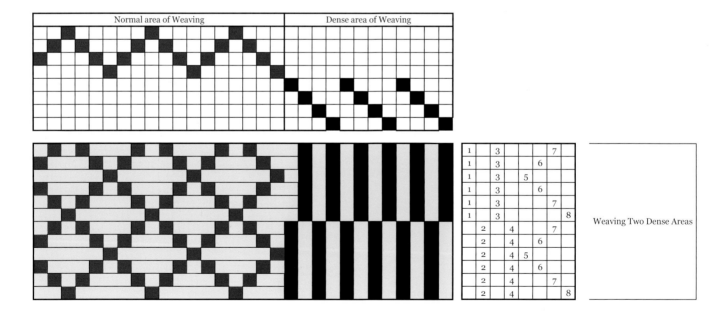

A weaving draft with a dense area threaded as tabby on four shafts: The dense areas can be woven with as many picks as necessary, although only six are shown here. Notice that the draft should always include a repeat of two dense areas.

Rule 3: *The dense area is always threaded as tabby but does not have to be threaded on just two shafts.* A minimum of two shafts are required for a tabby structure, but the dense area can be threaded on four shafts with a tabby or twill threading. For example, the dense area can be threaded as 1, 2, 3, 4, but woven as 1, 3 and 2, 4. This allows the dense area to be woven either normally as a twill or as a dense area, as the 3-D shape requires. It can be helpful to spread out the dense-area warp across more shafts if there are enough shafts available and the warp yarn is sticky.

It's especially useful to spread the dense area out on four shafts in order to weave the header. Remember that the dense area is threaded at a sett that is twice that of the adjacent normal area of weaving. If the dense area is threaded on only two shafts, the header will have to be woven as tabby. A double-sett area of tabby next to an area of normal weave will try to expand to the left and the right. If it's threaded on four shafts, it can be woven as twill and will not try to expand as much. The end of this chapter includes a more thorough discussion of the header options available to avoid this cloth distortion when weaving the header in a dense area threaded on two or four shafts.

Rule 4: *Each individual dense area is placed on a different tensioning device than the normal areas of weaving.* If you are weaving multiple dense areas and if your loom has a second warp beam, you can use the second warp beam to tension all the dense areas; however, doing this prevents the different dense areas from being advanced at different rates and limits your design options. I prefer to tension each dense area separately, since it's so easy to do with any of the tensioning options already discussed.

Rule 5: *If a dense area is placed at a selvage, you must use a floating selvage, preferably one with two pieces of yarn for strength.* Without a floating selvage the weft threads will slide out of the dense area and create little loops. In addition, the dense-area warp threads will be long, unwoven warp floats that hang free, and you will lose the ability to create a dense area.

The different areas of the warp are put onto the loom at different times, but each section must have its own lease sticks, to keep the threads in order. I usually put the largest part of the warp on a normal set of lease sticks, and I use Popsicle sticks or nails for the dense or expanded areas of the warp. These must be taped together to keep them in place on the small warp section. They can be tied to the normal lease sticks to help control them and keep them from twisting.

For the sample in this chapter, I warped the two normal areas onto my loom's warp beam, and the three dense areas onto individual spools on the rod beam. The dense areas at each selvage were threaded as four-shaft tabby on shafts 1 through 4, which are the shafts closest to the beater on my loom. The dense area in the middle of the warp was threaded as four-shaft tabby on shafts 5 through 8.

Weaving expanded areas versus dense areas: A ratchet-and-pawl system mounted on a rod beam works better to tension dense areas than do weights. A dense area requires more tension than is practical to provide with weights, the tension can be controlled more exactly with a ratchet and pawl, and it's easier to release the tension in small increments when needed. Weights are easier to use when weaving expanded areas because the weight moves a small amount when beating in the weft of an expanded area, preventing the expanded area from being beaten in too tightly.

This warp has three dense areas and two normal areas. The normal areas are wound onto the loom's warp beam; the dense areas are each on their own spool on a rod beam.

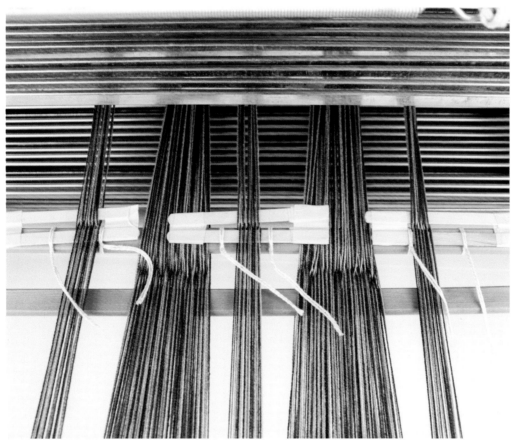

Popsicle sticks work well as lease sticks for the dense areas as each section is wound onto its own spool. The Popsicle sticks are taped together to hold the cross and then tied onto the lease sticks used for the normal-area warp before threading starts.

I prefer to place the dense-area sections of the warp on the shafts as close as possible to the beater. The double sett of a dense area can cause the warp threads to stick to each other, depending on the type of fiber you are using. If it's difficult to open a clean shed in the dense area, you can help clear the shed with your hand more easily if the shafts are close. Increasing the tension on the dense area also helps produce a clean shed.

The sample was designed with normal areas threaded as four-shaft tabby on shafts 9 through 12. All the warp threads alternated colors because a log cabin structure was used. Log cabin woven with dense areas can yield some interesting results.

I threaded the loom with four-shaft tabby to spread the warp out over more shafts, but you need only two shafts to do log cabin, or four shafts to do log cabin with dense areas. Once the header was woven, the first dense areas were started. At the beginning of this sample the two selvage dense areas were woven while the dense area in the center was woven normally. Later the two selvage dense areas were woven normally while the center dense area was woven as a dense area.

Chapter 4 discussed three options for tensioning the cloth while weaving an expanded area: pinning the gathers down, using leapfrogging tension rods, or using a cloth trap. Only the last two options are available if you are weaving a dense area. It does not work to pin the gathers down to the top of the cloth, because the extra fabric length created by the gathers is not consistent for the width of the cloth. This makes it impossible to try to create a straight fell by using pins alone.

The processes for using leapfrogging rods or a cloth trap are almost, but not exactly, the same whether you are weaving expanded areas or dense areas. The tools and the various required cinches work the same as described in chapter 4.

The project shown in chapter 4 involved weaving only one expanded area in the width of the warp. The example in this chapter involves weaving multiple dense areas, but they are not all woven at the same time.

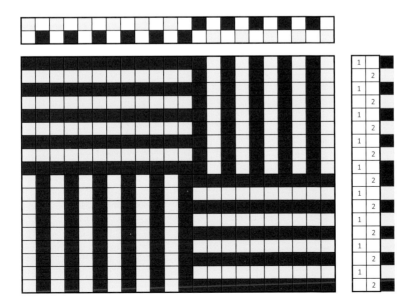

Log cabin: This is a simple structure that gives you many options on just a few shafts. Since the thread colors alternate, you can switch from horizontal to vertical lines by just reversing the thread colors either in the warp or the weft. Winding a log cabin warp is fast because you can wind both colors at once.

Dense-Area-Tensioning Options

ADVANCING AND RETENSIONING WITH
LEAPFROGGING RODS

It is necessary to weave a header before starting to weave a dense area. Review the first weaving draft in this chapter and notice that there are long floats on the first four shafts. In this example draft, even- and odd-numbered threads take turns floating over the top of six picks. In actuality, a dense area can contain any number of picks before the shed on the dense area is changed. The exact number depends on the number of picks in a repeat of the normal-area structure and the amount of gathering desired. See chapter 8 for suggestions about how to determine the number of picks in a dense area.

Again, you must use a floating selvage while weaving dense areas at the edges of the cloth. However, the floating selvage alone will not prevent excess pull-in at the selvage, because the weft pick is being extended to its full width by only one or two floating selvage threads. Those floating selvage threads are no match for many weft picks floating through a tunnel of warp threads. The weft will soon disappear into the shed if the picks are not long enough. And although it's easy to weave loosely at the dense area, it's not easy to do so consistently or without slowing down your weaving rhythm.

The solution is to pull the floating selvage outward with the hand closest to that selvage while tugging on the weft thread with the other hand. By pulling the floating selvage sideways by approximately the same amount, you ensure that the weft picks are all the same length.

Once you have woven the required number of picks in the dense area, change the entire shed, including all dense areas, insert a tension rod, and drop the shed. Using at least two bungee cords, catch the rod with the slightly unbent hooks, and hook the other end of each bungee cord to a piece of anchored Texsolv under the loom. Tension the bungee cords by moving the hook under the loom into the correct hole in the Texsolv. The process to tension the tension rod is the same as was described in chapter 4.

After the bungee cords are tensioned, the dense area must be captured before it can be pulled in. To capture the dense area, pull outward on the floating selvage to expose the weft loops in the shed. Insert a small crochet hook into the weft loops, following the path of the floating selvage. Create a capture thread by cutting an approximately 8-inch (20 centimeter) piece of the same yarn as used for the weft. If the weft thread is very fine or not very strong, use a double length.

By pulling on the floating selvage next to the dense area at a selvage, you ensure that the weft thread does not get lost inside the shed.

This is the first dense area after being woven and after the tension rod is inserted, but before being pulled in. For this sample I wove 30 picks in each dense area. The tension rod is inserted in the first shed of the *next* dense area. Note how the dense-area warp floats over the weft bundle.

Fold the capture thread in half and catch the fold of the capture thread with the crochet hook. Pull it through the weft loops and then pull the capture thread ends through the fold. Tighten the capture thread loop. Tie an ordinary knot in the ends of the capture thread but don't tie it close to the cloth.

The capture thread is a permanent part of the cloth and will not be removed later. Appendix 2 explains how to deal with the capture thread so that it cannot be seen.

Once the tension rod is tensioned and the weft loops are captured, release tension at the back of the loom. Release the tension only on the normal areas that are being woven at this time, but not on any dense areas being woven. The dense-area warp should remain under tension without being advanced while several dense areas are woven.

The dense areas don't all have to be woven at once if they are threaded on different sets of shafts. For this sample I wove three dense areas at the selvages while weaving the center dense area normally. Next, I wove the selvage dense areas normally while weaving the three center dense areas. Finally, I wove three selvage dense areas again. Whenever a dense area is being woven normally, it is treated as a normal area of weaving with respect to warp advancement.

As the tension is released at the back of the loom, the tensioned bungee cords pull on the rod and cause the long warp floats in the dense areas to pull in and tighten around the encased weft threads. This creates a weft bundle in the dense areas, as the weft threads bunch together.

If the weft bundle isn't tight enough, tighten it with the help of a comb. The best kind of comb to use is a pet comb with widely spaced metal teeth. Insert the comb into the warp at the dense-area fell and pull it toward the breast beam. Tighten the bungee cord nearest the dense area to help hold the tension rod as much as is practical. Don't worry if you can't get the bundle to stay as tight as you want. You can use the comb to tighten the dense areas more after the next ones are woven.

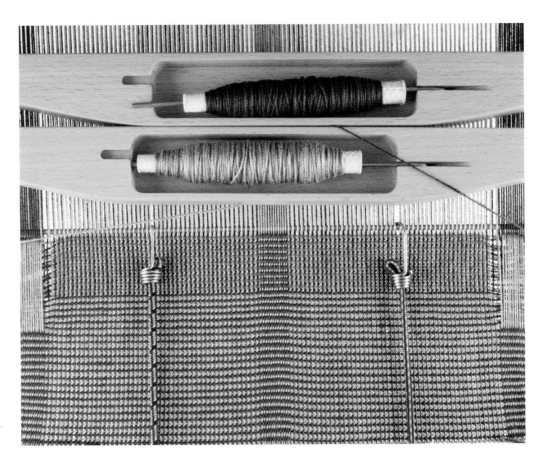

The tension rod is inserted into the shed and tensioned with bungee cords. Notice the long warp floats in the dense areas at the selvages.

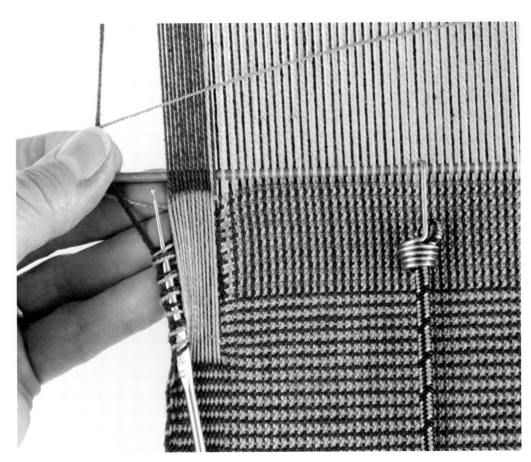

Pulling out on the floating selvage exposes the weft loops. Follow the path of the weft loops with a crochet hook.

Weaving expanded areas versus dense areas: One difference between weaving a dense area and an expanded area is the way in which the warp is advanced. When weaving an expanded area, both the normal and expanded areas of the warp are advanced, but the expanded-area warp is advanced at a slightly greater rate than the normal-area warp.

When you are weaving a dense area, the normal-area warp is advanced after each one or two dense areas are woven, but the dense area itself needs to be advanced only after weaving four to eight dense areas. The rate at which the dense-area portion of the warp is advanced will depend on the number of picks in each dense area and the size of yarn you are using. The dense area will need to be advanced more often if you use fewer picks in each dense area or if you use larger-sized yarn.

Once the dense area is pulled in, adjust the tension on the bungee cords so that the fell is parallel to the breast beam. You are now ready to weave the next dense area, but you might want to use a temple to help prevent your cloth from pulling in as you weave. A common weaving temple will not work if you have a dense area at a selvage, because the teeth of the temple will damage and distort the dense area. The mitten clip temple described in chapter 3 works well to help tension the cloth. The end of each ribbon or braid holds a mitten clip and an S hook. Attach the mitten clip at the selvage of a normally woven area. Use the S hook at the selvage with a dense area. The S hook is attached to the loop that you created when you tied a knot at the end of the dense-area capture thread.

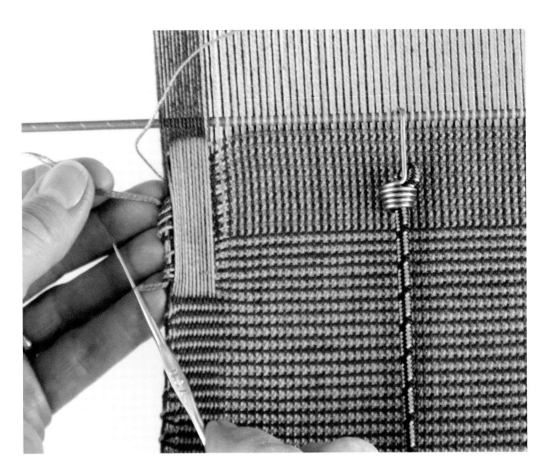

Pull the capture thread through the weft loops.

Pull the ends of the capture thread through its folded loop.

The tension rod will hold the tension as you weave the next dense area. Once it has been woven, change the shed, insert the second tension rod into the open shed, and drop the shed.

At this point the hooks of the bungee cords are holding the first tension rod in place. Remove these hooks from the first tension rod and move them onto the second rod. Pull out the first tension rod. As before, capture the weft loops with a capture thread, pull in the dense area by releasing tension on the area of normal weaving, adjust the tension on the bungee cords, and pull in the dense area by using a pet comb if necessary. Advance the mitten clip temple if you are using it, and continue weaving as before until you complete the next dense area.

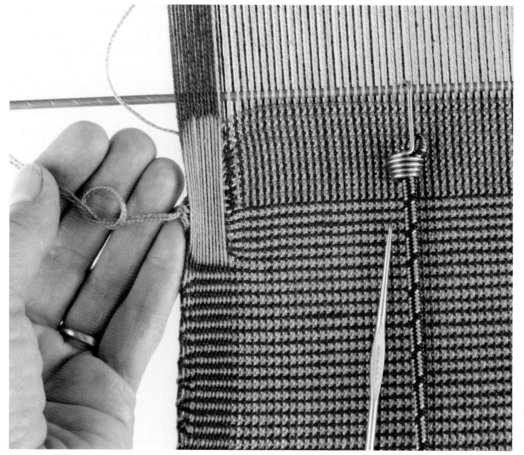

Pull the capture thread tight and tie a knot at the end. Do not tie the knot close to the selvage.

A pet comb with widely spaced teeth can be used to help tighten a dense area, or previously woven dense areas.

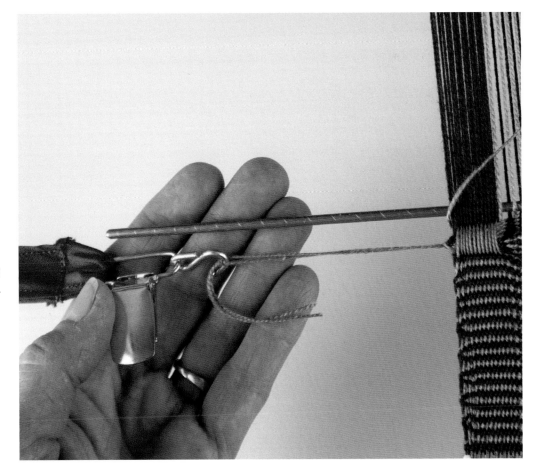

A mitten clip temple can be used when you are weaving a dense area at the selvage. A normal weaving temple cannot be used while weaving dense areas, since it will damage them. Notice how the S hook is used to pull on the capture thread that gathered the dense-area weft loops.

Weaving expanded areas versus dense areas: Another difference between weaving expanded areas and dense areas is the way in which the leapfrogging rods are used to tension the woven cloth. When they are used with expanded areas, the rod is placed only in the open shed of the expanded areas and not in the shed of the normal areas of weaving. When leapfrogging rods are used with dense areas, the rod must be placed in the entire warp shed. The rod does not leave a visible mark in the dense area, because it can be pulled in with a pet comb after the rod is removed. However, the rod does leave a visible mark in the normally woven cloth.

There is also a difference in how often the warp must be retensioned. While weaving an expanded area, the fell will bulge out and make beating difficult after only six to twelve picks, requiring retensioning of the warp. But a straight fell line is maintained when weaving a dense area because the weft picks are spaced out under the long warp floats until they are pulled in. This means that you can weave dense areas of almost any number of picks before pulling the dense area in and retensioning the warp.

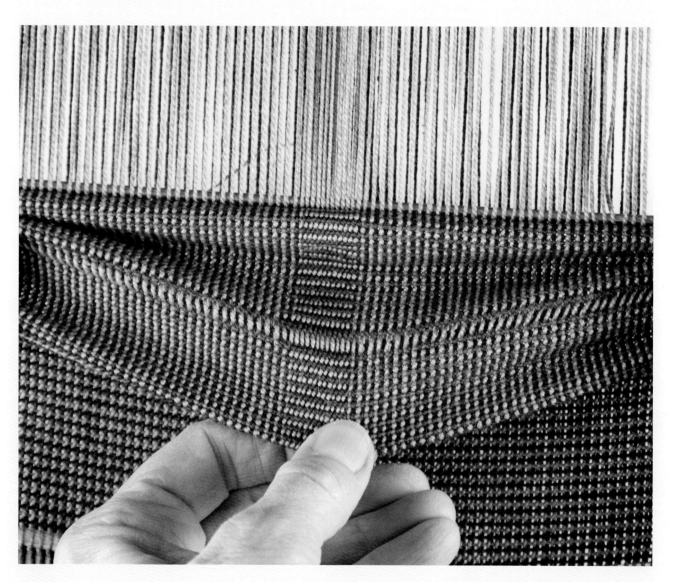

Leapfrogging rods are faster to use and a good way to learn the dense-area technique. Notice the gap left by the leapfrogging rod in the normal area of weaving. That gap can be disguised by a thick weft yarn or ribbon placed in the shed at the same time as the rod. You can use a cloth trap instead to totally eliminate this gap.

An even or odd number of picks can be used in a dense area. If there is a dense area at only one selvage, an even number of picks works better because the shuttle can start and stop at the normal selvage for each dense area. If there are dense areas at both selvages, the shuttle will have to stop at one side or the other when the dense area is completed.

In this case a choice must be made. Should the thread from the last pick be captured by the capture thread, or should it be captured with the next dense area? I've done it both ways, but it's slightly less visible if the thread from the last pick is captured with the next dense area, since it becomes a complete weft loop only after the next dense area is started. It is unlikely that anyone will notice, no matter which way you choose.

If a dense area is somewhere within the warp width rather than at a selvage, there is no weft bundle to gather, and the issue of using an even or odd number of picks is not important.

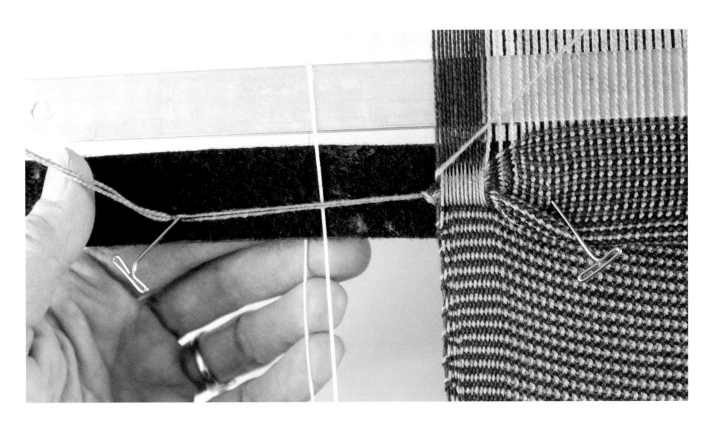

The tension bar cinch loop is in place at the left of the warp. Notice the dense-area loops captured by the capture thread and pinned to the bottom of the cloth trap.

ADVANCING AND RETENSIONING WITH A CLOTH TRAP

Using a cloth trap will prevent the creation of gaps in your weaving from the leapfrogging rods.

After the first dense area is woven, open the first shed of the next dense area and insert the tension bar into the shed. Drop the shed. Since the tension bar does not bend while the warp is being tensioned, and since it will not stay in place during the weaving, it's easier to use than a tension rod.

Slip the bottom of the cloth trap under the cloth so that the padded area is facing up. Install a tension bar cinch at each end of the tension bar next to the selvage on that side. For each cinch, the fine nylon cord loop captures the tension bar and the bottom of the cloth trap at that side of the warp.

As with expanded areas, the knotted end of the nylon loop is attached to one end of a bungee cord with a lark's-head knot placed just behind one of the hooks. The other hook on the bungee cord is slipped into one of the holes in a piece of Texsolv, which is itself anchored to a point under the loom.

Use a capture thread to capture the weft loops of any dense areas at a selvage, and remember to tie a knot in the end of the capture thread. The technique for capturing the dense-area weft loops is the same whether you use leap-frogging rods or a cloth trap to reposition the warp and the fell.

Release the tension on the normal area of the warp, but not on any dense areas being currently woven. If tension is great enough on the tension bar cinches, releasing the warp tension on the normally woven areas will allow the tension bar to pull in the dense areas. Use a pet comb to pull the dense areas in more if needed.

Pin the warp width onto the bottom of the cloth trap. The gathers created by the dense areas must be held under control by the pins before the top of the cloth trap can be installed. The knot tied at the end of the capture thread is pinned down to the cloth trap and helps pull the warp out at each side to prevent pull-in. The selvage on an area of normal weaving is also pinned down to the bottom of the cloth trap, since a normal weaving temple cannot be used with it.

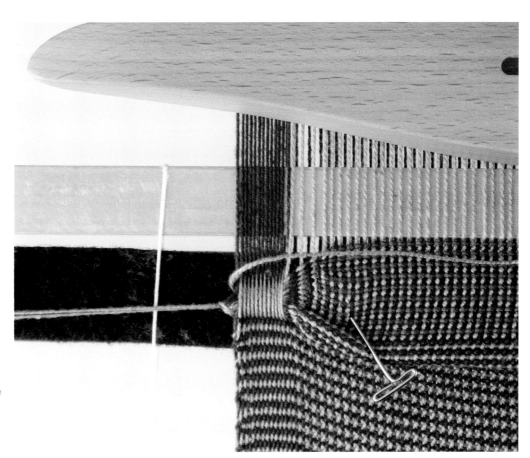

Notice how the gathers next to the dense area are pinned in place. The cloth trap should be a short distance away from the fell to prevent the beater from hitting it. The purpose of the pins is to create a straight fell and hold the normally woven areas in place while you position the top of the cloth trap. The dense area does not have to be exactly at the fell, because it can be tightened later if needed.

Because of the shape that the cloth is taking, the dense area will not be at the front edge of the cloth trap.

Position the top of the cloth trap on top of the bottom piece, with the tacks pointing down, and cinch it closed at each side with a set of cinches. Install and tension the cinches that pull the cloth trap parallel to the breast beam. Once the cloth trap is closed and positioned, it may be necessary to tension various sections of the warp again. Remove the tension bar and continue weaving.

Review chapter 4 for more-detailed instructions on how to set up and use the two sets of cloth trap cinches. The cinches are set up and used identically, no matter what you are weaving.

Weaving expanded areas versus dense areas: Expanded areas pull in evenly along the warp width so that the tension bar and cloth trap naturally end up parallel to the breast beam. However, when a dense area is being woven at only one selvage, the amount of extra warp length at the normal selvage can cause the cloth trap to be much farther away from the breast beam at that end. Don't worry about that at this point.

Pin the cloth down so that the fell is a short but equal distance away from the front of the cloth trap. Add the top of the cloth trap and cinch it down. Release more tension on the normal warp if necessary and then cinch the trap into place parallel to the breast beam. Finally, retension the warp as needed.

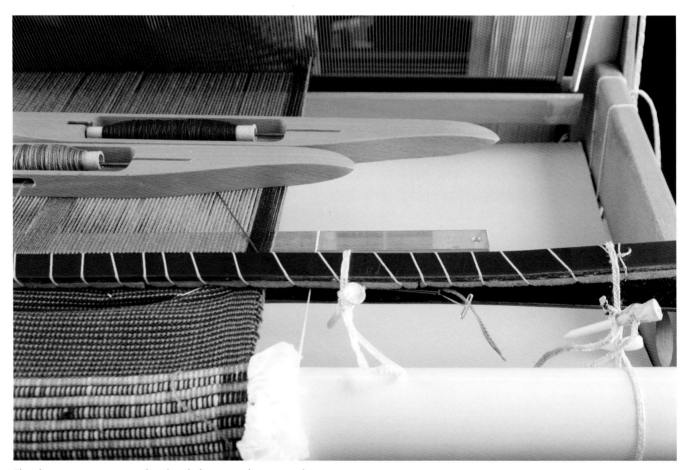

The dense area is captured in the cloth trap and positioned parallel to the breast beam. Weaving can begin again once the tension bar is pulled out.

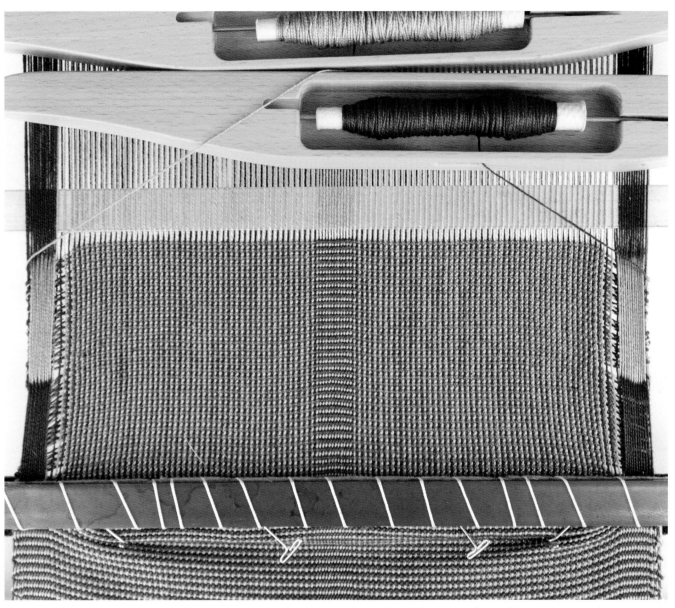

Retensioning the warp is faster if you weave two dense areas before pulling them both in at the same time.

From here on, the process is the same. Once the next dense area is woven, insert the tension bar and tension it. Use a crochet hook to help pull the fine nylon cord around each end of the tension bar.

Remember to release tension on the warp and pull out the pins that hold the cloth to the bottom of the cloth trap *before* removing the golf tees to release the cinches. If you don't remember to release tension and remove the pins first, your cloth may be damaged.

Repositioning the cloth trap after every dense area can be tedious, although it gets easier after you learn the process. The process will be faster if you reposition the cloth trap after weaving two dense areas, rather than just one. This works well for two dense areas, but not for more.

If you weave two dense areas, capture each dense area with its own capture thread and use a pet comb to help pull the dense areas in, in turn. You can also weave two dense areas before repositioning leapfrogging rods to reduce the number of gaps in the cloth created when the rods are removed.

Weaving dense areas can cause a lot of extra fabric to accumulate in certain sections of the warp. Once this happens, it's necessary to continue to use the cloth trap or leapfrogging rods to tension the cloth until it's removed from the loom. In an extreme case, I wove a fabric with a dense area at one selvage. The dense-area selvage was 11 inches (28 centimeters) long, and the normal-area selvage was 54 inches (137 centimeters) long. There was so much excess fabric hanging loose at one side that it started to get in the way of my treadling. I was forced to rig a kind of sling under the loom to hold the excess fabric out of the way.

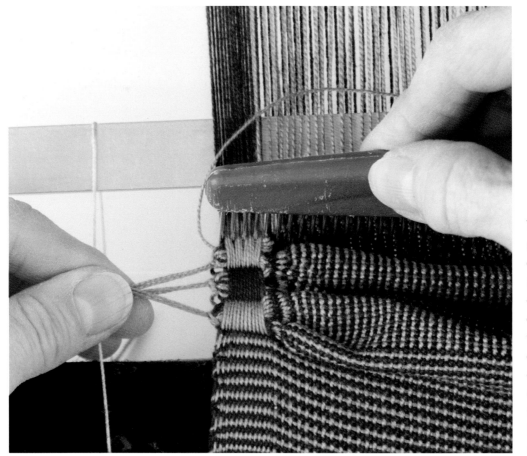

Two dense areas are being pulled in at once. (One dense area was pulled in previously.) If the two dense areas are at a selvage, you can pull on the capture threads as you use a pet comb to help the dense areas pull in. Notice the alternating thread colors in the dense-area warp created by the log cabin weave structure.

Here are the second and third dense areas after they are pulled in. Notice the gathers that are forming and how they are pinned to keep them out of the cloth trap as much as possible.

Remember to weave another header once you are finished weaving the last dense areas. If you don't weave some normal cloth, the last dense area will loosen and may even fall out of your cloth when you try to remove it from the loom.

USING LINGOS TO HELP WEAVE DENSE AREAS

Consider a dense area woven in the middle of a warp with normal areas of weaving on each side. The warp threads in the dense area are the shortest, but that isn't a problem because they are controlled independently by their own tensioning device. In addition, the dense-area warp threads are all the same length. The warp threads at each selvage in the normal area are the longest. But what is the situation with the warp threads that transition from being between the shortest threads in the dense area and the longest threads at the normal-area selvage?

The answer is that the threads very near to the dense area create small loops of excess warp length that can be seen on the surface of the cloth. These loops are created only on the first six to twelve warp threads nearest a dense area. The finer the yarn that is used in the warp, the more threads there will be that create these small, but visible, loops.

The way to prevent these loops from developing is to separately tension the six to twelve warp threads adjacent to a dense area, by hanging a lingo on each warp thread. Lingos must be hung at both sides of a dense area if it's positioned in the middle of a warp. The lingos should be hung after the first dense area is woven, but before it's pulled in for the first time. I also use lingos to tension my floating selvages.

The woven sample for this chapter includes three dense areas. It uses 5/2 cotton and six lingos for each area adjacent to a dense area, or 24 lingos. Each lingo weighs approximately 2 ounces (57 grams). Lingos have several advantages over other types of weights, such as fishing weights or small containers of pennies. Lingos don't easily get tangled up in each other even when they must be very close together. They are easy to hang because of their shape, don't abrade the warp threads in any way, and slide along easily without further adjustment as the warp is advanced. If you find that loops continue to develop even when using lingos, either weight additional threads or add an extra lingo to certain threads.

The lingos are hung at the back of the loom. Keep them from sliding down to the warp beam by installing a tight cord or hanging a lease stick between the sides of your loom at the back. After weaving for a time, you will discover that these lingos all hang at slightly different heights. The ones nearest the dense area will hang lower than the ones farther away.

Lingos can be purchased from stores that sell supplies for draw looms, or you can make them inexpensively from the instructions in appendix 1.

Weaving expanded areas versus dense areas: It's easy to forget that the cloth trap, and not the cloth beam, is holding the cloth tension. When weaving dense areas, never release the tension on the cloth trap until after you have inserted the tension bar into a shed and tensioned it. The results of forgetting are not terrible if you are weaving expanded areas. But if you are weaving dense areas placed asymmetrically in your warp, the result can be disastrous, especially if you are using weights to tension any part of the warp. In this case you will need to pull on the woven cloth with your hands to straighten out the fell as much as possible, open a shed, insert the tension bar, and then hold it in place by hand until you can capture the warp tension again.

This dense area in the middle of the warp was woven with lingos on only the right side. You can easily see which side had the lingos in place during weaving, and which did not.

Here you can see 24 lingos hung at the back of the loom and held back by the lease sticks. Six lingos hang adjacent to each dense area. I warp back to front and never remove my lease sticks. Instead, I slide them over the back beam and suspend them there.

Additional Dense-Area-Weaving Considerations

WEAVING A DENSE-AREA HEADER

Weaving a header before or after a dense area can cause the fabric to expand, since the dense area is set at twice that of the adjacent normal areas of weaving. If the excess fabric is at a selvage, it can be turned under and stitched down. If the excess fabric is in the middle of the warp and there are four shafts available for the dense area, it can be woven as twill to lessen the effect of the extra warp density.

What you are able to weave in the dense-area section of the header depends on how many shafts you have available for the dense area. If you have two shafts, you have two choices. You can either weave it as tabby and deal with the excess fabric, or you can omit weaving the header in the dense area for every two picks out of four. This works if you have a dense area at just one selvage. A dense area at two selvages is easily accomplished using two shuttles. One shuttle weaves the entire warp width for two picks, followed by the other shuttle weaving only the normal area for two picks.

A dense area in the middle can also be woven for just two out of four picks, but that will leave long floats on one side of the warp.

If you have enough shafts on your loom to weave the dense areas as double weave, more options are available. With four shafts you can thread the dense area as a simple twill and then weave a double-weave tube, or two independent layers of double weave. This gets more complicated if there are dense areas at two sides or in the middle of the warp. Because the dense areas and normal areas are on different sets of shafts, they can be lifted independently, allowing you to divide one dense-area weft pick into two parts, effectively reducing the sett in the dense area by half.

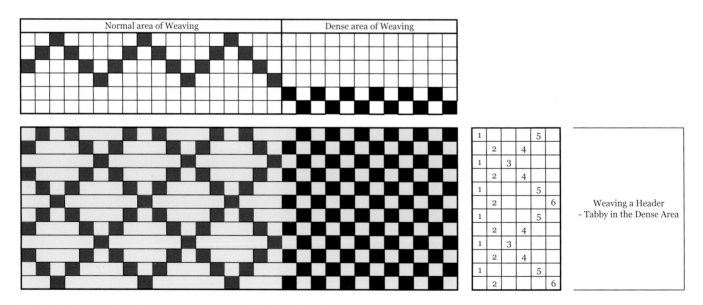

The draft, showing the dense area woven as tabby for a header

Weaving a Header - Tabby in the Dense Area

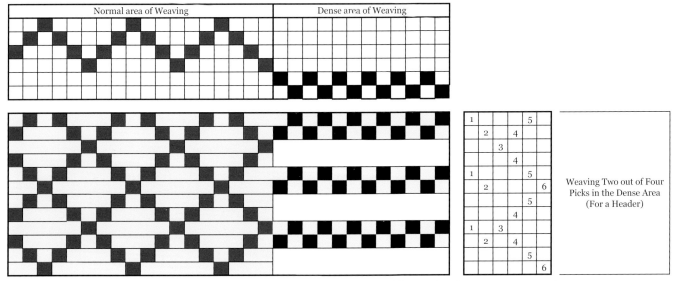

The draft, showing the dense area woven as tabby for a header for two out of four picks. This option requires that you start weaving on the left.

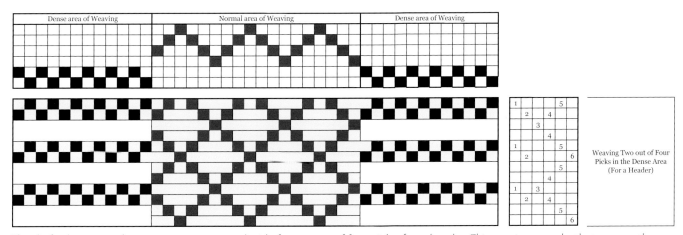

The draft, showing a dense area woven at each side for two out of four picks, for a header. This requires one shuttle to weave the entire warp width and another to weave just the normal area, since that shuttle doesn't start or stop at the selvages.

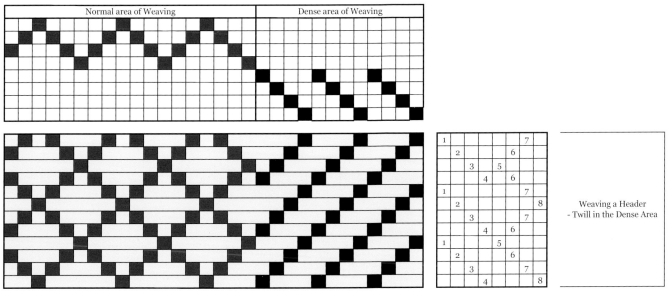

The draft, showing the dense area woven as twill for a header. One shuttle is required. How much this reduces the bulk in the dense area also depends on the weaving structure used in the normal area. In this draft the normal area has a float of five, and the dense area has a float of three. Weaving a twill will help, but only a little.

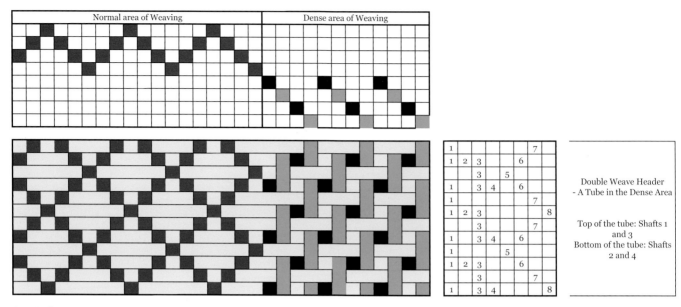

The draft, showing the dense area woven as a double-weave tube for a header. One shuttle is required.

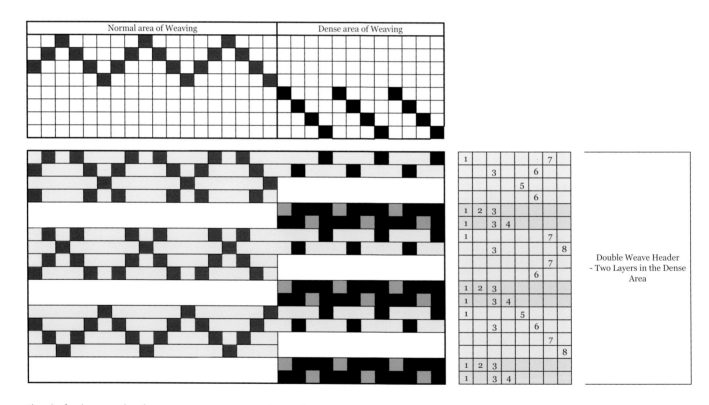

The draft, showing the dense area woven as two layers for a header. Two shuttles are required. Starting on the left, one shuttle with yellow weft weaves the normal area, the top dense area layer, and two picks of just the normal area. Starting at the right, the other shuttle with green weft weaves just the bottom area of double weave in the dense area. The bottom layer is not attached to the rest of the warp.

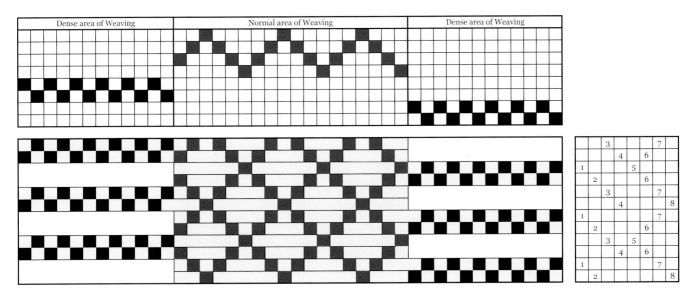

This draft shows one method for weaving the dense areas alternately, for a header. The two dense areas are on different sets of shafts, and the two shuttles start at opposite sides. This is not the only method that will work, but it's easy to understand.

WEAVING LOG CABIN WITH DENSE AREAS

The woven sample for this chapter used a log cabin structure. Each header was woven in such a way as to make the stripes travel in the same direction as the adjacent normal areas.

As threaded:	Dense Area	Normal Area	Dense Area	Normal Area	Dense Area
Shafts used:	1-4	9-12	5-8	9-12	1-4
Warp ends:	24*	94	24	94	24*
Sett:	40	20	40	20	40
Width in reed:	.6 inch 1.6 cm	4.7 inches 11.9 cm	.6 inch 1.6 cm	4.7 inches 12=1.9 cm	.6 inch 1.6 cm
	Header				
As woven:	Three Dense Areas	Normal Area	Normal Area	Normal Area	Three Dense Areas
	Normal Area	Normal Area	Three Dense Areas	Normal Area	Normal Area
	Three Dense Areas	Normal Area	Normal Area	Normal Area	Three Dense Areas
	Header				

*Plus floating selvage

This table shows how the sample for chapter 5 was planned.

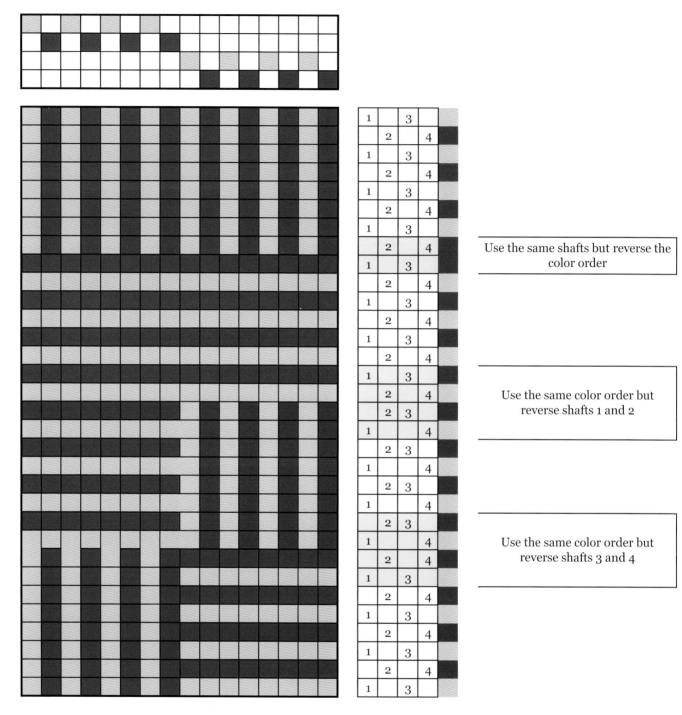

Use the same shafts but reverse the color order

Use the same color order but reverse shafts 1 and 2

Use the same color order but reverse shafts 3 and 4

The direction of the log cabin stripes can be totally controlled with the weft if different areas of the warp are threaded on different shafts.

Log cabin allows the stripe directions to be changed at will by using two picks of the same color in the weft, or two adjacent threads of the same color in the warp. But for this sample, simple alternating thread colors were used across the entire warp, including the floating selvages, with no adjacent threads of the same color. The weft was woven with two shuttles, using the same two colors as the warp.

It was not necessary to put two threads of the same color together in the warp because the dense areas were threaded on different shafts than the normal areas, making it possible to reverse the color stripes in the different areas independently. This can be done by using two picks of the same color, or by using the same shaft in one of the areas for two picks. For the second option the result is a small two-thread float in either the dense area or the normal area.

The ultimate tool for weaving 3-D shapes is the ability to individually control the tension and advancement on each warp thread. The next chapter explains how to set up and weave on an infinitely tensioned warp.

The completed woven sample

6 Weaving with Infinite Tension

The previous chapters discussed threading different sections of the warp onto different sets of shafts, and independently controlling their tensions in order to weave expanded areas or dense areas. The ultimate in 3-D weaving on a hand loom is to be able to control the tension on each thread individually, by hanging a lingo on each individual warp thread.

Infinite-tension control allows you to shape the cloth as it's being woven without having to plan the shape in detail prior to warping the loom. For example, as the weaving progresses you can decide to add an expanded area at will, with any width, and at any position along the warp width. This can be done without setting up the warp threads for the expanded area on a separate set of shafts. Using infinite tensioning, you can decide to add a series of expanded areas, at positions that overlap each other and that slowly migrate across the surface of the cloth, without the preplanning we have discussed up to now.

This would be very difficult to do with the techniques described previously. A separate set of shafts would be required for each individual expanded area or each section of the expanded areas that use the same warp threads. This little sample of eleven overlapping expanded areas would require thirteen sets of shafts to accomplish. Using infinite tensioning, no preplanning and no additional shafts are required. Weaving with infinite tension is a useful technique when you have a limited number of shafts available. All the sample shapes shown in this chapter can be done with only two shafts.

Additional sets of shafts are still required to weave dense areas, because they need a greater tension and because the dense area shed remains open while a dense area is being woven. The techniques discussed in the previous chapters can be combined with the infinite-tension technique, providing additional options to shape the cloth.

If you have four shafts, you can accomplish all the shapes shown in this chapter with two shafts left over for the inclusion of dense areas! But to weave with infinite tension, you have to be willing to add some parts to your loom.

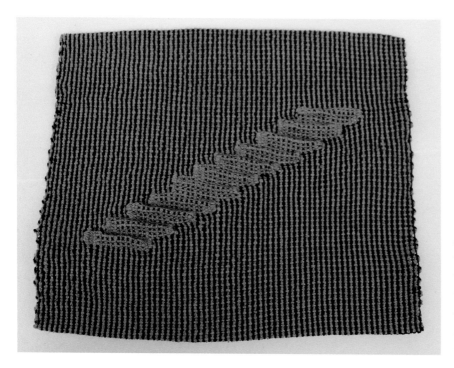

A series of expanded areas march across the cloth from one side to the other. These were woven with a single color of thread in the weft, but that is optional. They were also woven one after the other, without any areas of normal weaving between them, but that too is optional.

Setting Up the Loom to Weave with Infinite Tension

Infinite tensioning requires a lingo hung on each warp thread at the back of the loom. That requires a floor loom because the lingos have nowhere to hang on the warp of a table loom. Since infinite tensioning can be combined with normal weaving, it's not necessary to use it on the entire warp if you only want to shape a portion of the warp width. This reduces the number of lingos needed. The location that the lingos are hung cannot interfere with the loom's main warp beam or the path of the normal warp threads from the warp beam, around the back beam, and through the shafts to the front of the loom. To hang the lingos, it's necessary to create a horizontal path from the warp beam to the breast beam. Since the loom's normal warp path provides no place to hang the lingos, an additional warp beam must be added behind the loom.

Weavers who are familiar with second warp beams will know that an additional back beam is also required to separate the warp layers and to allow each warp layer to advance on its own. A second back beam is typically placed just behind and a little higher than the original back beam. The threads on the infinite-tension warp beam need to be held only a little higher than the loom's warp beam, and only when there is another section of warp under them.

The lingos cannot be hung in a single row, since seven of them hung in a row take up an inch of width. If the sett of your warp is 24 threads per inch (10 threads per centimeter), each inch of warp width requiring 24 lingos would spread out to 3.4 inches (8.7 centimeters) at the back of the loom. Multiple rows of staggered lingos allow a greater sett in the reed without expanding the warp width at the back of the loom.

A straight path for the warp and the extra space needed for the lingos can be created by adding an extension off the back of the loom. This extension includes an inexpensive ratchet and pawl attached to a wooden dowel to create a warp beam, and a place to hang the desired rows of lingos.

The back of the loom with the infinite-tension extension installed

The inexpensive ratchet and pawl as mounted on a wooden dowel at one end of the loom extension. These pieces create an additional warp beam. The pawl has holes so that a weight can be hung from it to keep the pawl engaged with the ratchet.

The final consideration is the weight of the lingos. Each one weighs about 2 ounces (57 grams). The warp that I used for the samples in this chapter contained 144 threads and the same number of lingos. That means I needed to hang a total of 18 pounds (just over 8 kilograms) of lingos off the back of my loom, just for this narrow warp. Since this much weight could risk either tipping the loom over or breaking some part of the loom, the extension required legs to carry the extra weight.

In addition to the loom extension with the added warp beam, there are a total of four pieces of aluminum *C channel* mounted parallel to the warp beam at the back of the loom. These act as spacers for the rows of lingos. I use four spacing bars plus a metal rod mounted directly above the loom's original back beam. The metal rod acts as a second back beam and prevents the warp threads on the infinite-tension warp beam from resting on any normal part of the warp underneath. This rod is easy to take off and put on for warping because it's held in place with eye screws.

The metal rod just above the back beam plus the four pieces of C channel allow four rows of lingos to be hung, spaced out. The spacing prevents the rows of lingos from interfering with each other. On my loom, I moved the original back beam a few inches closer to the back of the shafts to save a little room.

Each row of lingos requires an aluminum bar that can be raised to hold the weight of the lingos when needed to advance the warp. The aluminum bar has a hole drilled at each end. A piece of Texsolv passes through each of the holes, around the spacing bar above, and the end of the cord passes through a hole at the other end of the cord, where it's secured with an arrow peg. The arrow peg keeps the loop intact. By pulling on the pegged end of the cord, the loop can be made smaller or larger, raising or lowering the aluminum bar. A second arrow peg inserted into one of the holes in the Texsolv is used to set the desired height of the bar at each end.

When advancing the warp, a pair of knitting needles can be used, one at each side of the loom, to set the height of all the aluminum bars so that the weight of the lingos is removed from the warp. The knitting needles are inserted into holes on the Texsolv, just like the arrow pegs. Once the warp is advanced, the knitting needles can be easily removed, letting all the bars fall at the same time.

As each lingo is hung on a warp thread, it's also hung in such a way as to straddle one of the hanging aluminum bars. All the lingos are angled in the same direction to minimize the width of a row of them. My sample warp had a sett of only 12 threads per inch, so I used only two rows of lingos, alternating them on two aluminum bars. If you install enough spacers and suspended aluminum bars for four rows of lingos, you can accommodate a sett of between 28 and about 32 threads per inch (11–13 threads per centimeter).

I used wood and a heavy aluminum bar for the loom extension, C-channel aluminum for the spacing bars, and flat aluminum for the suspended lingo holders, but you can use any material that works for you. The creation of an infinite-tension extension is shown in detail in appendix 1, along with suggestions for mounting it on different types of looms. Instructions for making your own lingos can also be found there.

You may not want or need the ability to weave shapes on the entire warp. Or, you may not have enough lingos for the entire warp that you are weaving. Note that you can place part of your warp on the loom's warp beam and another part on the infinite-tension warp beam extension. If you are not weaving with infinite tension, the added warp beam can also be used as just a second warp beam, without hanging any lingos.

As a demonstration, the lingos have been hung in four rows. Note how the lingos straddle the aluminum bars suspended under each section, and how they are hung angled in the same direction.

Loom loss: Loom loss is the extra length of warp required to weave that can't be turned into cloth. Some amount of warp is required to tie it onto the cloth and warp beams. The length of warp that is required to pass through the shafts, front to back, can't be used to make cloth. It's not possible to weave right up to the first shaft because some extra warp length is required to open a shed wide enough for your shuttle to pass through. All these little warp lengths are included in the calculation for loom loss.

If you are using an infinite-tension warp beam and lingos, remember to plan for extra loom loss. I've woven more than one warp to the point where the rod on the warp beam was only a few inches from the last shaft. But the rod on the infinite-tension warp beam can get only as close to the last shaft as the last row of lingos. The amount of extra loom loss required by the infinite-tension tools will depend on your loom and where you place the lingos. Measure the distance between the last shaft and the spacing bar nearest the infinite-tension warp beam. This distance will be the additional amount of loom loss that cannot be turned into cloth.

The spacing bars can be placed inside the loom's back beam in order to reduce the amount of loom loss, but only if you will never use an area of normal weaving at the same time. The bars that carry the weight of the lingos while the warp is being advanced cannot operate correctly if they hang inside a normal area of weaving.

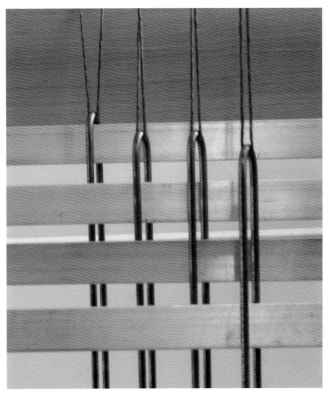

A view from under the back of the loom shows the lingos hanging on demonstration warp threads and straddling four aluminum support bars. The bars can be raised and lowered to carry or drop the weight of the lingos since the warp can't be weighted when it's being advanced.

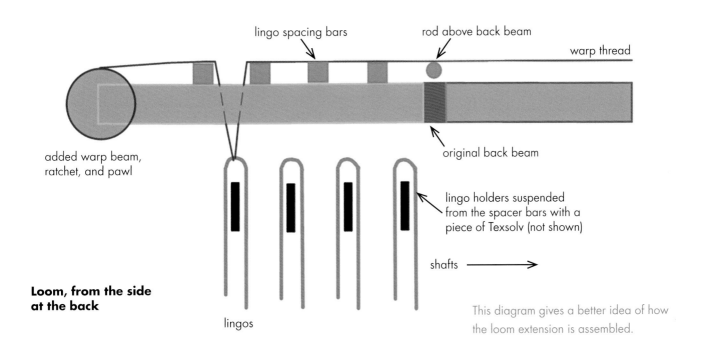

lingo spacing bars

rod above back beam

warp thread

added warp beam, ratchet, and pawl

original back beam

lingo holders suspended from the spacer bars with a piece of Texsolv (not shown)

shafts ⟶

Loom, from the side at the back

lingos

This diagram gives a better idea of how the loom extension is assembled.

Separate parts of the warp can also be placed on the rod beam or hung with weights. All the warp-tensioning techniques, including infinite tensioning, can be used independently or together, as needed. There are only two considerations to take into account. The first is that you use the techniques best suited for the project you are planning to weave. The second is to remember that weaving a dense area requires a second set of shafts and more tension than can be provided by infinite tensioning.

Setting Up the Front of the Loom for Infinite-Tension Weaving

My sample warp was set up on four shafts, but I could have used only two shafts to weave the series of expanded areas shown previously. Since the different sections of the warp aren't placed on different shafts, they cannot be raised and lowered independently. Another technique must be used to weave only a portion of the warp width.

Once the warp is beamed, threaded, sleyed, and tied on at the front, there is one more step required. The different groupings of threads must be marked to make the weaving efficient. For this sample warp, which had a sett of 12 threads per inch (eight threads per centimeter), I chose a grouping of four threads.

I placed a cone of heavy, strong yarn on the floor under the front of the loom and taped a long wooden dowel to the top of the beater. Starting at one end, I counted out four warp threads. I pulled the yarn up through the warp, around the entire beater (including the dowel), tied a knot at the top of the beater, and cut the yarn. I counted out the next four warp threads and tied another loop around the entire beater. This process continued for the entire warp.

The purpose of the dowel taped to the top of the beater is to ensure that the loops tied around the beater can be tied tightly and evenly without being too tight. If the loops are too tight, the yarn rather than the reed will beat your warp. After a time, the yarn loops will weaken and beat unevenly.

After the entire warp, or the section of the warp on the infinite-tension extension, has been marked in this way, the dowel is removed and the loops are taped to the top of the beater. The tape prevents the knots in the yarn loops from rotating around the beater and getting tangled in the warp or the reed as you weave.

Tying loops around the entire beater creates an easy way to remember how much of the warp is being woven on each pick. Whether the shuttle is passing to the right or to the left, it can be reliably raised out of the shed or pushed down into the shed on every pick. But it can sometimes be

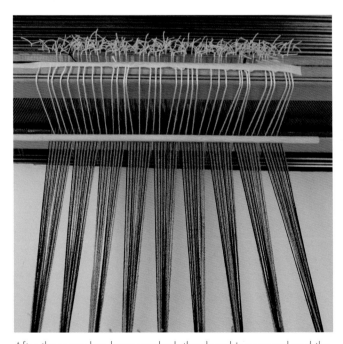

The entire warp has been marked, every four threads, with a loop of yarn that wraps around the entire reed. The dowel acts as a spacing tool, so that the individual loops are easier to tie consistently.

After the warp has been marked, the dowel is removed and the tails and knots in the cords are taped to the top of the reed. This prevents the marker loops from rotating and the knots and their tails from getting tangled in the warp.

difficult to keep your place and remember which grouping of weft threads is your starting and ending point on subsequent picks. The modified clothespins described in chapter 3 are perfect for helping you remember what part of the warp was woven last.

Because a dowel was used when tying the loops of cord around the beater, these loops have a small amount of slack in them. Pulling on this slack in one direction or another creates a gap in the top layer of warp threads when the shed is open. Several of these loops can be captured by clothespins to help you remember which groups of threads are being woven at any point in time. Be aware that *you must pull on this slack from the same direction on each pick*, or the gap created in the warp will be in different places on different picks.

Another way to mark your place in the groups of threads that you are weaving is to insert a thin knitting needle through the loops that mark the warp thread groups. Insert the needle and let it sit on top of your beater. As each group of warp threads is woven, slip that marker loop over the stop on the knitting needle. You will need to add an extra loop around the beater at the side of your warp to help hold the knitting needle in place when there are only one or two groups of threads left to be woven.

Clothespins are being used to help remember which groups of threads are currently being woven. It's an easy matter to release one of the loops from the clothespins as weaving progresses. I usually position the clothespins to pull the loops toward the selvages when using two of them, but anything will work as long as you are consistent.

As before, once the fell line is no longer straight and parallel with the reed or weaving has become difficult, the warp must be advanced. Once you decide to advance the warp, remember to insert either a tension rod or a tension bar in the next shed and secure it as explained in previous chapters. Either of the cloth-tensioning techniques, leapfrogging rods or the use of a cloth trap, can be used to straighten and secure the fell. Depending on the width of your warp and the number of lingos you are using, you can advance the warp in one of two ways.

The first method is to raise up each end of the aluminum bars that are hanging under each row of lingos. The bars must be raised enough so that the weight of all the lingos is being carried by the aluminum bars and not by the warp threads. To do this, shorten the loops of Texsolv used to hang the aluminum bars. Pull on the end of the Texsolv cord with the arrow peg, and when the bar is high enough, secure it with a golf tee or a second arrow peg. Do that at each end of each bar. Next, release the ratchet and pawl a small amount to allow the warp to be advanced.

Using the tension bar or rod at the front of the loom, secure the new fell line as appropriate for the technique you are using. The leapfrogging-rods and cloth trap techniques used to pull in and straighten the fell line work exactly the same with infinite tensioning as with expanded or dense areas. Finally, lower the aluminum bars to allow the lingos to again tension the warp threads.

The second method is a little faster but assumes that the lingos at the back of the loom are already hanging a few inches under the spacing bars, and that you have a tension bar inserted into the shed and tensioned with fine nylon cord. For this method, a tension bar works better than a tension rod. Pull the tension bar forward until the fell is again parallel to the breast beam. As you do this, individual lingos will automatically be raised as much as is needed. Adjust the tension on the tension bar so that it is sufficient to hold the fell line straight. Proceed with the needed adjustments as determined by the cloth-tensioning method you are using.

The second method of advancing the warp, by pulling the fell into a straight line by hand, won't work in all cases. For example, it will not work if you are weaving dense areas in addition to the infinitely tensioned area. It may not work if the shapes being woven are too extreme. And it may not work if the size of your warp and the number and weight of lingos you are using are too great.

Weaving!

Infinite tensioning allows you to weave any number of picks, for any warp width and for any length that you desire. But there are some techniques that work better than others. It will become obvious after you try to weave a few samples that you must think about how the weft is being beaten.

Consider two examples. In the first example, each pick is a little bit shorter than the previous one, and in the second example each one is a little bit longer.

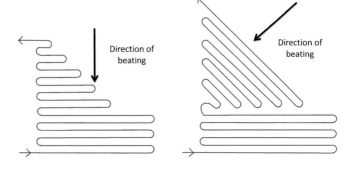

The way the picks are laid down can affect the action of the beater.

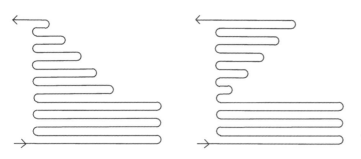

The plan for how the picks are woven starts at the bottom in this diagram. In the figure on the left, increasingly shorter picks are woven, while increasingly longer picks are woven using the plan on the right.

Each of these approaches looks like they work equally well, until you consider how they are beaten by the reed. In the example on the left, the reed remains parallel to the fell, although the area being beaten becomes shorter and shorter. In the example on the right, each subsequent pick grows a little longer as the beater tries to push the pick against the previous one and the last pick of the normally woven area. In addition, the cloth that was normally woven gets beaten time after time as each newly placed pick attempts to reach its original fell line. The result is that the beater wants to beat at an angle that is not parallel to the fell, and the picks get longer than they otherwise should be because the fell is developing on a diagonal.

Depending on how you look at it, my beater has the ability, or the problem, of being able to beat at an angle. Some loom beaters force the beat to be parallel to the breast beam.

Increasingly longer picks can work, sort of, if they are balanced across the warp. But in that case, other problems appear. To see the effect of a beater that forces a beat parallel to the breast beam, consider the example of increasingly longer weft picks that are symmetrically placed along the warp width.

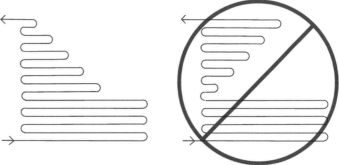

Weaving with increasingly longer picks that are not placed symmetrically along the width of the warp is not recommended!

The next sample is a weave that uses increasingly shorter picks in the middle of the warp until the picks were only a few threads wide. At that point the fell is pulled back into a straight line and the second half of the shape is woven in the mirror image, with picks that start small and get increasingly long but are still placed symmetrically with respect to the selvages. The pick plan would look like the following diagram:

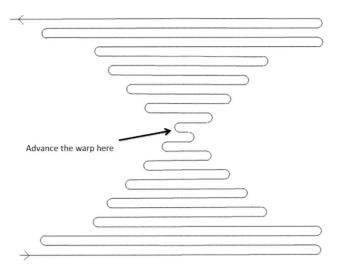

Advance the warp here

This pick plan is symmetrical with respect to the selvages. The first part of the plan works fine, since shorter and shorter picks are used. But will the second symmetrical part of the plan work too after the warp is advanced and the fell is straightened out?

The weaving done during the second half of the plan shows that even a symmetric plan cannot eliminate all the problems. In this case the beat of the reed was still parallel to the breast beam, but the cloth had difficulty reaching the fell as the plan progressed.

I was able to selvage this sample by using a pet comb to manually pull in the gaps in the warp threads on each side, before pulling the cloth into a straight fell line and continuing the weaving. This was possible because I used extremely strong yarn for the sample. Despite my best efforts, the two halves of the plan produced weaving of two different lengths. The second half produced a length of cloth 15 percent shorter than the first half, although both halves contained exactly 26 picks. To weave this sample I advanced the cloth tension only twice, once after the first triangle and once after the second. But if I had advanced tension on the second triangle more often, I may have had better results, without having to manually pull the picks into the fell.

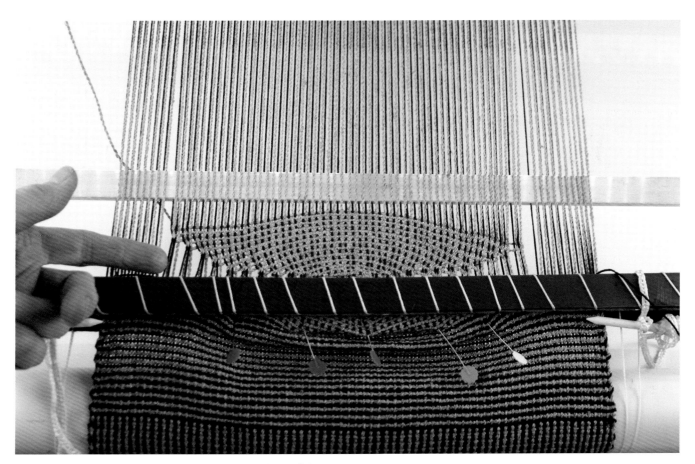

The beat is symmetrical across the warp, but the edges of the new weaving don't reach the fell line because of the accumulated bulk of cloth being woven. A cloth trap is being used to hold the woven cloth in place.

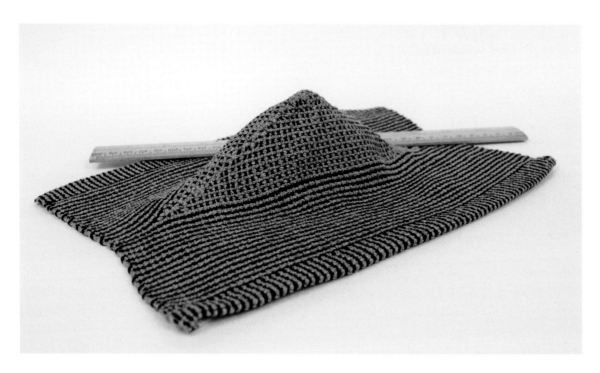

The resulting sample. Decide for yourself whether the difference in the woven lengths is worth it to weave this shape, remembering that you will need to manually deal with the warp threads at each side.

Overlapping wedges grow out of alternating selvages and are woven with a single color. The color lines created by the log cabin structure work to show off the wedges. The resulting cloth is not a rectangle!

From this discussion it's clear that inserting wedge-shaped pieces into a cloth as you weave is a simple matter, as long as you progress from weaving longer to shorter weft picks. The result is a more gently curving cloth than can be achieved with expanded areas or dense areas, and without the use of extra sets of shafts.

The next sample involves weaving cloth normally, but interrupting it at regular intervals with wedges that start at alternating selvages. A single shuttle was used for the wedges to accentuate them in the field of pink and black rows created with the log cabin structure.

The wedges reminded me of gores in a skirt. Since most skirts have waistbands, I wanted my next sample to test out the theory that I could weave a gored skirt with a waistband, as a single piece of cloth. I first cut the last sample off the warp. The first 28 warp threads at one selvage were pulled through the reed and rethreaded so that there were two pink threads beside each other. This allowed the lines in the log cabin to travel horizontally in the waistband but vertically in the skirt. After the 28 warp threads were resleyed and the entire warp was tied on at the front, weaving proceeded.

The plan for the skirt test sample is simple. It consists of a small distance that is woven normally, followed by weaving a wedge. The beginning of the wedge starts at the selvage opposite the waistband and reaches all the way to the waistband. While weaving the wedge, each successive pair of picks that travels toward and away from the waistband stops four threads sooner than the previous pair. Once the wedge is complete, another length of normal weaving is again followed by a woven wedge shape.

The log cabin structure that I used requires two shuttles of different colors. The woven wedges use only one color in an alternating sequence. The correct color of yarn needs to be at the correct selvage before weaving can progress.

While it's good to have the same number of picks in all the normally woven areas, no one will notice an extra pick or two in the finished piece. The easiest approach for managing the shuttles is to weave the normal area and then add a pick or two until the shuttle with the color of the next wedge is at that selvage, and the other shuttle is at the waistband selvage.

Cutting off the warp: Cutting woven cloth off a warp before it's complete is simple. Weave a short distance of cloth (1.5 inches or 4 centimeters), using some waste weft yarn. Open the next shed and insert a piece of unbendable material such as a metal rod, a metal bar, or a piece of wood similar to a lease stick. Drop the shed. Tie this item temporarily to the breast beam with a simple loop of cord at each end.

Apply a good layer of household white glue to the top surface of the area woven with waste yarn. Rub it in a little with your finger and let it dry completely.

Release the cloth beam and unroll the previously woven cloth. Remove it from the rod attached to the cloth beam. Cut through the middle of the glued section to release the cloth from the rest of the warp. Tie the unbendable material to the cloth beam rod. You may need to tie it on in several places. Retension the cloth beam and remove the temporary ties from the breast beam. You are now ready to weave again.

Warning! My sample required me to rethread and resley 28 warp threads. That meant that I also had to cut these threads off the glued section. Since they were tensioned with lingos at the back of the loom, I had to remember to raise the aluminum bars straddled by the lingos so that their weight was removed from the warp. If I hadn't remembered to remove their weight, the lingos could have pulled the cut threads out of the reed and out of the heddles.

This process works for any warp, but you must be careful of any extra weight that you have added to your warp threads. You may be weaving with infinite tension and have lingos hanging on all of your warp threads, or you may have just one small weight at the back of your loom that was placed there to repair a single broken thread. You must remember to remove any thread weights before you cut them away from the glued section.

Here is the resulting test for weaving a gored skirt with an attached waistband. For a life-sized version, the length of the skirt would be equal to the width of the warp less the waistband.

Here you can see how the gores look when spread out.

It is also possible to weave the wedges with two shuttles, changing the direction of the log cabin color lines between the normally woven areas and the woven wedges. However, that results in either a turn for both shuttles on the surface of the cloth or a break in each color weft thread every two picks.

Note that the waistband is woven normally throughout the sample. If the goal is to weave a full-size skirt, it's not necessary to warp the waistband on the infinite-tension warp beam or to use lingos to tension it.

Looking at the hanging lingos, it's easy to imagine that some of them will eventually reach the floor. This would release the tension on those threads and make the lingos useless. One option is to wind the warp forward onto the cloth beam, adjust it at the warp beam, and wind it back onto the warp beam. There is a faster and easier option that avoids all of that work. This option makes use of the space between the infinite-tension warp beam and the last aluminum C-channel spacing bar.

Only a portion of the lingos will be in danger of hitting the floor, so only a portion of them will need to be adjusted higher. Count the number of lingos that you want to raise and calculate their weight. Fill a water jug until it's approximately the same weight. Gather the threads of these lingos into a carabiner. Attach the carabiner to the water jug handle with a piece of Texsolv and an arrow peg. By lowering the jug, you can raise the group of lingos all at once. Since the group of lingos and the water jug are about the same weight, they will be in perfect balance with each other.

Another option is to totally change the warping process itself. I usually attach my warp to the warp beam rod by slipping the rod through the loops created when I wind my warp, rather than tying the warp onto the rod as I do at the cloth beam. But I can tie the warp on with a surgeon's knot at the back also, and I don't need to cut the loops to do that. This lets me adjust the lengths of groups of threads at the back when they become too long from weaving many wedges in a row. It doesn't require any extra warp length to do if the loops are not cut at the back, since they can always be placed on the extended warp beam rod later in the process.

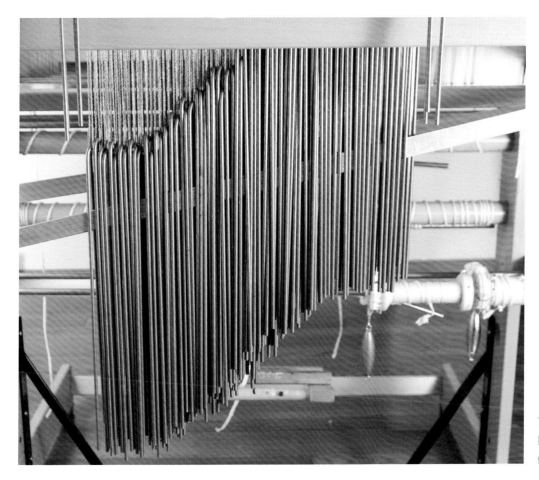

The pattern created by the height of the lingos mimics the shape being woven.

Remember that the warping process is designed to equalize the tension on all the threads in the warp width. But if there are lingos hung on each and every warp thread, the tension is equalized automatically. That means that the warping process can be changed dramatically and still work.

For example, the chained warp bouts can be simply hung at the back before being threaded through the heddles, through the reed, and then tied on at the front. Groups of threads can then be tied onto the rod on the extended warp beam, at the back of the loom. After the lingos are hung, all the warp threads are at equal tension without being wound onto any beams, front or back. If the lingos are allowed to hang low to the floor, the groups of threads would need to be only occasionally retied at the back of the loom, allowing you to adjust the hanging heights of groups of lingos at the same time. The benefits of this approach will be obvious once you try to weave a circle, where one side of the warp uses its entire length and the other uses very little.

There are many other shaping options that can be explored using infinite warp tensioning. Wedges of different dimensions can be woven and combined into more-complex shapes, including curves. Shapes other than wedges can be woven and combined with each other or with wedge shapes.

The transitions between shapes can be more gradual or more rapid or can be combined with areas of normal weaving in interesting ways.

An infinitely tensioned warp can be combined with expanded areas and dense areas. The traditional techniques of double weave, and structures such as waffle weave, honeycomb, and deflected double weave, add still more choices. And don't forget to consider the use of specialty fibers such as elastic or metal wire!

At this point you may feel overwhelmed. In addition to the three 3-D techniques, there are the choices of fiber, weaving structure, color, and the different combinations of all of these. In the face of all these choices, my suggestion is to first play with each of the techniques by itself. That will give you experience with what works and what doesn't, and your own ideas will flow from there. The loom modifications that I have described were developed in the service of weaving natural shapes. The shape is the end goal, while the tools and techniques are just a way of achieving it.

My personal goal is to be able to weave the shapes found in nature; the shape of a human body or the form of a butterfly. Your goals will be different.

If the lingos are in danger of hitting the floor, a hanging water jug can be used to raise them. This image looks down at the last aluminum C-channel spacing bar and the infinite-tension warp beam.

The next chapter deals with using a combination of fiber and metal wire to weave sculptural pieces. Although the shape is created while being woven, it's held in place by wire once the piece is off the loom.

Ruff Five, woven with the infinite-tensioning technique using green magnet wire, rayon, and a piece of armature wire at the neck

7 Weaving with Copper or Metal Wire

Wire Basics

There are metal yarns developed specifically for knitting and weaving that consist of fine wire covered by some sort of fiber. This type of yarn works much the same as any other yarn and is not discussed here.

The basic process of weaving with wire is almost the same as weaving with any fiber, but there are a few important differences and some additional things to learn. If you have never used wire in your weaving, the best approach is to try it with a sample warp.

My favorite wire for sculptural pieces is magnet wire, which is an enamel-clad copper wire that is used to wind the magnetic core of a motor. It usually comes in red, green, or copper colors and in many different gauges. The enamel cladding acts as an insulator and prevents the copper from oxidizing. Other colors of enamel-clad wire are available from companies that sell to jewelers and artists; see appendix 1 for sources.

The gauge of a wire describes its size, and like weaving yarn, the larger the number, the smaller the size. I recommend the use of wire gauges from about AWG (American Wire Gauge standard) 26 to 30 (0.404 mm to 0.254 mm diameter) for the warp. Wire with a gauge smaller than 26 is too inflexible, whereas wire with a gauge larger than 30 is too delicate and will break. As with nonmetal fiber, the gauge used in the weft is more forgiving. Note that US gauge standards are not the same as metric or European standards.

The most troublesome aspect of weaving with wire is its tendency to kink. Whether in the warp or the weft, kinks in the wire will cause it to catch on the other fibers. Kinks are sharp bends in the wire that look like small loops. They cause the metal to fatigue and make it more likely to break at that point.

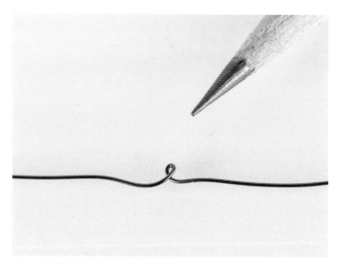

This small kink in the wire will catch on the other yarns and will not pass smoothly through a fine reed. If it's in the weft, it will catch on all the warp threads as the shuttle passes through the shed. Kinks also weaken the wire.

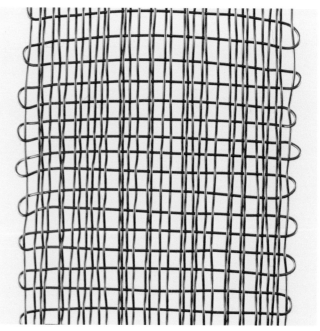

Wire warp and weft: The weave structure is difficult to control when wire is used for both the warp and the weft. AWG 27 wire was used for this experiment. The wire was set at 24 wire ends per inch (nine per centimeter). Notice that the wire wefts are spaced out because beating a wire warp is difficult. The wire warp threads have a tendency to drift out of place.

If you find a kink, carefully untwist it to remove the loop. Never pull on a kink to straighten it out. That will only make the kink smaller and weaken the metal even more. Once the kink is untwisted, tightly hold the wire a few inches on either side of the kink. Slide the wire back and forth lengthwise against the edge of a hard piece of wood to straighten it out again.

Weaving with wire is different from weaving with other yarns in the way the wire bends as it's being woven. If wire is used in just the warp or just the weft, this won't be as obvious. But if wire is used in both the warp and the weft and the goal is a balanced weave, the weaving will be difficult and the results will be somewhat uneven unless great care is taken.

Weaving with a wire warp is different in the way the wire packs as it's being beaten with the reed. A wire warp woven with a fiber weft results in a tightly packed surface, and the wire disappears altogether. The fiber bends easily around the wire, allowing the wire to bend very little. This causes the fiber to pack tightly against itself, and the result is a weft-faced weave, unless the warp is set very closely. A weft-faced weave that can be bent and will hold a shape

without any visible metal structure may be just what you want for a sculptural shape. Some experimentation will be necessary to achieve the desired effect.

A fiber warp woven with a wire weft is more satisfying if you want the wire to be visible. Because the fibers bend more easily around the wire, fiber fills up some of the space between the wire picks and prevents them from being packed too tightly against each other. The result is that the wire picks show on the surface of the cloth.

The sculptural pieces that I have woven use a fiber warp of fine wool plus a short magnet wire warp used for the dense areas. The dense-area wire warp is typically set at 100 ends per inch (40 ends per centimeter). The weft is also magnet wire.

Since the weft is wire that does not bend as easily as the wool, it's important to find the correct sett for the wool being used. The wool will easily shift side to side if the sett is not correct. My general rule is to set the wool at twice what I would normally use for the same fiber warp. It is useful to add a few extra fiber weft threads into the sett at the selvage to fill out the loops created by the wire weft.

Wire warp and fiber weft: The result is a weft-faced weave unless the wire is closely spaced. Depending on the wire gauge used, it would need to be set very closely to result in a warp-faced weave.

Fiber warp and wire weft: Both the warp and the weft are visible. The sett was 24 ends per inch (nine ends per centimeter), woven as tabby. To see more of the wire weft, either space the warp out more or weave a twill structure.

Setting up a warp this dense can be tedious but is faster and easier if you wind two ends at once and then thread and sley the two ends as one. The results are also better, as the following samples show. The black fiber is a wool and nylon blend. Wrapping this fiber around a ruler resulted in approximately 32 wraps per inch (13 wraps per centimeter). All samples used US gauge 27 magnet wire.

These samples illustrate three points. First, wire and fiber used together don't weave like either a totally wire cloth or a totally fiber cloth. Second, until you have some experience with the materials, sample! Finally, none of the samples are right or wrong. Even a woven piece that looks much too loose, or too tight, is right if that is what you intended.

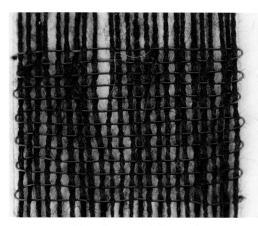

A fiber warp, set at 16 ends per inch (six ends per centimeter) with a magnet wire weft, woven as tabby. The resulting fabric is loose.

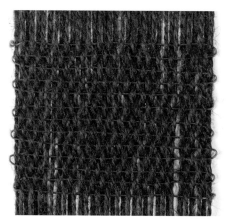

A fiber warp, set at 24 ends per inch (nine ends per centimeter) with a magnet wire weft, woven as tabby. The warp threads still slide side to side a little.

A fiber warp, set at 24 ends per inch (nine ends per centimeter) with a magnet wire weft. Every two warp threads are sleyed and threaded together. Notice how the warp threads lie side by side with minimal sliding right to left.

A fiber warp, set at 24 ends per inch (nine ends per centimeter) with a magnet wire weft, woven as twill. Every two warp threads are sleyed and threaded together.

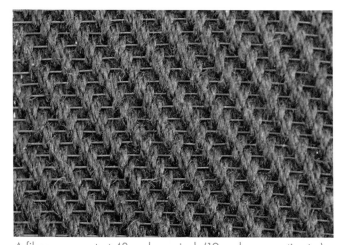

A fiber warp, set at 48 ends per inch (19 ends per centimeter) with a magnet wire weft woven as twill. Every two warp threads are sleyed and threaded together. Notice how doubling the number of ends reduces the amount of wire weft that is exposed.

Creating a Wire Warp

The wire warps that I use most often are narrow and not longer than a few yards, since they are woven as dense areas in combination with a fiber warp. If your wire warp is very wide, I suggest winding it in several bouts, each a couple of inches wide, so that there is less to manage at one time.

Winding a wire warp uses almost the same process as winding a fiber warp. The warp must be planned so that you know how many warp threads and how long a warp to wind. The warp is wound on a warping board or warping mill in almost the same way as a fiber warp, although the small wires may be a little more difficult to see as you wind the warp. You create a cross in the same way, and you tie choke ties in the same way. The choke ties should be tied tightly so they don't slide along the wire, and they should be tied more frequently than for a fiber warp.

When you remove the warp from the warping board or mill, don't chain it. Trying to chain a magnet wire warp only provides many opportunities to create kinks. Instead, coil the length of the warp into a circle and secure the ends and the circle with the modified clothespins, as discussed in chapter 3.

The wire warp is beamed like a normal warp, but some special techniques can be used to deal with the slippery wire. I usually don't cut the ends of the warp that go around the rod on the warp beam, but I tape them onto the rod to keep them from sliding around. The lease sticks can be the same ones you use for the entire warp. Popsicle sticks or nails that are taped together can be used as lease sticks if the warp is very narrow.

I usually beam from back to front. That means that I wind the warp onto the warp beam with the help of lease sticks, a raddle, and packing between the warp layers on the warp beam. The warp must be held under tension while winding on, but the wire is too slippery to allow you to hang weights onto the warp bundle in the normal way.

The solution is to use a wide rubber band. Make a lark's-head knot around the warp bundle at the front of the loom with the rubber band. Attach the loop of the rubber band to a weight, such as a jug of water, with a piece of Texsolv and an arrow peg. The rubber band will provide enough friction to keep the lark's-head knot from slipping along the wire bundle. As the warp is wound on, the choke ties can be cut off one by one until the end of the warp bundle is reached.

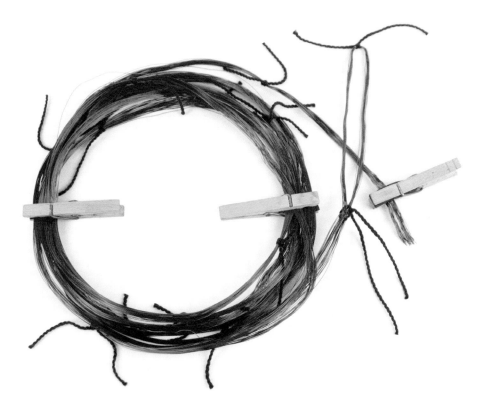

Modified clothespins secure this magnet wire warp, capturing the cut ends and the looped warp length. The warp has a cross, and tightly tied choke ties, every few feet.

Leave a length of the warp at the front of the loom so that there is enough wire to thread the heddles and sley the reed. If you remove the weight, the wire may start to unwind itself from the warp beam. To prevent this, use masking tape to temporarily tape the wire warp to the back beam before removing the weight. The tape will keep the wire from unwinding itself like a watch spring that has just been released from tension. Secure the wire ends at the front of the loom either with modified clothespins or tape, until you are ready to thread and sley them.

You are now ready to thread the heddles and sley the reed. Since the wire ends are stiff, it's not necessary to use a threading tool or a sley hook. You can use these tools if you want, so do what works best for you. At each step, it's easy for the wires to escape and slip out of the heddles or the reed. Use the modified clothespins to control the wires or groups of wires.

Once the wire warp is threaded and sleyed, you are ready to tie it onto the cloth beam. Here again the wires need to be controlled. I like to tie wire onto a piece of threaded rod because the threads keep the wire from sliding off. Sections of wire are wrapped around the threaded rod and twisted together, since knots don't work well in wire. The rod can then be attached to the cloth beam rod with two pieces of Texsolv and arrow pegs.

This method has the advantage of allowing you to attach different sections of the warp to the cloth beam, using different methods. I prefer attaching fiber sections of the warp by lashing them on, but that doesn't work very well for wire sections of the warp. In this way I can use the best method for each section of the warp without the different methods interfering with each other.

The wire section of the warp was wrapped around a piece of threaded rod, and the ends were twisted together. The threads in the rod prevent the wire from sliding along the rod, which is itself tied to the cloth beam rod with pieces of Texsolv and arrow pegs.

In this example, a wire warp is tied on to a threaded rod, which is itself attached to the cloth beam rod. A wool warp can be added on top, or underneath, using the lashing method. If a section needs to be moved or removed, or a threading error needs to be corrected, the other sections of the warp are not affected because they are tied on separately.

Tying on versus Lashing on: Most weavers use one of two methods to tie their warp onto the cloth beam rod. In both cases the warp is divided into sections of about an inch each (2–3 centimeters). I find it easier to lash on, because the tension between the sections of the warp is easier to adjust, and because it creates less warp waste than tying on. For both methods, threading and sleying errors can be corrected without retying the entire warp.

If the warp is tied on, the warp threads for each section are divided into two approximately equal parts. The threads pass over the top of the cloth beam rod and then under it. Each half of the section comes up beside the outside of the section being tied on, and the two halves are tied together using a surgeon's knot. A surgeon's knot is a simple overhand knot, but one where the ends pass around each other twice instead of just once. To correct a threading mistake, release tension on the warp, untie the appropriate knot and make the correction, retie the knot, and retension the warp.

If the warp is lashed on, a simple knot is tied at the end of each section of the warp. The knot must include all the warp ends in that section. A cord is tied to the rod on the cloth beam. This cord passes through the approximate center of the first knotted section of warp threads, around the rod, through the second knotted section, around the rod, and so on until all the knotted sections have been captured in turn. Finally, the cord is tied onto the cloth beam rod at the other end. I use Texsolv and an arrow peg for the cord used to lash on. To correct threading errors, release the tension on the warp, untie the appropriate knot, and make the correction. Retie the knot, making sure that the lashing cord is in the same position with respect to the knot, and retension the warp.

Tying on with a surgeon's knot

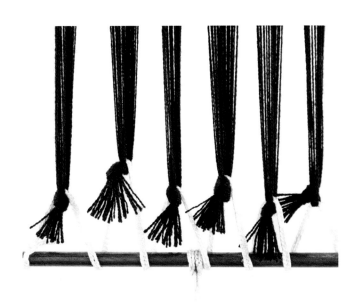

Lashing on

Weaving with a Wire Weft

Once the correct sett has been determined, weaving with a wire weft is the same as weaving with a fiber weft except for two small differences. The first difference is in the process of starting to wind a bobbin or pirn. Since wire is slippery and has a bit of a spring to it, I find it helpful to use a small piece of tape to attach the wire to the bobbin or pirn, to make it easier to wind tightly.

The second difference involves dealing with the bend of the wire at the selvage. If the wire isn't bent at the selvage, small loops will form. I don't like the look of these loops, but that is an aesthetic choice of mine. To prevent the loops, the wire must be bent at the selvage. There are two ways to easily accomplish this.

The first method is to wear the rubber thimbles, described in chapter 3, that are fitted with blunt weaving needles. As each new pick is woven, the wire can be bent around the needle while you are tugging on the wire with the opposite hand.

The second method is to use a strong selvage thread to bend the wire weft. After a pick is woven, pull the selvage thread opposite the shuttle out to the side of the warp and tug on the other end of the wire. This will cause the wire to bend around the selvage thread, eliminating the loop. A floating selvage works well for this because it's easier to find with your fingers than an ordinary warp thread. If you plan to use your selvage thread in this way, make sure it's strong enough that the wire doesn't cut into it and cause it to break.

The only difficulty, which applies to both methods, is that it's challenging to place the bend in the wire at the correct location and to do it consistently. Adding a few extra warp threads to the sett at the selvage helps because the extra threads will spread out and fill up any extra wire at the bend.

One surprising way in which fiber and wire are the same is that both can stretch as they are woven. Although I've never attempted to measure the stretch of the copper magnet wire that I use, I estimate that it stretches about the same amount as tightly woven long-fiber cotton. This makes sense when you remember that metal is often stretched slightly to strengthen it.

In addition to copper magnet wire, I like using a fine wool or a wool and nylon blend for my sculptural pieces, because of the stretch provided by the wool and the strength provided by the nylon. The fact that the wool stretches allows the copper to become a framework for the wool and makes the shaping process easier. The wool fills in the framework, and the copper provides a sparkle and a shimmer for the whole piece.

Bending the wire warp around a weaving needle fitted into a thimble

Bending the wire warp around a strong selvage thread

We have now discussed the technical aspects of weaving in three dimensions on a hand loom. You probably have ideas for shapes that you would like to try to weave, but aren't sure which techniques to use or how to plan your project to accomplish those shapes. The next chapter describes how to design and plan to weave the exact shapes you have in mind.

Ruff Four: A neck ruff woven with a black wool and nylon warp and a red magnet wire weft. This piece was woven for chapter 8, using the infinite-tensioning technique with double weave.

8 Design Considerations and Planning to Weave a Shape

The technical aspects and some examples for weaving a 3-D shape on a hand loom are discussed in the previous chapters. This chapter describes the finer points of designing and planning to weave your own shapes. Some of the concepts apply to all three techniques—expanded areas, dense areas, and infinite tensioning—and any type of material that you plan to weave. Other concepts apply to only one of the techniques. For all the 3-D techniques, you must remember to plan which shafts to use for the various parts of the warp.

Weaving Software

No matter what you plan to weave and whether you use a dobby loom or not, you will want to develop a weaving draft to help you plan and execute the weaving. It doesn't matter whether your draft is done by hand or with weaving software. However, weaving software assumes that the entire warp width is woven on each pick, and that is not always true with these techniques. The draft diagrams in this chapter illustrate how the weaving is actually accomplished versus how it will look in the software. Consider the following example of a weaving draft where only shafts 1 and 2 are woven on the first four picks, followed by weaving all the shafts on the next four picks:

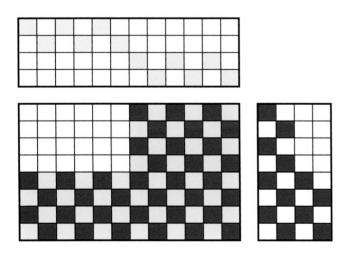

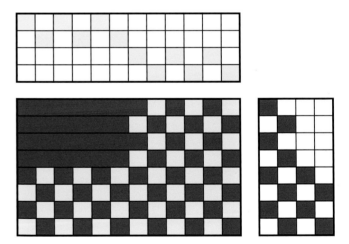

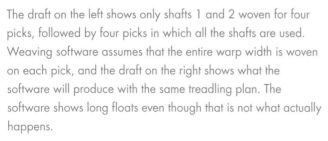

The draft on the left shows only shafts 1 and 2 woven for four picks, followed by four picks in which all the shafts are used. Weaving software assumes that the entire warp width is woven on each pick, and the draft on the right shows what the software will produce with the same treadling plan. The software shows long floats even though that is not what actually happens.

All the draft examples in this book show what actually happens. You must ignore the inaccuracy of the weaving software.

Think about weaving double-weave layers with different structures, layers with different widths, and layers that are not all woven at the same time. A weaving like this can get very complicated. Eventually it can get so complex that the weaving structures are all but impossible to see in the software. Complicated drafts make it difficult to see if there are errors in the structure prior to actually weaving the cloth. The solution to this is something that I am embarrassed to say I did not realize for much too long.

That is, *the threading draft and the treadling draft do not have to be the same draft!*

In the following example a narrow double-weave layer is woven for two picks, alternating with two picks of the base layer, for a distance of eight picks. After that, the narrow double-weave layer is woven independently and floating on top of the base layer for several picks. In the threading diagram the weave structure will be pretty messy, even when just tabby is used. Consider how much more confusing it would be with more-complex structures.

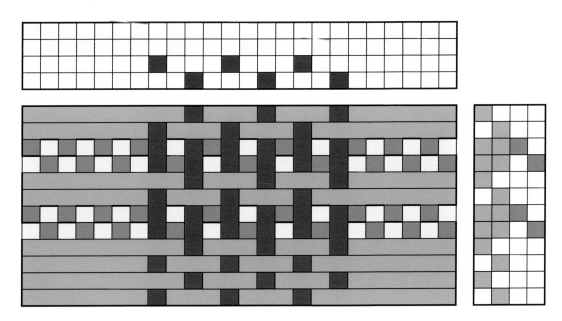

Threading for double-weave layers woven at the same time, using weaving software: Two picks of the top double layer (the red warp threads) on shafts 1 and 2 are followed by two picks of the base layer (the yellow warp threads) on shafts 3 and 4, while both shafts 1 and 2 are held up out of the way. This continues for a total of eight picks. After that, shafts 1 and 2 are woven by themselves for four picks. It's messy looking.

Once the threading is done, there is no reason to use the threading draft for the actual weaving. It's easier to follow if there is a separate treadling diagram that separates the layers out like this:

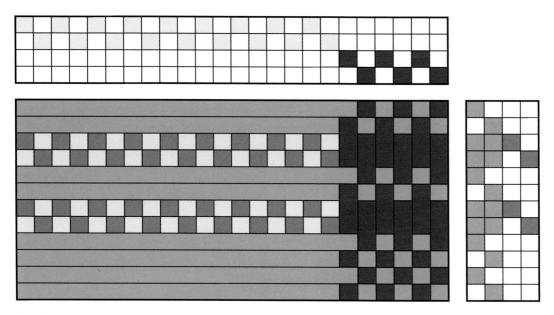

Simplified threading, using weaving software: This draft is much easier to look at, even in the software. It's easy to see that the top layer on shafts 1 and 2 is woven for two picks, followed by two picks of shafts 3 and 4, while both shafts 1 and 2 are held out of the way. After that, shafts 1 and 2 are woven by themselves for several picks.

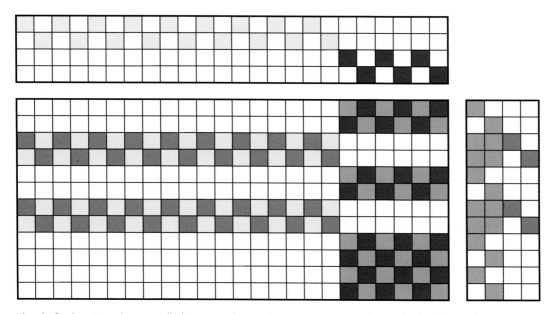

The draft, showing what actually happens: the two layers are woven independently. The top layer is not woven but must be held up while the bottom layer is woven. Your weaving software won't look like this.

Threading and Treadling Pattern Repeats

One design complication involves the number of picks in a repeat for the pattern being used. For example, if you are weaving double-weave layers that exchange places at some point, and the two layers have different weave structures, they should have the same number of picks in a repeat. If they don't, one pattern will be incomplete when it comes time for the layers to exchange places.

Depending on what you are weaving, this may also hold true for the number of warp threads in a threading repeat. If two structures don't have the same number of threads or picks in a repeat, one should be a multiple of the other. Sometimes it's possible to experiment with the structure and add or remove a thread or a pick to get the desired number in a repeat.

Whether you are weaving double weave or not, it's important to think through how the weaving pattern will look on the finished cloth so that it doesn't look like you made a mistake. Fancy twills are less forgiving than tabby or simple structures such as log cabin. Weaving software can be a great help in visualizing the resulting cloth, and in helping you make changes if you need to add or drop a thread or a pick from a pattern repeat.

SAMPLE, SAMPLE, SAMPLE!

No matter which technique you employ, it's essential that you understand how your cloth will weave up. Your results will vary depending on the size of yarn and the sett that you use. The technique you use to beat the cloth can affect how tightly it's beaten. For example, if you change the shed while the reed is held against the fell, your results will be more consistent.

The yarn size and sett are things that are decided before setting up the loom. Sampling will provide information on the number of picks in a given length of woven cloth or in a repeat of the pattern structure. The length and width of a repeat will determine the appearance of the resulting pattern, which may be important information for the shape you want to weave.

It's also important to sample using the specific technique that you are planning to use. If you are weaving wedge-shaped pieces with infinite tensioning, your beating at the end of the triangle—when there are fewer warp threads being beaten—may cause the cloth to compact more than it does when many warp threads are woven. That will reduce the length of the cloth at that point and may affect the resulting shape you are weaving.

These general concepts apply to all the 3-D weaving techniques, but there are also some specific design concerns that apply only to individual techniques.

Design Considerations for Weaving Expanded Areas

Expanded areas are the easiest to weave, but they require some thought to plan. The amount of extra warp length required will depend on what you plan to weave with regard to the size and number of expanded areas, and where the expanded areas are located in the overall warp. If they are all placed at the same location on the warp width, they will require more warp length than if they are scattered around on the surface of the cloth. Scattering them around requires less extra warp length but more sets of shafts.

One consideration is the ratio of normal weaving to expanded-area weaving. A one-to-two ratio of normal to expanded-area weaving provides some extra cloth on the surface, but is it enough? Is a ratio of one-to-three too much? In addition to adding some extra warp length for sampling, it can be useful to make a mockup with different ratios by pinning or sewing patches of gathered cloth onto a piece of scrap fabric. This technique is especially useful for planning clothing pieces that feature expanded areas, such as the jacket woven in chapter 4. A mockup is a valuable tool to help determine the placement of expanded areas in an overall design.

Once the number of expanded areas has been determined along with their size and location, the expanded-area warp length can be calculated. As a practical matter, expanded areas don't usually require as much extra warp length as the other techniques. It's often sufficient to add a half yard (46 centimeters) to the length of the normal warp for the expanded areas unless a large number of them are planned.

It's always better to have more warp left over at the end than to run out before you are done weaving, so plan for the longest warp you think you will need. A slightly longer warp will provide the opportunity to weave more samples or to try out other ideas that you have for weaving shaped fabric.

An expanded area of the warp that is threaded on a separate set of shafts and uses a rod beam or weights for its tension can also be used to try out weaving dense areas. Unless you resley the reed, the sett will not be dense enough, but it can still be useful to determine the length of selvage created by a given number of picks.

Think about the weave structure that you are planning. The expanded area does not have to use the same threading or treadling as the normal area, but since they will be seen together, the patterns will interact with each other visually. The patterns being woven should be kept intact when it's again time to weave across the whole warp, and the expanded-area pattern should be pleasing when it's woven by itself.

Weaving software can make this easier to figure out. In the following examples of a simple twill, the expanded area (the blue weft) is woven on shafts 1 through 4 and the normal area (red weft) is woven on shafts 5 through 8.

But notice the pattern that emerges when just the expanded area is woven. The motif in the expanded area is not complete. This problem is easily corrected by adding a single thread on shaft 1, at the far left of the expanded area. But that causes a float when the expanded area is woven along with the normal area of weaving. A different way to approach the problem is to totally change the treadling pattern in the expanded area. The only requirement is that the new treadling pattern must work with the threading pattern when all the shafts are woven.

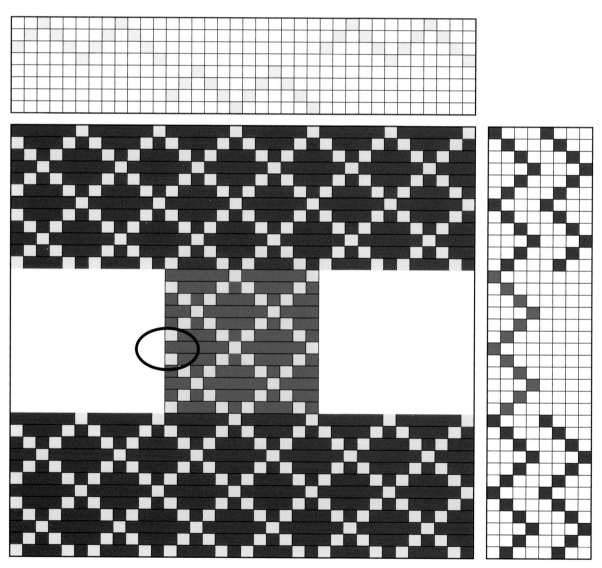

The circled area shows that the motif is not complete when just the expanded area is woven.

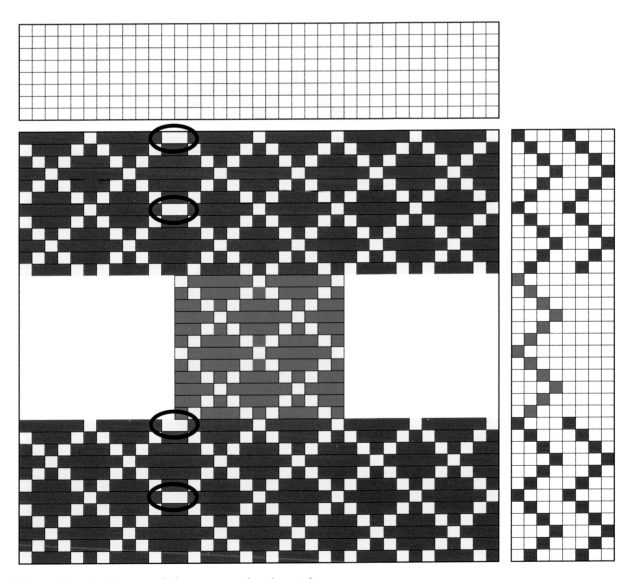

Adding a thread to the expanded area to complete the motif
causes a float when the normal and expanded areas are
woven together.

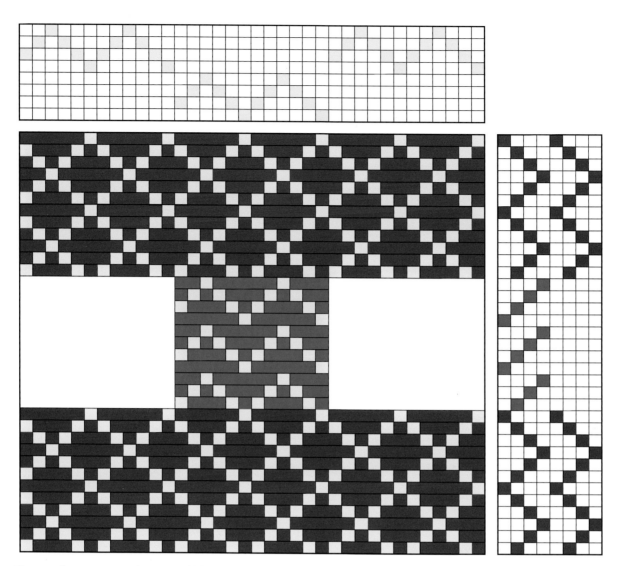

The treadling pattern in the expanded area can be changed
altogether to avoid the problem.

The easiest approach is to first plan the draft with the desired threading on the various sets of shafts. Add the treadling sequence for the normal-area shafts and review the woven pattern for errors. Add treadling rows for just the expanded area into the draft. Review how the normal and expanded areas interact, and fix any problems that you find. Once the draft is complete, simplify the threading by separating the various sets of shafts out into their own sections. Thread the loom by using the original draft, but use the simplified threading while weaving.

After you start weaving, carefully look at the woven cloth for errors or unpleasing results. Errors during sampling don't always need to be corrected, but you will want to correct them before you start weaving the actual project.

Design Considerations for Weaving Dense Areas

Dense areas require weaving a header at the beginning and end of the weaving, and the options for doing that are explored in chapter 5.

The best way to determine the number of picks needed in a dense area is to measure the required selvage lengths for the shape being woven, and then weave a sample. To sample, weave three or four dense areas. Each time the dense-area shed is changed to insert either a tension rod or a tension bar, also place a short contrasting-colored marker thread into the shed at the selvage opposite the dense area. If there are dense areas at both selvages, place the marker thread in the middle of the warp at its fullest point. The marker thread needs to be only a few inches long, but remember to leave the tails hanging out of the shed so that it can easily be removed later.

Measure the length of the cloth at both the dense area and the fullest part of the normal area of weaving. These two numbers will give you the ratio of the normal weaving to the dense area of weaving, for the yarn and number of picks being used. If the normal-area cloth is too short, add more picks into each dense area, and if it's too long, use fewer picks.

When weaving a shape that is flexible, such as a ruffle for a piece of clothing, the exact dimensions may not matter as much, as long as the warp is long enough to weave the fullest part of the normal weave. However, it's still useful to know the dimensions of the fabric in order to determine how long the warp should be. The easiest way to make this determination is to construct the desired shape from inexpensive cloth. Use gathers to mimic the dense-area gathers, then measure the amount of cloth used.

In other cases, the shape and dimensions are not very flexible, as, for example, when using dense areas to weave a cylinder shape for a pillow covering. In that case the circumference of the cylinder will be the warp length, and the height of the cylinder plus the diameter will be the warp width. Don't forget to add extra width and length for loss on the loom, pull-in, some header fabric to hem at both ends of the weaving, and shrinkage from laundering.

Once the warp lengths are determined, think about the pattern being woven. As a practical matter, if two adjacent dense areas contain slightly different numbers of picks, no one will notice the difference.

For example, think about a normal-area pattern repeat of 50 picks with a dense area at one selvage. One dense area can contain 24 picks and the next one can contain 26 picks, enabling the shuttle to start and stop at the selvage opposite the dense areas. The first dense area can be woven with the even-numbered dense-area shafts raised, and the second can be woven with the odd-numbered shafts raised. This difference won't be visible in the finished cloth unless the warp was advanced using the leapfrogging-rods method, and even then, it will be barely noticeable.

No matter how many picks there are in the pattern repeat, the overall draft repeat must contain an even number of dense areas, since the dense area is always woven as tabby. Multiples of the pattern repeat can be used in a single dense area, or partial pattern repeats can be used, but each entire repeat of the draft must have an even number of dense areas.

WEAVING DENSE-AREA SHAPES

Consider three different shapes: the shape of a globe, the shape of a lantern, and the shape of a cylinder. Each shape consists of a dense area at each selvage, with an area of normal weaving in the middle. Each of these three shapes uses the same overall weaving plan, but with some important differences.

The globe shape uses very narrow dense areas, with as large a number of picks in each dense area as possible. This plan causes the cloth to pull in a great deal at the north and south poles, where the gathers will be extreme.

The lantern uses wide dense areas at each selvage, with a medium number of picks in each one. A medium number of picks is 20 to 50, depending on the weight of the yarn. The dense areas create the vertical collar found at the top and the bottom of the lantern. The collars are shaped like flat rings because the dense areas are wide and contain a relatively small number of picks. The normal area of weaving creates the bulge at the center of the lantern.

The cylinder shape is woven like the globe shape, with one important difference. The middle of the normal area of weaving uses a different kind of yarn than what is used for the top and the bottom of the cylinder. When a heavier and stiffer type of yarn is used in the area of normal weaving that will become the height of the cylinder, the cloth will naturally bend to form a cylinder shape.

Differences in the width of the normal areas of weaving can be used to change the shape of the final piece. If an area of normal weaving has a dense area on both sides, or a dense area on one side and a heavy-yarn floating selvage on the other, the amount of shape expansion contributed by the normal area will be determined by its width. The wider the warp of the normal area, the more that area will bulge once the piece is off the loom.

If you use a heavy wire for the floating selvage, it can be pulled in after the cloth is off the loom, creating gathers much like a single-thread dense area. Consider the warp plan for a geisha-style headdress:

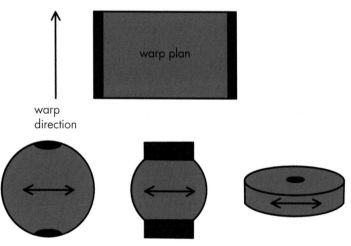

The black areas represent the placement of dense areas. Note the direction of the warp in the warp plan and on the woven shapes.

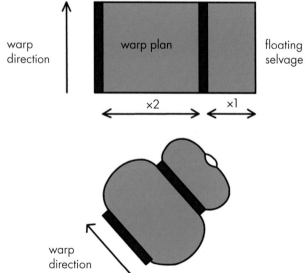

The black areas represent the placement of dense areas. Note the direction of the warp in the warp plan and on the woven shape. The wire floating selvage at the right edge of the warp is pulled in after the warp is off the loom, creating a loop at the top of the headdress form.

Dense areas at the selvages can be woven alternately to create triangles. Changing the weft thread color at the same time makes the triangles more visible. While the dense areas are woven at one selvage, the dense-area section of the warp is woven normally at the other selvage. Because the dense area is set at twice the number of threads per inch, the selvage that is woven normally bulges out a small amount. That small bulge either can be turned under during the finishing process, dealt with in one of the ways described in chapter 5, or regarded as a feature.

Dense areas can be set up at various locations in the width of the warp on the same or different sets of shafts. When they are set up on different sets of shafts, they can contain different numbers of picks and be advanced at different rates. There are obviously a lot of options and combinations available to create shapes by varying the number of picks in the dense and normal areas, their widths, the rate and method by which the cloth is advanced in the different areas, and the weight and physical characteristics of the yarn used in both the warp and the weft.

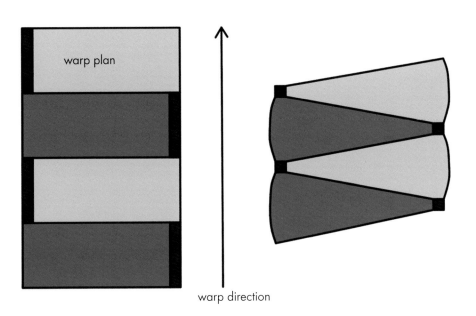

warp plan

warp direction

Dense areas are placed at each selvage, represented by black. Triangles are created by weaving dense areas alternately at the selvages and changing the color of the weft thread at the same time. The two dense areas must be placed on different sets of shafts since they are not woven at the same time. While a dense area is being woven at one selvage, the dense-area shafts at the other selvage are woven normally.

Design Considerations for Infinite-Tension Weaving

As with expanded areas and dense areas, weaving software is unable to depict what actually happens when a wedge-shaped piece is woven using the infinite-tensioning technique. If the weave is balanced and the number of warp threads woven is reduced by two for each two woven picks, the resulting triangle should have two equal sides. If the warp has an area of normal weaving at the right and the software could depict weaving with infinite tension, it would look like this:

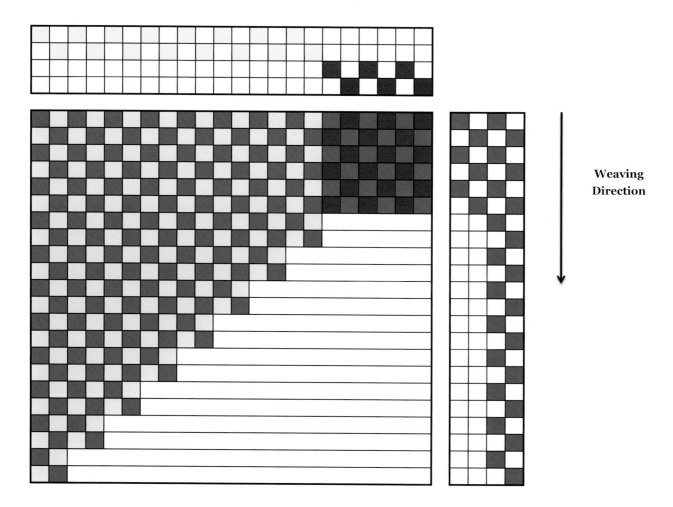

Weaving Direction

An area of normal weaving is at the right, starting at the top of the draft. After it's woven for six picks, the infinite-tension-area wedge is woven. If the weave is balanced, the woven triangle will have two equal sides.

Weaving software is not helpful when determining the exact number of warp threads to weave with each set of picks to create a triangle of a given shape, but graph paper is useful. Weave a sample to determine how many warp threads and picks are woven in a square dimension. Using graph paper, plot this result to determine how to arrive at the desired shape. Remember that to prevent floats along the diagonal of the triangle, picks need to start at a selvage and be woven in pairs to return the shuttle to the same selvage.

Weaving will be easier and faster if, for example, six picks are woven capturing a given number of warp threads, followed by weaving six fewer warp threads for the next six picks. The difference on the cloth won't be seen if the yarn is fine and closely set. But if the yarn is heavy and not closely set, the number of threads captured by a set of picks should be reduced more gradually.

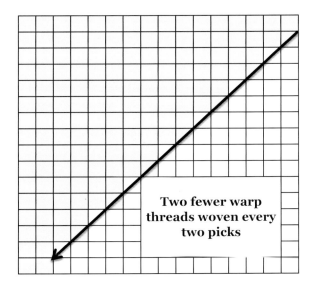

Two fewer warp threads woven every two picks

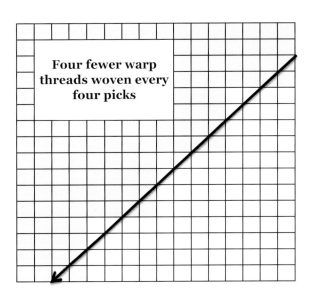

Four fewer warp threads woven every four picks

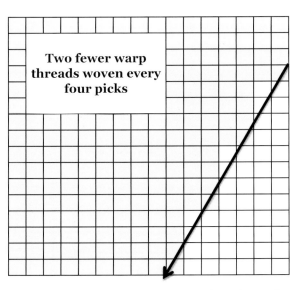

Two fewer warp threads woven every four picks

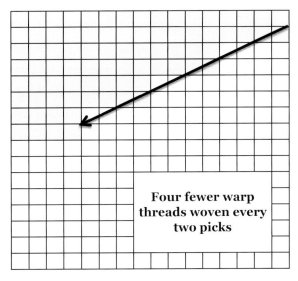

Four fewer warp threads woven every two picks

The number of picks in a set and the number of warp threads captured by each pair of picks can be varied independently to arrive at triangles of different shapes. Each set of picks should be an even number. In a balanced weave, reducing the number of warp threads captured by an equal number of picks results in a triangle with two equal sides.

The above examples use tabby. But if you are weaving a pattern, you should also consider where that pattern will be cut off by your infinite-tension weaving plan. Consider a balanced weave with a nine-thread pattern repeat in the warp and a seven-pick pattern repeat in the weft. In this case, reducing the number of warp threads by two for every two picks will cut the pattern motif at an angle. In addition, the infinite-tension section of the warp would need to contain a multiple of 63 warp ends ($7 \times 9 = 63$) to allow the infinite-tension wedge being woven to be completed at the same time as the end of a pattern repeat.

Weaving software is useful for determining how the pattern will look once woven, but it will not show how it will look as the weft picks become more and more narrow. Print out the weaving drawdown and use a piece of paper to hide the part of the pattern that will not be woven. This will give you an idea of how the weaving will look, but weaving a sample will be more accurate.

WEAVING INFINITELY TENSIONED SHAPES

The shapes you weave using infinite tensioning can be combined with rectangles to create an overall shape. Mockups are useful in determining how the weaving plan will turn out. Cloth can be used for the mockup, but paper is easier to work with if your shapes are primarily geometric.

The copper wire and fine wool piece shown at the end of chapter 7 includes a double-weave section in the infinite-tension weaving area. The piece was intended to be a neck ruff and needed to fit on a body shape. The mockup was created directly on my dress form out of aluminum foil, newspaper, and tape. This allowed me to measure the dimensions of height and circumference around the vertical neck portion, and the longest selvage dimension of the abbreviated cape portion that rests on the shoulders.

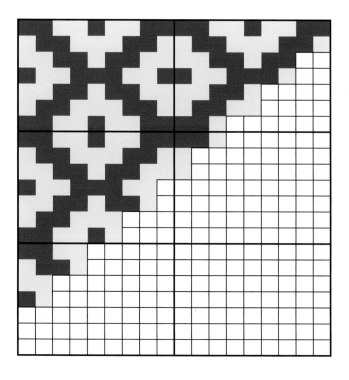

Notice how the infinite-tension weaving plan cuts across the pattern. Notice also that the infinite-tension part of the weaving completes before the pattern repeat is complete.

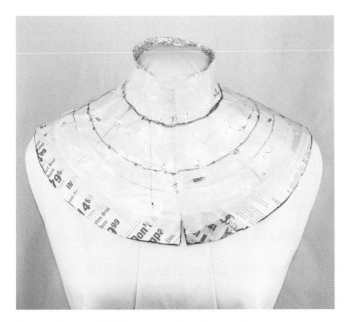

The mockup for *Ruff Four*, woven for chapter 7

Using these measurements, I was able to calculate the warp length for the infinitely tensioned sections and the normal-weave section at the neck. Double weave was used to weave expanded areas that were open on each side. These measurements allowed me to calculate the different warp lengths. The double-weave layer was a little longer since it was going to weave the expanded areas.

Once the loom was warped and a sample was woven, I determined that each infinitely tensioned triangle contributed about 2.5 inches (6.4 centimeters) to the selvage on the edge of the cape section. That information allowed me to devise a plan that would produce the overall shape and dimensions on the mockup, using a combination of triangles and normal areas. I added a small amount of normal weaving at the beginning and end for finishing.

Once it was woven, I placed the finished piece back onto the mockup to see how closely it matched the shape I had planned.

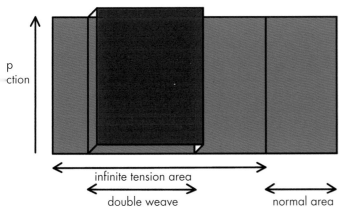

The warp plan: The neck normal area was placed on its own set of shafts. The warp was black wool and nylon. The double-weave area was red wool and nylon. An extra half yard (46 centimeters) was added to weave an infinite-tension sample before the piece was started.

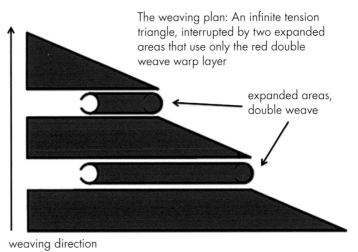

The weaving plan: The original plan was to alternate between weaving a normal area on the entire warp width, with a triangle containing two expanded areas. The sample informed me that I would need to weave several triangles alternately with the normal weaving to achieve the selvage lengths required for the shape. The double-weave layers were woven together as one, except for when the expanded areas were being woven. This worked because the weft was copper wire.

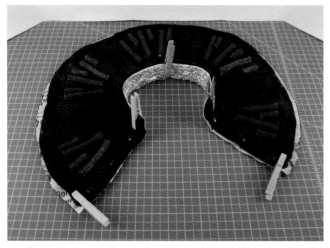

The finished piece matches the mockup very well!

The red double-weave warp was woven together with the rest of the black warp except when it was being used to weave the expanded areas. That worked because I used a copper wire weft. The copper allowed all the warp threads from both of the double-weave layers to slide together against each other, as explained in chapter 7. This would likely not have worked with a fiber weft. As a part of the finishing process, the expanded areas were held up off the surface of the piece with the help of black beads strung inside them.

The combination of triangles and rectangles can be used to weave many different shapes. The neck ruff just discussed uses a triangle with a normal area of weaving at the point of the triangle. What shape would result if the normal area was placed at the other side of the triangle? If the infinitely tensioned area was woven normally before you start to weave the triangle, what would be the result? And what shape would result if only the first portion of the triangle was woven and then stopped? What would happen if only triangles were woven?

By playing with geometric forms and imagining them together and remembering the direction of the warp, many interesting shapes can be created. The number of lingos required can be reduced by considering the shapes in different ways. In the following examples, the gray represents normal areas of weaving that do not require lingos. The red represents infinitely woven areas of the warp: areas that do require lingos.

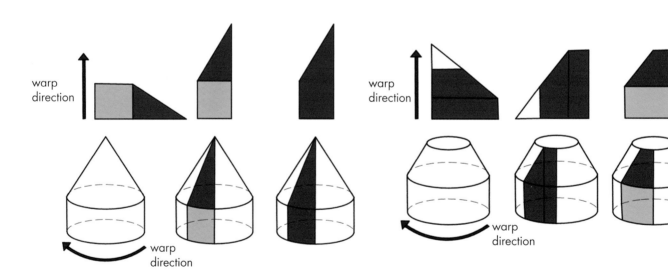

Weaving a cylinder topped by a cone. The normal area is at the left, and the infinite-tension area is at the right. Technically, a normal area isn't needed to create this shape, but using one will reduce the number of lingos required. Not using a normal area will provide the flexibility to weave additional shapes.

Weaving a cylinder topped by a truncated cone. This shape illustrates weaving a rectangle followed by a partial triangle. Note that using a normal area for the cylinder reduces the number of lingos required.

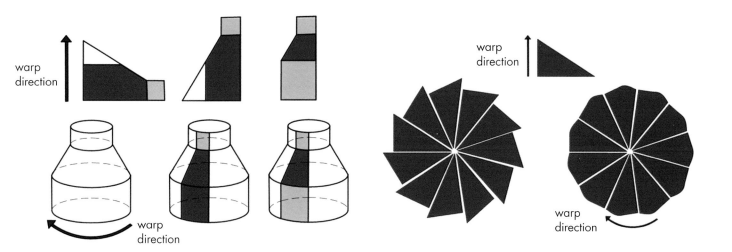

Weaving two cylinders with a truncated cone between them. Since the cylinders are different diameters, the two normal areas should be on different sets of shafts if possible. The shape can be woven with all the areas on one set of shafts if you tie marker threads around the reed to mark off certain areas, as explained in chapter 6.

What is the result of weaving only triangles? The result is not a pinwheel, because the triangle diagonal is forced into line with the selvage each time the warp is pulled in. The actual result will be more of a flower shape, depending on the yarn used and the shape and number of triangles woven.

If you have trouble thinking about how to weave the shape you want to create, build it out of construction paper and consider it from different points of view. You will be surprised at how many shapes can be constructed out of just triangles and rectangles. Remember that paper is stiff and fiber is not. The shape you weave may vary from your paper model as a result. Thinking creatively can help reduce the number of lingos that you need to use to create your shape.

Don't forget to consider the warp length. The flower shape in the last illustration will result in impossibly short warp threads at the center of the flower. Your lingos will be hanging on the floor after a very short amount of time if you wind the entire warp onto your infinite-tension warp beam. Consider dividing your warp into thirds. Wind the outside two-thirds of the warp onto the beam, but hang the last third over the beam with weights that equal the weight of the lingos on that part of the warp.

Your triangles don't have to be all the same shape. Some can use a short amount of the warp length but use the full warp width, while others can use a lot of the warp length but little of its width. The number of fewer warp threads woven for each set of picks does not need to be the same across the hypotenuse of the triangle. If you vary the rate by which you reduce the warp threads woven, your hypotenuse can sink into or bulge out of the shape woven.

The projects shown up to now may be more than you want to try as a first attempt. In the next chapter there are three beginning projects, with complete instructions for each one. Completing the projects in chapter 9 will give you experience weaving expanded areas and dense areas, and weaving with infinite tension. The projects have been designed to minimize the equipment you will need to try these techniques. Have fun!

First Projects to Try

AN EXPANDED-AREAS PROJECT: A Jabot Neck Ruffle

The goals of this chapter are to allow you to try each of the techniques on a four- or eight-shaft loom, with a minimum of new tools to build or loom modifications to make, and to make an actual project rather than just a sample. It is not possible to try the techniques with no new tools. The infinite-tension project requires lingos, and the dense-area project requires small thread weights or lingos.

Hanging weights can be used rather than a rod beam, and leapfrogging rods can be used rather than a cloth trap. The simple tools required are described in chapter 3. In order to reduce the sett and speed up the setup and weaving time, the yarn used for these projects is heavier than what you might normally use, or the warp is very narrow.

I personally wove all of the projects in this chapter. When I found that there were changes that would make the project turn out better or be easier to weave or to sew, I describe the project with those changes so that you will have the benefit of my experience. Some sewing or finishing work is required for each of the projects, but it's minimal.

This jabot is woven as a scarf with ruffles at each end. I used fine gold rayon for the entire warp and the normal-area weft, while the expanded areas were woven. I used dark-gray 2/20 linen for the expanded-area weft and the area between the two ruffles. The rayon and linen are approximately the same size.

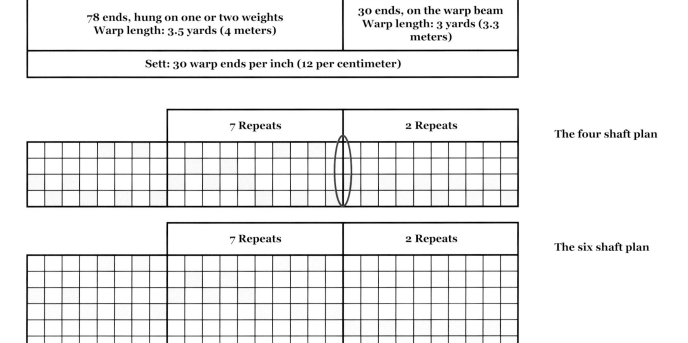

78 ends, hung on one or two weights Warp length: 3.5 yards (4 meters)	30 ends, on the warp beam Warp length: 3 yards (3.3 meters)
Sett: 30 warp ends per inch (12 per centimeter)	

The four shaft plan

7 Repeats   2 Repeats

The six shaft plan

7 Repeats   2 Repeats

The project details are shown using either four or six shafts. The red figure shows where to wrap a marker cord around the whole beater if you are using only four shafts.

A jabot is a good project to try if you like to weave cloth for clothing but don't want to make something complicated for a first project. The jabot can be worn independently or attached to the garment like a collar.

Normally, the area of weaving with the most warp ends is placed on the warp beam. This piece is an exception because the widest part of the warp is woven as an expanded area and must be tensioned with weights. The expanded area consists of the leftmost 78 warp threads, while the normal area on the right is only 30 warp threads wide. The warp is set at 30 ends per inch (12 ends per centimeter) for a warp width of only 3 inches (7.5 centimeters) in the reed. The suggested yarn sizes and colors are what I used, but you can use whatever you want or have on hand, with the limitation that this project works better with fine yarns. Linen works well because of the stiffness it provides to the ruffles.

The suggested weaving structure is a huck lace, but any lacy structure will work in the expanded area. The normal area of weaving is tabby. The entire piece, exclusive of the headers, is 37 inches (94 centimeters) long. The ruffled areas at the ends are each 7 inches (18 centimeters) long. Note that I occasionally use different colors in the diagrams than I use in the actual woven piece, to make the structure visible.

This project can be woven with two shuttles on either four or six shafts. If you used only four shafts, wrap a marker cord around the beater between the expanded-area and normal-area warp threads. Start by weaving a header with either tabby or the lace structure.

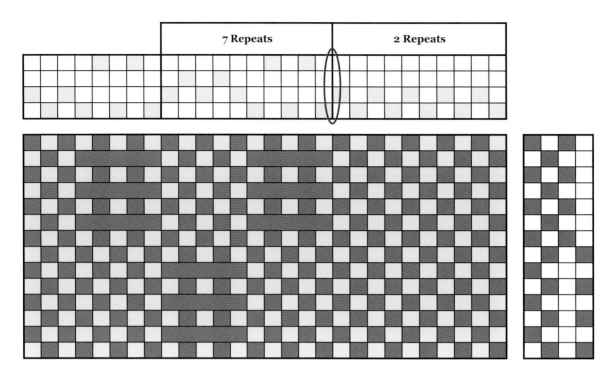

Weaving the header on four shafts: Headers and the normal area of weaving between the two ruffled areas can be woven as tabby on shafts 1 and 2 or as lace on all four. I threaded the normal area as tabby, but you could use the lace structure there also, which would produce tighter ruffles in the expanded area.

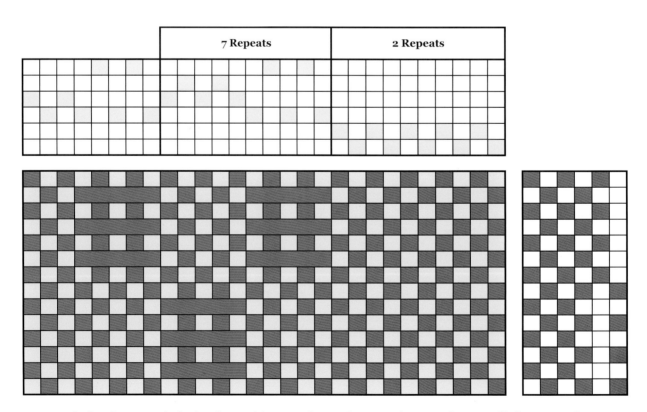

Weaving the header on six shafts: headers and the normal area of weaving between the two ruffled areas can be woven as tabby on shafts 1 through 4 or as lace and tabby as shown.

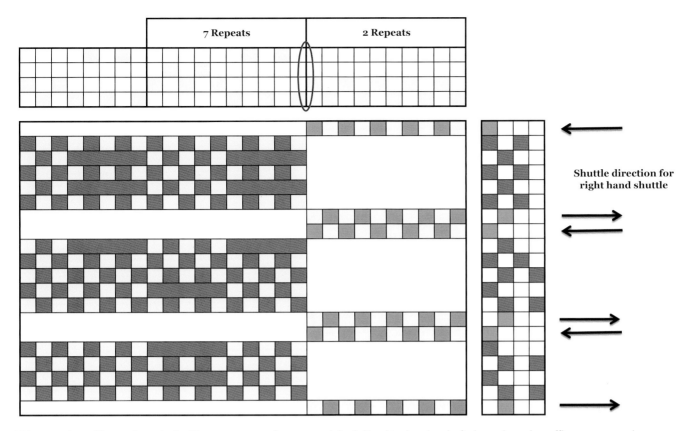

Weaving the ruffles on four shafts: Your weaving software won't look like this, but the draft shows how the ruffles are created. Remember to clasp the weft threads from the right and left shuttles whenever they meet. Two different colors are used to better illustrate the weave, but my sample used the same gold rayon yarn in both the warp and the weft of the normal area.

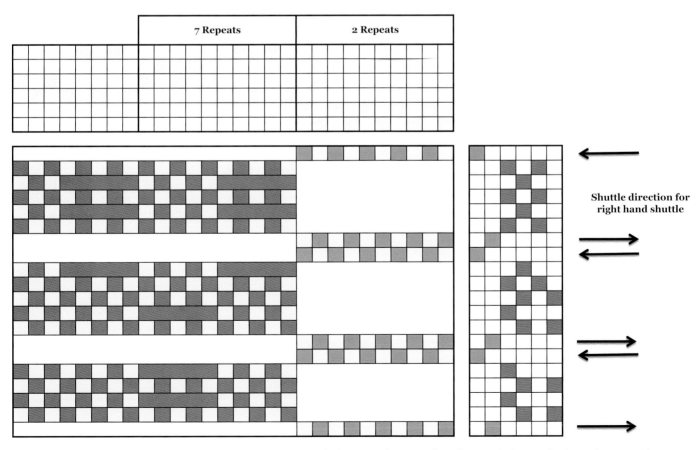

Weaving the ruffles on six shafts: Weaving is easier on six shafts because the normal- and expanded-area sheds can be opened in turn. Your weaving software won't show this. Two different colors are used to better illustrate the weave, but my sample used the same gold rayon yarn in both the warp and the weft of the normal area.

The first ruffle can be started once the header area is woven. Using the leapfrogging rods will be cumbersome on such a narrow warp, in addition to leaving marks in the cloth. Because the total warp is only a few inches wide, there is another option available in addition to using a cloth trap. Small areas such as these ruffles can be tensioned by using the type of weights used with knitting machines. These weights come in various widths and have a series of hooks that can be hung on the knitted fabric as it comes off the knitting machines. In our case, the hooks can be inserted into the warp just beyond the fell with the help of a tension rod inserted into the shed.

Since a weaving warp is parallel to the floor, the knitting weights cannot provide the cloth tension that we need to weave. They must be used in a different way. By drilling holes in the weights or by wrapping cords around the weights, they can be attached with a piece of Texsolv to an anchor point under the loom. I use my weights by attaching a small piece of Texsolv through two holes in the weight to make a loop. I use a second loop to connect the weight loop and the Texsolv anchor cord. The second loop provides the tension adjustment for the knitting weight.

I prefer to use a tension bar to pull in the warp when retensioning my warp, but if you use a tension rod instead, the knitting-machine weights are easier to use. Simply insert the tension rod into a shed and drop the shed. Adjust the tension on the warp as needed to pull it in, and insert the hooks from the weight into the warp, capturing the rod. Adjust the tension on the weight but don't make it so tight that the rod is difficult to pull out. Pull the rod out to one side through the hooks of the knitting weight and tighten the tension on the weight a little bit more. After weaving some distance, the ruffle can be pulled in a little more without repositioning the weight.

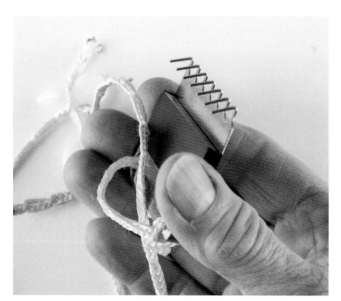

My knitting-machine weight was cut from a larger piece, but you can purchase inexpensive weights in different widths. The weight itself is not used in the weaving process, but the hooks are quite useful. Multiple weights can be used at the same time, but each one requires its own anchor point under the loom in addition to the anchor points used by the tension rod or bar you are using.

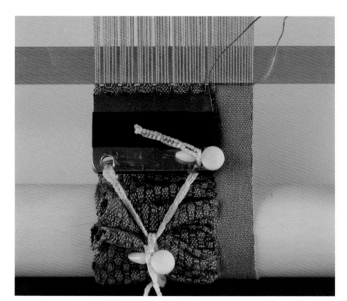

This knitting weight happened to be just the right width for the project, but a slightly wider one would work too. Once the hooks were inserted into the warp, the position of the fell can be adjusted once or twice before it needs to be reinserted.

Knitting machine cast on combs: Similar to weights, the knitting machine cast on comb has a series of bent teeth and is available in different lengths up to about 24 inches (62 cm) long. Some kinds can be attached together for even longer lengths. It's even possible to use a cast on comb instead of a cloth trap if your warp is not too wide. I have just started to experiment with them and find that they are not as sturdy as knitting machine weights. To use them for weaving widths over about 10 inches (25 cm), you will need to stiffen the comb by attaching a flat metal bar to the top with two-sided sticky tape.

If you want to try them, purchase the 4.5 mm comb (the bent teeth are 4.5 mm apart) in the length you need. Use combs as described for the knitting machine weights, but instead of drilling holes in them to hold the Texsolv tensioning cords, loop a cord around the entire comb between a set of teeth, one at each end. You can also use a tensioning cord in the middle if needed. As with the knitting machine weights, the tensioning cords are attached to an anchor point under the loom.

Compared to using a cloth trap on a wider warp, the combs are a little more difficult to use because you must use a metal rod rather than a flat bar to pull in the entire warp width when advancing. And it can be difficult to catch all the fell with the comb's bent teeth. On wider weaving widths, the tension rod can be difficult to pull out once the warp has been tensioned.

Cast on combs have the advantage of being readily available with no required construction, except for making them stiffer, and don't require side pieces on your loom for support. You don't need a temple with a cast on comb because you can insert the teeth into your unwoven warp at a diagonal, which will force the weaving width you need.

If you are weaving with four shafts, the entire warp width will be raised with every pick, so the weaving draft shows which part of the warp to actually weave. Your weaving software will look different. The marker cord wrapped around the entire beater will tell you where the shuttles should leave and enter the shed. See chapter 6 for a more thorough explanation of the use of marker cords.

Whether you are using four or six shafts, start weaving the ruffles with the normal-area shuttle on the right. Weave the normal area, from right to left, for one pick and put the shuttle down. Weave the expanded area of the weaving draft with the left shuttle for the number of picks shown, remembering to clasp the threads of the two shuttles whenever they meet. Weave two picks in the normal area with the right shuttle, which will again position it at the left edge of the normally woven area. Continue this way, pulling in the warp and adjusting the tension as needed, until the normal area on the right is 7 inches (18 centimeters) long.

Once the first ruffle is woven, weave both areas normally for 23 inches (58–59 centimeters). This area can be woven as all tabby or with the lace structure on the left. Finally, weave the second ruffle in the same way as the first, and end by weaving another small header.

I used different colors of weft thread in the expanded and normal areas. I like how that looks, but if I had planned to use the piece as a collar it would be more practical to use the same color in these two areas. Since I planned to use the piece as a jabot-type scarf, I wish I'd woven a larger header area so that I could make a loop of fabric that I could slide the two ends into, eliminating the need to tie it at the neck. See appendix 2 for more options.

This project took a little under two days to warp and weave. I used a shorter warp than I am recommending, and was barely able to weave the piece with the measurements I'd planned, with no extra warp available for experimentation. If you plan to experiment as well as weave the piece, you should make the warp even longer than recommended.

Here you see the jabot just off the loom, with no finish work other than a row of stitching at each end. The jabot was finished by turning the normal-area selvage under and stitching it to the inside edge of the ruffled area. In the neck area, the fabric was folded in thirds and stitched.

A DENSE-AREAS PROJECT:
A Bustier Apron

This bustier apron is easy to weave. The skirt and cloth for the pockets are woven first, using just tabby, after which the top is woven for a short distance with three dense areas, using a combination of tabby and twill.

Warp length - 2 yards (2.2 meters)
Sett: 24 threads to the inch (9 threads to the centimeter)

Threading on 4 Shafts (yellow heddles are empty):

Dense area - 24 heddles, 12 threaded initially.	Normal area Repeat for 252 warp ends	Dense area - 24 heddles, 12 threaded initially.	Normal area Repeat for 252 warp ends	Dense area - 24 heddles, 12 threaded initially.

Threading on 8 Shafts (yellow heddles are empty):

Dense area - 24 heddles, 12 threaded initially.	Normal area Repeat for 252 warp ends	Dense area - 24 heddles, 12 threaded initially.	Normal area Repeat for 252 warp ends	Dense area - 24 heddles, 12 threaded initially.

The project details for the apron, using either four or eight shafts. Use black 5/2 cotton for the warp and the same size of pink cotton for the weft. Note the reserved heddles that are not initially threaded in each of the three dense areas.

A 2-yard (2.2 meter) warp is suggested for this project. That should give you enough warp to weave the apron and to experiment a little either before or after. I haven't given exact dimensions for the amount of cloth to weave for a certain length of apron, and I leave that to your personal preference. My cloth was approximately 23 inches (58–59 centimeters) from the start of the tabby area to the start of the bust area.

This apron is woven from the bottom of the apron up to the top. The bottom is folded up over the front to create the pockets at the bottom of the apron. The selvages at each side are turned back to create a finished edge. A small amount of black commercial braiding or ribbon is used for the neck strap and the ties. A decorative bit of pink ribbon was added into one of the last dense areas, as will be explained.

Wind the warp in five bouts: three dense-area bouts and two normal-area bouts. The three dense-area bouts of 12 threads each can be the same length as the normal-area warp sections, because the bust section of the apron is not woven for very long and the dense areas are narrow. The normal areas are beamed onto the loom's warp beam. If you happen to have a second warp beam on your loom, use it to tension the dense areas. If you don't have a second warp beam, use heavy weights to tension each of the dense areas individually. As explained in chapter 5, an actual warp beam or a rod beam will work better than weights, which must be quite heavy to weave dense areas. The yarn you use must be strong enough to withstand being woven as a dense area.

When threading the normal areas, remember to leave 24 heddles in place for the dense areas on shafts 1 and 2 between the two normal areas and at each selvage. Initially, the dense areas contain only 12 warp ends that are threaded 1, 2, empty 1, empty 2, and so on. Depending on the number of shafts available to you, the normal areas are threaded on shafts 3 and 4, or shafts 3 through 8. I used 8 shafts for the pattern shown in the normal area of my bustier, so I modified it to 6 shafts for this project so that you could weave it on an 8-shaft loom. If you use a different weaving pattern, remember that two shafts have to be reserved for the dense area.

The dense areas are initially sleyed with the same sett as the normal areas, and no skipped dents. This lets the normal area of tabby weaving for the apron skirt proceed without a change in the sett across the width of the warp. Floating selvages are required at each side because there is a dense area at each selvage, although they are not woven as dense areas until the bust area of the apron is being woven.

Can you weave a joke? I originally wove this piece as a sort of weaving joke. Once it was done and on my dress form, it made me laugh. Wanting to share the joke with my husband, I called him into the room. He took one look and his face dropped! "You aren't going to actually wear that, are you?" was his reaction. And yes, I have worn it in public, over my other clothes. It makes a great apron to use when serving cocktails to guests.

Once enough cloth is woven with tabby for the pockets and the skirt of the apron, the bust area can be started. But before starting, the dense areas must be created. Open the next tabby shed and insert a leapfrogging rod, but just let it rest there without tensioning it yet.

Optionally, lift shafts 1 and 2 and slide a piece of cardboard or a weaving sword under these warp threads in front of the beater. This step is optional but will help you see what you are doing.

Release the weights, or tension, on the dense areas and measure the distance from the cloth fell, through the loom, to the ends of the warp in the dense areas. Cut a total of 18 warp threads that are *twice that length*. These pieces of thread will be used to double the sett in the dense areas.

Start threading at the back of the loom. Bring the end of one of the 18 warp threads through the back of one of the reserved heddles on shaft 1, making sure that it's next to a thread on shaft 2. Bring it through the same dent as the adjacent set of threads on the right, over the top of the leapfrogging rod and through the fell of the warp, capturing one or two picks. These picks will help anchor the thread once it's tensioned. Pass it back under the leapfrogging rod, through the same dent, through the reserved heddle on shaft 2, and, finally, to the back of the loom. In this way you will add 12 ends to each dense area while doubling the sett. Make sure that your threading preserves the tabby threading structure.

Sleying the dense areas to weave tabby: 12 ends

Sleying the dense areas with the additional dense area threads: 24 ends

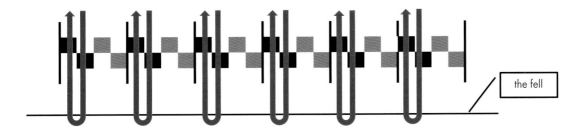

the fell

The sett in each of the dense areas is doubled just prior to starting to weave the bust area of the apron.

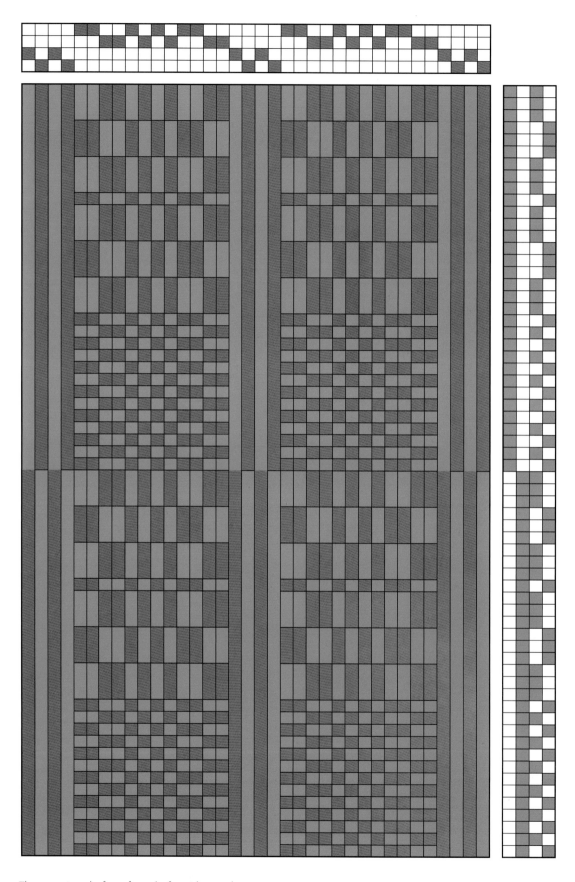

The weaving draft on four shafts with two dense areas

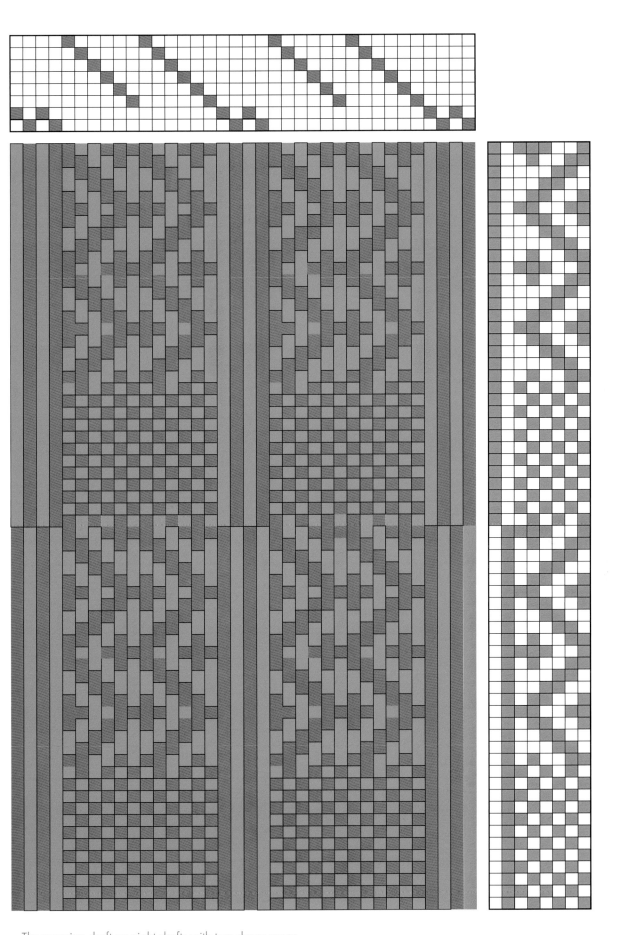

The weaving draft on eight shafts with two dense areas

Once all 18 threads are added in this way, remove the cardboard or weaving sword if you used it. Tension the leapfrogging rod in the usual way. Adjust the lengths of the added warp ends for each of the three dense areas in turn. Reattach each dense area to its hanging weight. The tensioned leapfrogging rod prevents the newly added warp threads from pulling out the first few captured picks once the dense areas are again weighted or tensioned.

After you hang lingos or other small weights on each of the four or six warp threads next to the dense areas, you are ready to weave the bust area of the apron. The drafts both for four and eight shafts are shown. Note that each draft includes the treadling pattern necessary to weave two dense areas of 32 picks each. After each dense area is woven, insert a new leapfrogging rod, pull in the warp, and tension the rod, as explained in detail in chapter 5.

The space left in the cloth by the leapfrogging rods is minimal because a twill is woven immediately after the rod is inserted. For this reason, I did not need to lay a piece of ribbon in with each leapfrogging rod. However, if you have only four shafts available and use the suggested weave structure, you may need to lay in a ribbon with each leapfrogging rod to hide the space it leaves in the cloth. Either way, you do need to add a ribbon to the shed along with the last leapfrogging rod to create the bow on the apron. For my apron I wove a total of eight dense areas, but you may want more or less depending on your required amount of fullness in the bust area. Remember to weave a header of tabby after the last dense area, so that you have an area to fold over and sew.

The bow in the center dense area

Tip: Before adding the ribbon and the bow, securely tie the bow in the middle of a length of ribbon. After the shed is open and the leapfrogging rod has been placed in the shed, thread one end of the ribbon through the open shed. Exit the top layer of the warp on one side of the middle dense area. Pull the ribbon and bow through so that the bow sits on top of the middle dense area. Push the end of the piece of ribbon back into the shed and let it exit at the other side. The ribbon now sits in the shed at each side, but the bow sits on top of the middle dense area. Later, while you are doing the finishing work, the bow can be invisibly hand stitched to the front of the apron to secure its position.

Chapter 5 explains how to use capture threads with dense areas at a selvage, to prevent the dense-area weft threads from sliding into the warp. For this project, a quadrupled length of the weft yarn is pulled through all the captured bundles and used to attach the apron ties. The original capture threads can then be removed altogether. This creates a nice semicircle at the sides of the piece. See appendix 2 for more information.

The needle shows where the leapfrogging rods were placed in the selvage. Areas of tabby and twill woven alternately are especially successful in hiding the space left by leapfrogging rods.

A quadrupled thread runs through all the dense-area groups at the selvages. This creates a semicircle at the edge of the cloth, and a way to attach the apron tie.

This little evening purse can be set up and woven over the weekend. Pick the yarn to match your favorite evening clothes and then add some fancy knitting yarn for a bit of bling.

Warp plan		Left edge area	Infinite tension area	Right edge area
Width:	inches	1	5	1
	centimeters	2.5	12.7	2.5
Sett:	inches	12	12	12
	centimeters	5	5	5
Warp ends		12	60	12
Lingos		optional	60	optional

Warp length:	yards	2.5
	meters	2.2
Structure		log cabin

The project details for the evening purse

The loom modifications required to weave with infinite tensioning involve adding an extension at the back of the loom, fitted with a warp beam and a ratchet and pawl. In order to make the technique easier to try without having to modify your loom, a slightly different setup is suggested. This alternative setup will work for narrow warps and will allow you to try the technique without making the permanent modifications to your loom. However, it will likely not work with wide warps or warps that are longer than 2 to 3 yards (2.2–3.3 meters).

The plan for this project involves heavy yarn to minimize the required sett and number of lingos required. The rightmost and leftmost inches of the warp width don't require lingos and are tensioned with weights. These sections are needed to sew the piece together during finishing. Fancy knitting yarn that contains approximately 93 yards (85 meters) of yarn in 50 grams is ideal, but any yarn of that approximate weight will work. Using a log cabin structure, the project warp requires four 50-gram balls of yarn of each color for the entire project; the warp and the weft. The most-effective colors are one dark color used with one light color. Since the project uses leapfrogging rods, some ribbon or other fancy yarn is woven in to hide the spaces left by the rods.

The suggested warp length and amount of yarn is sufficient for some extra warp in which to weave samples, the evening purse, and a little extra fabric for a handle loop or a flap closure. The purse is backed with heavy fusible interfacing and lined with a colored fabric. The closure can be a zipper or a flap with a snap.

AN ALTERNATIVE SETUP

Instead of adding an extension with a warp beam onto the back of your loom, pieces of wood can be securely clamped to each side at the back. Use at least two clamps or wood screws to attach each piece of wood. Your goal is a surface parallel to the floor on each side of the loom, on which you can place a piece of metal pipe and lease sticks. The point of the pipe is to provide a second back beam that is a little distance from your loom's back beam. In this way, you can hang half of your lingos between the extended back beam and the lease sticks, and the other half between the lease sticks and your loom's own back beam. The loom's back beam prevents the lingos from sliding toward the shafts.

The lease sticks take the place of the C-channel spacing bars described in chapter 6. Here they are not required because the warp is narrow and their weight is small enough to be supported by the lease sticks. A wider warp or one that is set more closely and uses more lingos does require the use of aluminum spacing bars.

The clamps holding the temporary side pieces must be very tight to hold up the warp weights. Wood screws will always work better than clamps to prevent the wood from sliding toward the floor. If your loom has an X-shaped frame, consider attaching the wood pieces to the sides of the loom and the castle frame. In addition to the clamps and with a little creativity, you can use Texsolv or other strong cord to also help tie the wood pieces to your loom.

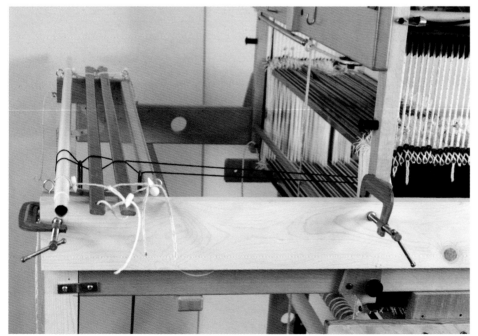

Where you clamp this piece of wood will depend on your loom. Use wood screws to attach the wood if at all possible. A smooth pipe and the lease sticks rest on the pieces of wood at each side. (My loom does not require the clamped wood because it has a permanent surface used to attach the extended warp beam for infinite

Any smooth piece of material, such as a pipe, metal rod, or broomstick, can act as a temporary back beam. The pipe used here is actually a piece of a tent frame. It's prevented from sliding off by eye screws installed at the ends of the pieces of wood. The eye screws also provide an anchor point that can be used with Texsolv to keep the pipe and the lease sticks in place.

Two jugs are used to weight the normal part of the warp, because the first 12 and last 12 warp threads at each selvage advance at different rates from each other. But because *each set of 12 warp threads* advances at the same rate, they don't require lingos. The warp does not need to be wrapped around a warp beam, because it's short. Instead, it can be hung over the temporary back beam and weighted directly. The warp can be chained or wrapped around a piece of cardboard, secured, and attached to the jug with a lark's-head knot, as explained in chapter 3.

Your exact setup will depend on the length of your warp and the dimensions of your loom. Remember that this setup is not ideal but is devised to allow you to try out a small infinite-tension project with minimal loom modifications. The permanent mechanism described in chapter 6 will always work better.

WEAVING THE EVENING PURSE

The cloth for the purse uses a log cabin structure so that the rectangular areas of normal weaving and the triangles can be woven with the color lines traveling perpendicular to each other. In addition to adding a ribbon into the shed when the leapfrogging rod is added, add a ribbon on the last pick of the normal area before the first pick of the next triangle. The log cabin structure is explained in chapter 5.

For the normal areas, the entire warp width is woven for 12 picks. To cause the log cabin stripes to run horizontally from one selvage to the other, the pick in the shed should

The entire warp hangs over the white pipe, weighted by water jugs. The lingos hang before and after the lease sticks.

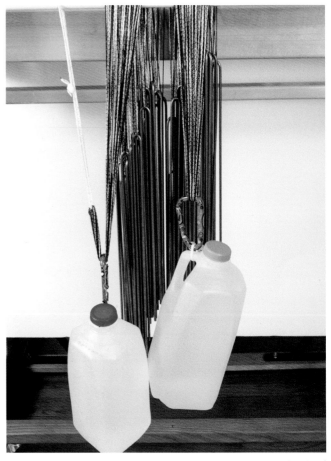

The normal-area warp is hung on two water jugs, at the back of the loom. The warp can be advanced by lifting the jugs.

be the same color of yarn as the raised warp threads. When the pick is a different color, the stripes run parallel to the selvage.

In order to preserve the log cabin stripes in the infinite-tension triangle, both colors of yarn must be used in the weft. Since the two shuttles each start at the selvage and return to it, four picks are woven in each set of picks. Each subsequent set of picks weaves four fewer warp threads than the previous one. Only the middle 60 warp threads are marked, so the marker threads that wrap around the entire beater are placed every four warp threads, starting and ending at the 12th warp thread on each side.

Place the ribbons as shown in the weaving plan, into a shed for which the raised threads most closely match the color of the ribbon you are using. My purse contains four triangles and four rectangular normal areas of weaving, but yours can contain more. Remember to weave some extra cloth for the seam allowance, and some extra to use to make a small handle or a flap to use when closing the purse. Once

the cloth is off the loom, iron it and use a stiff fusible interfacing on the backside. Cut a piece of lining cloth the same shape as the woven cloth. Since there are no special sewing techniques for this project, it's left to the reader to assemble the purse with either a zipper or a flap and snap closure.

The finished purse will hold a small cell phone, but not my larger-sized new one. If you need the purse to be a little larger, the warp will need to be an inch or two wider. That will also require more yarn and more lingos.

I didn't include the weaving draft for this project because the log cabin structure is so simple; it's just tabby with alternating color yarns in both the warp and the weft. If you decide to use a different structure, remember that the normal area of weaving and the infinitely tensioned area are sometimes woven together and sometimes woven at different times. Any pattern structure you use will need to plan for this, as explained in chapter 8.

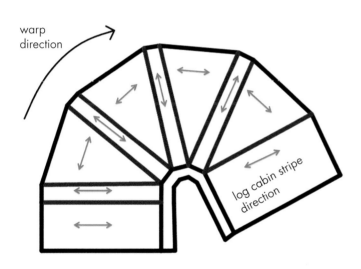

The evening-purse weaving plan: Note the direction of the log cabin stripes. The red lines show where a ribbon is inserted in the same shed as the leapfrogging rod, and in the last shed of the normal area of weaving.

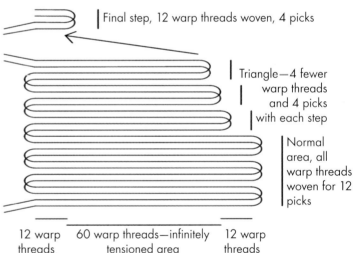

The evening-purse weft pick diagram: All picks are woven for the rectangles. The triangles are woven with the middle 60 picks plus the 12 picks on the left. The number of warp threads woven is reduced by four every four picks, allowing both shuttles to start and end on the left.

The projects described in this chapter were designed to be simple and fast, so that you could try out the different techniques with as streamlined a set of weaving tools as possible. In the next chapter we look at more-complex projects.

Survey of Advanced Projects

RUFF 2: Tabby with Double Weave, Leno, and Dense Areas

This chapter describes a variety of the projects that I've woven over the years, with the goal of inspiring you to design your own pieces. Enough of the details are shown to let you understand my approach, but the weave structures and some of the specifics are not shown.

A dense-areas project: Copper wire and wool work together to create this neck ruff. Double weave creates the woven accordion shape, and copper wire springs hold the accordion structures open.

This neck ruff used a tabby structure throughout. The warp consisted of a single layer of white wool for the neck ruffle, next to a dense area of enameled copper wire, next to a double-weave layer of wool for the accordion shape. I attached the tubes together by weaving the top and bottom layers together for two picks, which returned my shuttle back to where it started. Usually double-weave layers exchange places to weave tubes like this, but because every other top layer of the double-weave tubes included a simple leno structure, I was able to use the same set of shafts for the leno throughout. Copper wire was used exclusively for the weft.

The front copper tie was created by weaving just the dense area for some length before and after the ruff itself was woven. Because the copper dense area was made from 50 wire ends set at 100 ends per inch (40 ends per centimeter), it can be tightly woven.

Leno: Weaving leno requires a weaving sword, which is a smooth, flat piece of wood with a point at one end. Its width is about the height of an open weaving shed, and swords are available in different lengths, although many weavers construct their own. The point of the sword is inserted into the warp while manually manipulating the warp threads in various ways to force the threads to exchange places. Once the desired pattern is achieved, the sword is tipped so that its width is vertical. This creates a shed through which the shuttle can pass. Leno creates an open lacy weave, so be careful to beat gently so as to not destroy the effect.

There are many different ways in which the warp threads can be made to exchange places, using both single- and double-weave layers. When leno is being woven on only the top layer of a double weave, all the top-layer threads must be raised while the warp threads are being manipulated to insert the weaving sword.

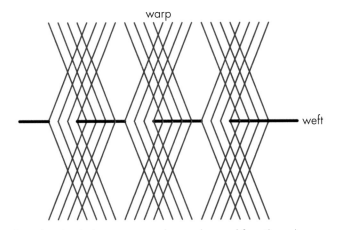

warp

weft

I used a simple leno structure that exchanged four threads at a time.

The tubes that created the accordion shape in this piece do not stay open on their own and don't create a diamond-shaped opening without help. Each one of the tubes was fitted with a spring to hold it open and create the shape. These springs consisted of a piece of heavy-gauge copper wire folded in half into a V shape, leaving the ends about 2 inches (5 centimeters) apart. The bent end of a copper spring was inserted into each tube. The wire spring stays in place because the cut ends of the wire catch on the wool and don't allow it to slide out easily.

Despite my using the simple tabby structure to weave this piece, it required a total of ten shafts! I used shafts 1 and 2 for the neck ruffle, and shafts 3 and 4 for the copper dense area. Shafts 5 and 6 were used for the bottom double-weave layer, and shafts 7 through 10 for the top layer. I used four shafts for the top layer because the inside and outside borders of the top layer were woven as tabby, without weaving leno.

By using shafts 7 and 8 for these borders, I could weave six picks of just the borders, using two shuttles. This was followed by two picks, using shafts 7 through 10 and a weaving sword to manually manipulate the central leno area. I wove two picks in the leno shed, using both shuttles, in order to return the shuttles back to their beginning locations. This was followed by six more picks of just the borders. The dense areas were pulled in after each tube was completed.

The entire top layer of each tube could have been woven with just two shafts, but by using four I was able to weave the borders independently from the leno area. By wrapping two marker threads around the entire beater to mark the leno area, I was able to ensure that I manually manipulated only the threads I wanted for the central lace section.

The display stand: I created a display base for this piece from copper pipe, copper tubing of the type used for refrigerator ice makers, heavy copper wire, and a mahogany wood base. The copper pipe elevates the ruff above the base. Once the copper tubing and wire were formed and soldered together in the desired shape to hold the piece, all the parts were carefully polished to remove all dirt and oxidation. I dipped the polished copper into a hot water solution that included dissolved liver of sulfur to create a black-brown patina. The final step was to spray the patina with lacquer to set the color.

A dense-areas project: This vest has two shoulder ruffles and a neck ruffle. All the ruffles were woven together as one piece.

This vest used a huck weave structure. The ruffle consisted of two different huck ruffles on the shoulder with a third huck ruffle at the neck. The two huck ruffles on the shoulder are a different-width double weave. The dense area was placed between the shoulder ruffles and neck ruffle. Dark-gray 2/20 linen was used in the warp, with a cream-colored linen weft. I used a commercial silk fabric to line the vest; the back also used a commercial cloth. The ruffles were attached to the vest with a series of snaps rather than being sewn on. This allows me to easily remove the ruffles in order to launder and iron them.

The entire vest was woven on one warp. The ruffles were woven first, followed by the body of the front of the vest. Weaving the body required that I spread all the warp threads out into one layer, and change the sett of the dense area to match the rest of the warp.

I planned ahead and placed the upper shoulder ruffle on the lowest-numbered shafts at the front of the loom, and left extra heddles for the upper shoulder ruffle at the right of the warp. When I finished weaving the ruffles, I cut them off the loom. I separated the shoulder ruffle layers, inserted lease sticks at the back of the loom for just the upper shoulder ruffle, and tied knots in the lower shoulder layer in front of the reed to prevent them from escaping through the reed.

Next, I carefully pulled the upper ruffle layer out of the reed and heddles, and back behind the shafts used on the lower layer. These warp threads, which were independently tensioned, were now independent from the rest of the warp and could be repositioned.

The neck ruffle and dense area had to be resleyed anyway, so those threads were pulled out of the reed but left threaded through their heddles. The heddles that had been reserved for the upper shoulder ruffle at the right of the warp and on the frontmost shafts could now be slid into place between the lower shoulder ruffle and the dense area and threaded. I resleyed the threads for the upper shoulder ruffle beside the lower ruffle, resleyed the dense area at the normal sett, and resleyed the neck ruffle. After the ruffle layers were spread out in this way, I wove the rest of the warp normally for the front of the vest. The patterns in the woven fabric that became the front of the vest echoed the huck designs woven in the ruffle layers.

This may still sound like a lot of work, but by planning ahead I had to rethread only one of the three ruffles and resley just part of the warp. The alternative would have been to put on an entirely new warp or rethread a greater portion of it.

Warning! It's worth repeating that whenever you are using weights to tension separate sections of a warp, rather than a ratchet and pawl, you must remember to remove those weights before cutting off the warp. If you don't, the warp will end up in a pile at the back of your loom.

Weaving the ruffles:

Top shoulder ruffle About 115 warp ends Six shaft huck Shafts 1 - 6		
Bottom shoulder ruffle About 170 warp ends Eight shaft huck Shafts 9-16	**Dense area** 24 warp ends Tabby Shafts 7 and 8	**Neck ruffle** about 60 warp ends Eight shaft huck Shafts 17-24

Weaving the front body of the vest:

Bottom shoulder ruffle About 170 warp ends Eight shaft huck Shafts 9-16	**Top shoulder ruffle** About 115 warp ends Six shaft huck Shafts 1 - 6	**Dense area spread out** 24 warp ends Tabby Shafts 7 and 8	**Neck ruffle** about 60 warp ends Eight shaft huck Shafts 17-24

The warp plan: the upper shoulder ruffle is woven as double weave along with a wider lower ruffle. The bottom diagram shows how the warp was spread out to weave the body of the vest.

The treadling isn't as difficult as it might look. You can develop the threading plan and the treadling plan separately to make it easier. Think of every two picks as weaving the top and then the bottom of the layer of cloth.

The first pick weaves the top of the neck ruffle, the dense area, and the top of the upper shoulder ruffle.

The second pick weaves the bottom of the upper shoulder ruffle, up to but not including the dense area.

The third pick weaves the top of the lower shoulder ruffle. The entire top shoulder ruffle must be lifted out of the way to weave the third pick.

Pick 4 weaves the bottom of the lower shoulder ruffle, the same dense-area shed as pick 1, and the bottom of the neck ruffle. Remember that all of the upper ruffle must be raised whenever the lower ruffle is woven.

After 52 picks the dense area was pulled in and the next one was started. Since four picks were required to return the shuttle back to where it started, the number of picks in a dense area must be a multiple of four. This process was repeated until the dense-area portion of the weaving was about 12 inches (30.5 centimeters) long.

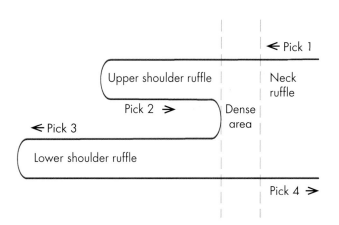

Treadling: There are 52 picks in each dense area. Because of the double weave, the shuttle requires four picks to return back to where it started. The dense area is woven only on picks 1 and 4.

A dense-areas project: weaving alternating dense areas at the selvages, with different weft colors, creates a series of triangles.

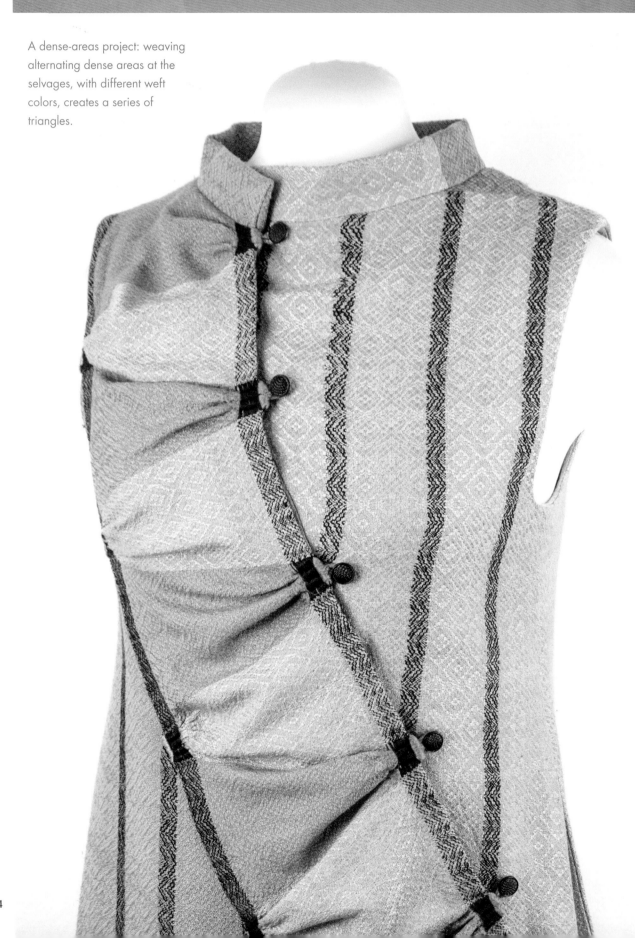

This triangles vest was woven with a twill structure, using a turquoise silk for the warp and either gold or silver-gray silk in the weft. The black vertical stripes on the front are black linen. The diagonal section of weaving, containing the triangles, was woven on one warp and the rest of the vest on another. I did two warps for this vest because I had a limited amount of the silk I wished to use, and the different pieces of the vest were of different widths. Commercial silver-colored silk fabric was used to line the vest.

The triangular part of the vest consisted of a twill structure of silk turquoise warp with a black dense-area linen warp at each selvage. I wove the triangles by alternately weaving four dense areas on one side of the warp with one weft color, and then four dense areas on the other side of the warp with the other weft color. The result was a series of triangles with a black border on each side.

I always determine the sewing pattern that I plan to use before I plan the warp, and it was especially important to plan ahead for this piece. My plan for this vest required black vertical stripes that intersected with the dense areas at the points of the triangles. The only way to figure out where to put the stripes in the normally woven warp width was to create the sewing pattern, weave the diagonal piece for the front of the vest, and then lay the finished weaving across the pattern. The weaving that contained the triangles started at the right shoulder, ran diagonally across the front,

and ended at the left seam hem. Once I had determined exactly where this diagonal section was to lie, I was able to determine the location of the black stripes. I had to remember to space the stripes out to make up for the natural weaving draw-in, but this wasn't difficult because I could measure it on the already woven piece.

The second warp, with appropriately positioned black stripes, was woven for the vertical parts of the vest front. Once the front of the vest was finished, I cut it off the warp. I removed the black-stripe warp threads, resleyed portions of the warp as needed, and wove the rest of the warp for the back of the vest. I used the silver-gray weft for the back of the vest except for the yoke, which used the gold weft color.

Sewing the collar was a challenge because it needed to be sewn onto sections of the body of the vest that used both weft colors. I finally decided to piece the collar so that it matched whichever weft color it was sewn next to. That created seams that don't usually exist in a collar, so I had to use a heavy interfacing material to make the collar stand up correctly.

The triangles for this vest could have been woven with the infinite-tensioning technique instead of using dense areas. The overall design would be the same, but the surface of the cloth would have been flat, without the gathers created by the dense areas.

I start planning a piece of clothing with this simple line drawing.

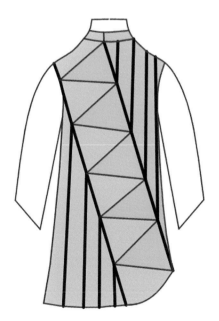

Once the sewing-pattern pieces were created, I was able to lay the woven triangles across the pattern to determine the location of the black vertical stripes.

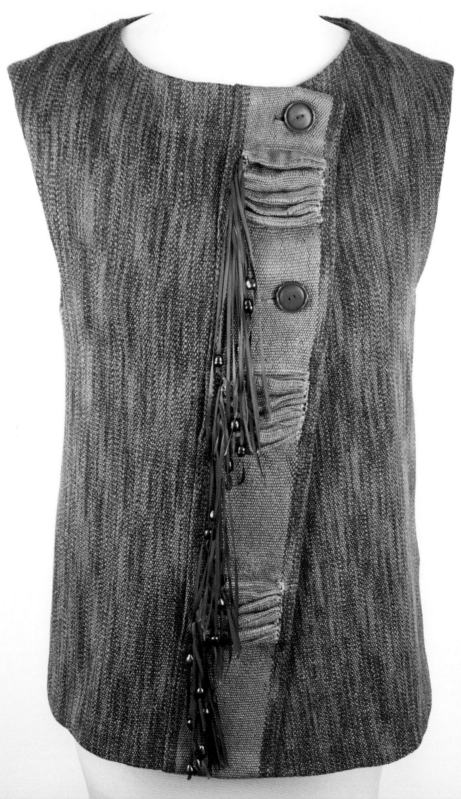

An expanded-areas project: This simple vest features only three expanded areas. Ribbons, with pearls hung on some of them, hide the spaces left by the leapfrogging rods.

This vest was woven using a tabby weave structure. The cloth was woven with a red variegated cotton and rayon warp and a red cotton weft. I added a 3-inch-wide (8 centimeter) section of tan rayon warp 3 inches from the right selvage. The tan rayon warp was used for the expanded areas and was placed on its own set of shafts, with its own tensioning. A blue narrow ribbon was added to the shed along with a weft thread whenever a tension rod was inserted.

After the expanded-area side of the front of the vest was woven, it was cut off the warp. The tan warp threads were removed and the rightmost red variegated warp threads were resleyed to be adjacent to the rest of the warp. The balance of the vest was woven normally.

The ribbons were originally centered in the 3-inch-wide expanded areas. Once the warp was off the loom, I pulled the ends of the ribbons that were closer to the selvage through to the backside of the cloth and then pulled the tails on the front to one side. That left a short ribbon tail behind, on the back of the cloth close to the selvage. A short length of sewing-machine stitching added right next to the expanded areas kept the short ribbon tails from sliding out. Some of the ribbons had to be cut off so that they didn't hang down past the vest hem.

After the vest was sewn and finished, I added the pearls. Adding a pearl to each ribbon would have made the vest too heavy, so I added them to only a few ribbons in each expanded area. I tied a small knot in each ribbon holding a pearl, to help position the pearl and keep it from falling out.

With the addition of the pearls, the front of the vest is heavy enough to pull itself down on the hanger. To help the vest hang correctly, I looped a bit of ribbon around the hanger and the top button. This loop supports the weight of the pearls while the vest is hanging in my closet.

A knot tied in the ribbon helps position the pearls so that they hang at different heights and don't bunch up.

A dense-areas project: A commode, or fontange, is a 17th-century headdress. Perhaps this one more closely resembles the old Dutch Volendam-style headdress.

This headdress was woven with a fine dark-green wool warp, and a weft of copper wire clad with red, green, or clear enamel. A copper-colored-wire dense area was placed at each selvage. I wove both dense areas normally for some distance before and after weaving the headdress, to create four lengths of woven copper that I used to finish the piece.

I didn't have a particular plan for the weft colors. Instead, I wove for a distance and then changed the weft color, making no attempt to place the colors symmetrically or in any particular order.

Once the weaving was off the loom, I shaped the piece. I gently folded the weaving in half lengthwise at the beginning of the normal area of weaving. I knotted the warp threads together in groups of four, starting with two threads from the far right and two from the far left of the warp.

After the first knot, I gathered the next two threads from each side to create a group of four, then knotted them. In this way I tied the left and right sides of the normal area together until I reached the center of the warp. These knots were placed directly against the fell of the first copper weft pick.

This created the cone shape at the end of the warp. I cut off each of these tied groups of warp threads to just a few inches and, using a crochet hook, pulled the warp ends through to the inside of the cone to hide them. The same process was used at both ends of the normal area of weaving, to create a cone at each end. Blue is used to depict the location of these knots in the diagram.

Next, I gently folded the warp in half lengthwise in the opposite direction from before, shaping it into a semicircle.

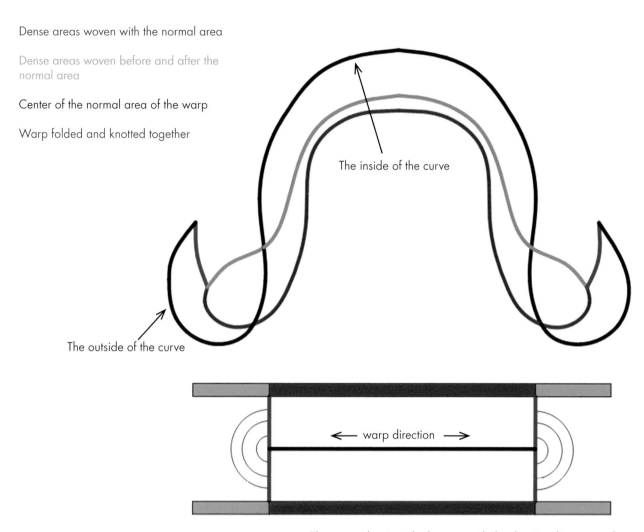

Dense areas woven with the normal area

Dense areas woven before and after the normal area

Center of the normal area of the warp

Warp folded and knotted together

The inside of the curve

The outside of the curve

← warp direction →

The warp plan is at the bottom, with the shaping diagram at the top.

The curve in the cones created in the last step bends in the opposite direction of the curve in the middle of the piece.

To visualize this, imagine drawing a line at its longest length in the warp, at the center between the two dense areas at each selvage. It will start at the point of one cone and continue it to the point of the cone on the other side. The middle part of the line will be on the outside of each cone, but on the inside of the curve at the top of the head. This imaginary line is in black on the diagram.

I folded the dense areas at right angles to the normal-area warp, creating the area that sits directly on top of the head. The dense areas at the sides of the warp became the front and back of the headdress. The weight of the piece tended to make it unfold, so I used several pieces of copper wire to connect the two sides of the normally woven part of the

warp together, at a distance of about 4 inches (10 centimeters) at the top of the head on the inside. The dense areas woven along with the normal area of the warp are in red in the diagram.

Finally, the lengths of the copper-wire weaving that were created before and after the normal area of the warp, in green in the diagram, were pulled together and attached at the top of the dense-area arc, front and back. These pieces pull the sides up to support them and keep them in place.

Whenever I weave a headdress, I plan enough length in the copper-wire dense areas to allow me to weave lengths of copper bands. Sometimes I end up cutting them off or using them in a different piece, but they often come in handy while I'm doing the final headdress shaping.

A dense-areas project: this project was woven with two different double-weave warps—one for the headdress and a second for the crown.

This headdress was woven with a tabby structure, using a dark-brown wool in the warp and blue-enameled copper wire in the weft. In order to depict the rows of braided hair that I wanted for this piece, I wove pleats. I put two normal areas of double-weave wool on either side of a central dense area of clear-enameled copper wire. The central dense area creates the part in the hair on either side of the head.

Double-weave pleats are created by weaving more picks in the top layer than in the bottom layer, pulling in the top layer, exchanging the layers, and weaving the next pleat by using the layer that was previously on the bottom. In this way, the same amount of warp is used in each layer over time. If the two double-weave warp layers contain different colors of yarn, the colors of the pleats will alternate.

The crown for the piece was woven on a separate warp of clear-enameled copper wire in the warp and the weft, with a dense area at one selvage. I wove double-weave tabby for the normally woven area next to the dense area, in order to create a series of pockets that were open on one end. I planned to insert a glass test tube into each pocket after the piece was off the loom. To make sure that the pockets were the correct size to hold the test tubes, I inserted a piece of cardboard into the pockets as I wove. Each piece of cardboard was just a bit wider than half the circumference of the test tubes.

Queen Shammuramat: This piece was inspired by the carved images of Ashurnasirpal II of Assyria, but I wondered what kind of headdress his queen, Mulisu, might have worn. Sadly, there are no images of Mulisu, but there is a carved figure of Shammuramat, the wife of his grandson who ruled Assyria as regent, approximately 811 to 808 BCE, until her son came of age.

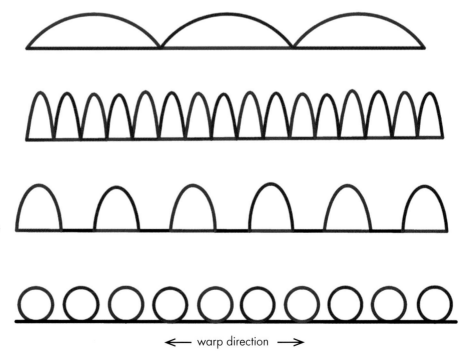

Double-weave pleats: The different colors depict the different double-weave layers; black can be either layer. Different effects can be achieved by weaving different numbers of picks in each layer or spacing the pleats differently.

← warp direction →

After the headdress was off the loom, it was shaped. The copper wire in the weft allowed me to create the curves at the back of the piece. After shaping, the crown was sewn on to the headdress with copper wire. Warp threads at the face created the bangs, and warp threads at the back created the hanging hair. Both the plume at the front of the crown and the structure holding the curled portion of the headdress up in the back were made from the copper-wire warp ends of the headdress dense areas.

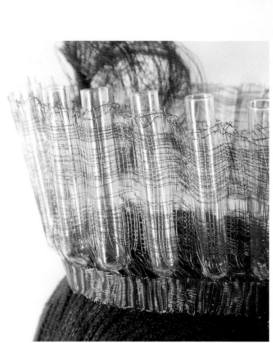

The detail of the crown

The back of *Queen Shammuramat*

Conclusion

You have learned so much! You've learned new terms that I had to invent to describe my processes and have learned about the new tools required—and how to use them. I hope you have started to view what can be accomplished on a hand loom differently, too.

The processes I describe for weaving expanded areas, dense areas, and infinitely tensioned areas evolved over time. When I first started trying to weave three-dimensional shapes, the tools were much more rudimentary and difficult to use. My first cloth trap device required that I keep an electric hand drill fitted with a nut driver nearby, to loosen and tighten the bolts that held it together. And that cloth trap was an improvement over just using leapfrogging rods that left a mark in the cloth after they were removed!

I hope that my tools and techniques for 3-D weaving will continue to evolve and improve. For the future, I plan weaving adventures that involve using more than just one of these techniques in a single woven shape. And I hope to find ways to make the tools easier to build. Not everyone has both metalworking and woodworking shops in their basement, as my husband and I do.

But most of all, I hope that I have inspired you to challenge your own weaving processes. I hope that you have learned different ways to control the tension on your loom. And even if you have decided to continue weaving rectangles and use your sewing skills to shape your handwoven cloth, rather than trying to weave the shapes themselves, I hope you have been stimulated to experiment a bit more and break some rules from time to time. Weaving is too much fun and life is too short to always do things the same old way.

Finally, I would welcome your comments, questions, and ideas. This has been a solitary road for me to tread, and I would very much welcome your company. Please contact me through my website (www.sallyeyring.com) to see what I've been working on or just to stay in touch.

A cylinder-shaped purse, woven using the dense-area technique

Appendix 1

Sources and Tool Construction

The technical information described in this section will, by necessity, have to be more generic than I would like it to be. I don't have access to information about all the tools and materials available around the world, or about all the types of looms available. The exact size of wood screw or the exact size of a piece of wood that I used on my looms may not be available to you, and it might not be the right solution for you if it were. Up to now I have tried to always give measurements both in the English system used in the US and the metric system used in most of the rest of the world. That would be difficult to do here, and somewhat useless since the materials you can access will vary greatly by locality. In many cases, it doesn't matter what size of wood screw you use to attach one thing to another as long as it works for you.

Over the years I've made many changes to many looms, adding pieces, replacing broken or twisted parts, or changing the loom mechanics. I've changed the shedding mechanism on several looms, built one loom from scratch, and built my own 32-shaft electronic dobby loom from an eight-shaft countermarche loom.

I will give only one caution, based on experience. The most common mistake I've made over the years is to underestimate the forces at play on a weaving loom.

For most of the tool construction procedures described, you will need to determine the details of the materials used.

Whenever possible, use the larger screw or the thicker piece of wood. Looms are usually made from hardwood such as maple, but you will probably be using softwood such as pine to construct parts. In general, hardwood requires slightly larger holes than does softwood. Always predrill your holes in any wood and carefully determine the size of the holes. A hole that is too small in hardwood can cause the screw to break as you try to put it in. In softwood, a hole that is too large can prevent the screw from grabbing the wood. If you are in doubt, experiment on a piece of scrap wood. Follow the old adage, *measure twice, cut once*.

In some cases, you will need to drill holes into aluminum stock. Aluminum is a soft metal, and drilling will be easy if you use a nail and hammer to first tap a little dent into the metal where you will be drilling. Always buy (or borrow) the strongest and best-quality drill bits that you can. They will be able to drill metal and will work better on wood too.

Please work safely. Wear glasses or goggles to protect your eyes while drilling holes or cutting materials. Remember where your fingers are and where the tool will go before you start. Make sure that the material you are drilling is secured, so that the drill bit can't grab the material and swing it around to hit you. If you want to drill a large hole in metal, start by drilling a small hole first and then work your way up. If you are uncomfortable using hand tools such as electric drills or saws, find someone to help you.

Sources

The sources listed here are almost all US-based companies. I apologize to my weaving friends in other parts of the world. Perhaps knowing the name of a part or source will help you locate your own best options.

3-D-printed ratchet-and-pawl sets: The ratchet-and-pawl sets mentioned in this book are 3-D printed on demand and available from Shapeways. You may need to set up a free account to make a purchase. The link for the page with the ratchets contains a link for the pawls. There are two different finishes available, but the strength is the same and the difference in the finishes is negligible. I paid to have these designed for me, but only the designer and Shapeways profit; I receive nothing. The ratchets can be attached to any dowel or piece of wood that is at least 1½ inches in diameter. The ratchets (part number SSJ2TXEAP) and pawls (part number FWPMV8J29) are purchased separately. Their website is www.shapeways.com/product/SSJ2TXEAP/.

braking systems for looms: If you are making a warp beam of any kind, large or small, and prefer to have a metal braking system, purchase *beam ends* from the Canadian supplier Camilla Valley Farm. They sell Leclerc looms and repair parts. Loom parts that work on one kind of loom will often work on other looms as well. If you need help, they are happy to talk with you about repair parts. Their website is www.camillavalleyfarm.com/.

fine nylon cord: The fine nylon cord mentioned in this book is white, 0.9-millimeter, miniblind cord that I get from a wholesale drapery company. One spool contains 1,000 yards, but it's so useful to have around that I have purchased two or three of them over the years from Textol Systems, Inc. The part number is 11601. Their website is www.textol.com/.

hardware: My favorite source for screws, nuts, bolts, and many other things is an online source known as Bolt Depot. They carry a wide variety of products and ship quickly. Their best feature is that you can purchase exactly what you want in exactly the quantity you need. For the items they carry, they have every size and length you could need in stock, and you can purchase one item or 100, and any number in between. Their website is very helpful because it provides full specifications for the parts. For example, it's useful when purchasing eye screws to know the inside diameter as well as the outside diameter of the eye. Their website is www.boltdepot.com/.

lingos: I buy the cut rod that I use to make lingos from Philip A. Rand Co. Inc. They are very close to my home and will ship orders, so if you can't find a local source, they may be your best option. Ask for AWG (American Wire Gage standard) wire no. 9, cut into pieces 25 inches long. Two hundred lingo pieces will weigh 25 pounds, so expect to pay shipping charges. If you are purchasing locally, ask the supplier for wire that is approximately 17.05 feet per US pound, or 0.05866 US pounds per foot. If you buy heavier wire in shorter lengths, it will be more difficult to bend. Their website is www.philiparandwireropeandslings.com/.

metal stock: You can purchase many of the lengths of metal you will need from your local hardware store. The chain hardware stores don't all carry the same stock, even when owned by the same company. If you can't find something in the length you need at one store, shop around. If you need lengths of metal longer than 48 inches, you will probably have to find a local metals specialty store or order the parts online. Stainless steel will be more expensive, and it isn't necessary if you are willing to apply a coat of paste wax and polish the metal. Hardware stores also sell screws, nuts, and bolts, but you may have to purchase more than you actually need because of the way that they are packaged, their prices are sometimes high, and they might not carry the exact lengths and sizes you need.

Texsolv: Texsolv is available from many online weaving and yarn stores. I don't have a favorite source, and I shop around for the best price before I order. You can purchase Texsolv in the normal weight, which is usually sufficient, or in a heavier weight for attaching the long rod on a warp or cloth beam. It comes in spools of different lengths. There are two types of connectors available for use with Texsolv. One type is called an *arrow peg*, or just a *peg*. The other type is called an *anchor*, and it's used with countermarche weaving loom tie-up systems. The arrow pegs are the ones used and described in this book.

Velcro: Velcro is the trademarked name for *hook and loop* tape. You can purchase it online or in most hardware stores. The loop half of the tape is used on the bottom of my cloth traps. The heavy-duty version that I recommend is utilized to hold carpets to the floor. You can find it in the carpet section of stores that sell flooring.

wire for weaving: You can find wire for weaving by doing an online search for *magnet wire*, or *craft wire*. I like the wire sold by the Paramount Wire Company, commonly referred to as Parawire. Craft stores and beading stores also carry wire, but usually not in the quantities needed for weaving. Make sure you understand the wire gauge recommendations in chapter 7 before you purchase any wire for weaving. Their website is www.parawire. com/.

MAKING LINGOS

Lingos are useful as thread weights in a variety of weaving applications. They are made by bending a length of steel rod in half. The metal you use will depend on what you have available locally, but each lingo should be approximately 12 inches long once bent, and weigh about 2 ounces (57 grams). My lingos use a 25-inch-long, American Wire Gauge no. 9 piece of wire.

If at all possible, buy the lingos already cut into pieces. My local source cuts to size for me and I can buy 400 lingo pieces for around $90 US. When I get them, they are oily because a film of oil was put on to prevent them from rusting. I clean and seal them from rust in one step by using a rag to apply a coating of paste wax. After letting the paste wax dry for a few minutes, I rub the excess off with a clean rag to polish them and get them ready to bend into lingos. This cleaning and waxing process is my least favorite thing to do, but it's necessary.

To bend the lingos in half in a consistent manner requires two different jigs and a bench vise. The first jig folds them into a V shape, and the second jig folds them the rest of the way with the help of the bench vise. Using these two jigs together, I can fold 60 lingos per hour.

The first jig consists of a piece of wood the same length as the metal rods that will become the lingos. This piece of wood has a groove cut down the center, lengthwise, large enough to contain the rods. The easiest way to cut the groove is on a table saw, but if you don't have a table saw you can construct the groove by attaching two thin pieces of wood to the top of a third piece of wood, with enough space between them to accept the rod.

Cut the grooved length of wood in half and attach a door hinge to the top, perpendicular to the cut and on top of the grooves. Attach a piece of wood at one end as a stop so that the rods cannot slide out of the groove once inserted. I use two wood screws at the half of the jig with the stop to attach this jig to a work surface while I use it.

The second jig consists of two small pieces of wood or plywood. The top piece should be only 3/8 inch thick, and it's attached perpendicularly to the bottom piece with wood screws. The top piece is placed so that one end is at the corner of the bottom piece, as shown in the image. There are two holes in the top piece, and each one contains a nail. These nails are just far enough away from the bottom piece to allow the partly bent lingo to slip under them.

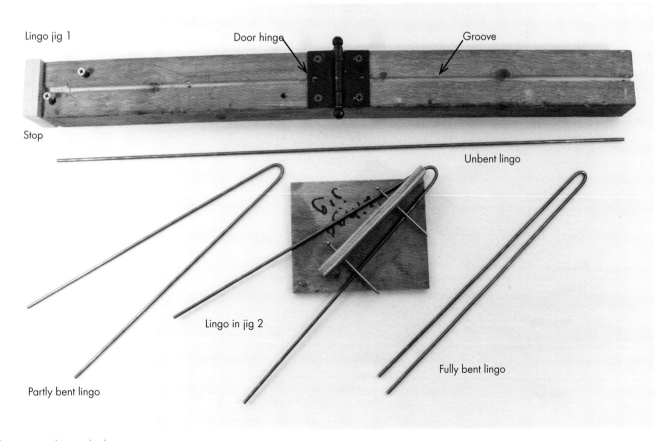

The jigs used to make lingos

To bend a lingo, slip one piece of polished metal rod into the open-ended groove of the first jig and push it all the way through, under the door hinge, to the stop at the other end. Lift up the half of the jig not attached to a work surface and fold it over, bending the jig and rod at the same time. The rod is now folded into a V shape. Let go of the jig to allow the partly-folded rod to slip out just a bit at the fold. Using any screwdriver, insert it into the fold of the rod and pull it out, away from the partly folded jig.

Use the second jig and a bench vise to bend the lingo into its final shape.

The second jig helps hold the lingo in place and the nails keep it from twisting on itself for the final bending. Insert the folded end of the lingo into the second jig under the nails and put the fold into a bench vise as shown. Tighten the vise to bend it the rest of the way. After finishing two or three lingos, you will learn exactly how much to tighten the vise so that the two sides of the lingo are bent parallel to each other.

LOOM TYPES AND MOUNTING OPTIONS

Unless you plan to use only leapfrogging rods and weights, you will need to add some type of device to your loom in order to use the techniques described in this book. There are many types of hand looms available in the world, but they all have the same basic components. While considering how to add additional components to a loom, we need to consider how the existing loom parts operate, the path that the warp travels, and the space used by our body while weaving.

It doesn't matter whether you plan to use a table loom or a floor loom. The only difference for our purposes is that the table loom does not have the room for an infinite-tension warp beam because there is no place to hang the lingos. Even a small table loom can hold a rod beam with multiple ratchet-and-pawl sets. My favorite table loom, which has a rod beam, is the Leclerc Dorothy loom, which is pictured in chapters 1 and 3.

Adding components to the back of the loom is more straightforward than adding them to the front of the loom. In order to support the weight of a cloth trap, the loom needs to have pieces of wood at the sides of the loom, parallel to the floor. But the reed and beater also need to be able to operate normally. If the beater sits *inside* the frame of the loom and *inside* any existing side pieces, the cloth trap can be easily supported. It can either be supported by the existing side pieces or by ones that you add.

Some looms don't have side pieces. Where side pieces exist but the beater is wider than the loom frame, they are placed too low to be able to support a cloth trap, and they cannot be raised without getting in the way of the beater. Another solution is needed.

We will look at four different types of looms in order to determine where various pieces might be added. The diagrams are not necessarily to scale, and not all components are shown. In the diagrams the looms are tan colored, the cloth and warp beams are represented by a circle that is dark brown as it's seen from the side, and the path of the warp is blue. Green is used for the added infinite-tension components. Red is used for the rod beam, and the rods in the rod beams are black. These rods are sometimes mounted on existing parts of the loom frame rather than on an added frame of their own. The special cloth trap supports are also green but are explained in a later section.

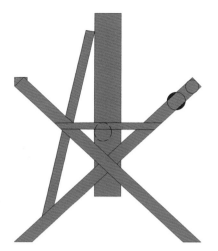

The basic profile of an X-shaped loom, with the beater inside the frame

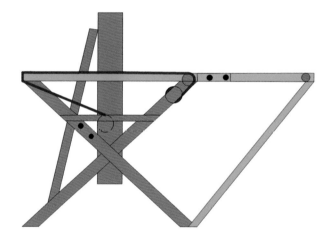

The additional parts will actually make the loom frame stronger, but these parts will have to be removed to fold the loom for storage or transport.

There are many popular jack (raising shed) X-shaped looms on the market. Generally, the beater sits inside the loom since they are built to be folded up for storage and for transport to weaving classes. Because the beater is on the inside of the loom frame, side supports for the cloth trap can be added easily. Note that the two sides of the X-shaped loom frame are attached one on top of the other, and they are not in the same plane. As a result, you need a small wooden spacer for each side to attach the cloth trap supports to the inside legs. This wooden spacer is the same thickness as the loom's legs.

If you make the side cloth trap supports long enough and add a support leg to the back, they can also serve as the loom extensions for an infinite-tension warp beam.

The rod beam at the back requires no additional wood, since the sides of the combination cloth trap support and infinite-tension warp beam can be used to mount the rods. If you want a rod beam but not the infinite-tension warp beam, the side cloth trap supports need extend only far enough at the back of the loom to mount the rods. Remember to plan enough space for the normal warp between the rod beam and the loom back beam.

The rods for a front rod beam, or just one rod to use as an anchor point under the loom, can be easily added just by drilling holes in the top front leg of the X-shaped loom frame. The rods will have to be removed to fold the loom. When deciding exactly where to place the rods, be careful to remember where your knees will be while you are weaving.

THE BOX-SHAPED LOOM

Adding parts to these heavy and strong looms is easy. An extension off the back provides a location for the rod beam and, if made long enough, an infinite-tension warp beam. Support legs will be needed to handle the weight of the lingos. The front rod beam can be placed on the low side pieces in the front, but make sure to stay out of the way of the braking mechanism, and remember where your knees will be while weaving.

The only problem is that the cloth trap will need to be supported in a different way. The special cloth trap supports are shown on the diagram, but these are explained in a later section.

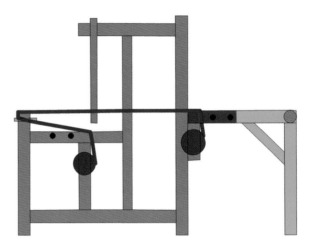

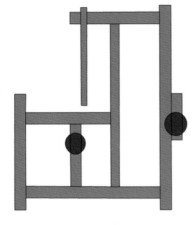

The generic profile of a box-shaped loom. These wonderful looms come in many sizes and can operate perfectly for hundreds of years. They usually feature hanging beaters.

The side supports are too low to support a cloth trap because the hanging beater is wider than the frame of the loom.

THE T-SHAPED LOOM

Note that the back rod beam can be mounted independently, or, if you are including an infinite-tension warp beam, the rods could be placed on the infinite-tension extension instead. Again, the special cloth trap supports are shown on the diagram but are explained in a later section.

The generous widths of the typical box-shaped or T-shaped looms can make it difficult to get the right diameter of metal rods long enough to reach from one side of the loom to the other, with a little extra length at each side for mounting. In the US we can easily get rods up to 48 inches long, which will work on a loom with a 40-inch weaving width at most. If this is an issue, it may be necessary to design a special rod holder to accommodate the shorter rods that are available to you locally. Or, longer rods can be special ordered, locally or online.

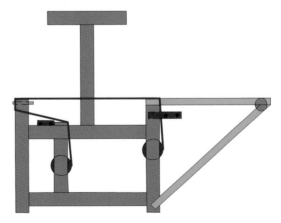

The generic profile of a T-shaped loom. These wonderful looms usually include a floor-mounted beater on the outside of the loom frame.

Because the beater is floor mounted outside the frame of the loom, the front rod beam, or a single rod for an anchor point, must not extend out far enough to get in the way of the beater, which was removed from this diagram for clarity.

THE MACOMBER LOOM

The Macomber loom is a well-designed and strong folding jack loom. It's one of my two favorite floor looms and has many fans in the US. The beater sits outside the loom frame, so it is not possible to add side supports to this loom. This is the loom that I used when designing the alternative to the side supports required to support a cloth trap.

The profile of the popular Macomber jack loom

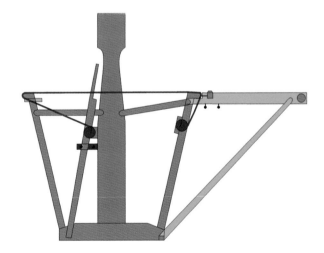

The compact nature of this strong folding loom presented challenges for mounting the necessary parts. The floor-mounted beater sits on the outside of the loom frame.

The 3-D loom: Although my Macomber loom is my favorite loom for normal weaving, my favorite 3-D loom is my 24-shaft Louët Magic Dobby, which is the loom pictured in most of the images in this book. Technically it's a table loom that can be attached to a stand, as mine is. With a weaving width of 27.5 inches (70 centimeters) and a floor stand, it operates like any other floor loom.

I've made many modifications to this loom over the years, and these additions have added weight, requiring me to also add structural supports to the floor stand. The images of my loom will not match any other Magic Dobby that you might see.

My Leclerc Dorothy table loom is pictured in chapters 1 and 3. I find these folding table looms easy to work on and to use. Maybe that is why I have two of them!

When I decided to add the 3-D weaving components to my Macomber, there were additional challenges. I'd previously added a second homemade warp beam and a second back beam to the loom. These additional parts needed to be accommodated along with the basic loom structure. The infinite-tension warp beam became the loom's third, full-width warp beam, not counting the rod beam.

I decided that it was unlikely for me to need three full-width warp beams, so I planned the 3-D additions with the assumption that the bottom warp beam would not be used at the same time as the 3-D components. For that reason, if warps were placed on the rod beam and the lower warp beam at the same time, each would get in the way of the other. But I could have placed the rod beam farther away from the second back beam to make them compatible; I simply chose not to.

The rear rod beam is also mounted differently from the other rod beams described up to now. Usually the two metal rods that make up the rod beam and hold the ratchet-and-pawl sets are mounted to the loom either by adding pieces of wood with holes for the rods at each side, or by drilling holes into the structure of the loom frame itself. The option I used here was to install eye screws into the underside of the infinite-tension extension at each side. These eye screws have an inside diameter a bit larger than the diameter of the rods used for the rod beam. They are easy to install and easy to reposition if needed. Once the eye screws are installed, the rods slide easily through the eyes and are well supported by them. The only downside is that the infinite-tension warp beam extension must be installed to use the back rod beam.

The front rod beam is installed in the typical way, with pieces of wood containing holes for the rods. The diagram may make it look like the beater and the rod beam are in conflict with each other, but they are not because the beater sits outside the loom frame and the rod beam is on the inside.

The Macomber beater has an advantage over some other looms because it can be easily lifted off the loom. The ends of the beater legs each have two slots cut into them. These slots slide onto bolts attached to the bottom of the loom frame at each side. The slots are of different heights, allowing me to choose the operating height of the beater.

Being able to lift the beater off the loom makes threading easier but also provides an advantage for 3-D weaving. The beater has a shuttle run on one side, making its approach to the cloth trap farther away. But by lifting the beater off and turning it around, the shuttle run is eliminated and the beater can make a closer approach to the cloth trap.

CONSTRUCTING A CLOTH TRAP

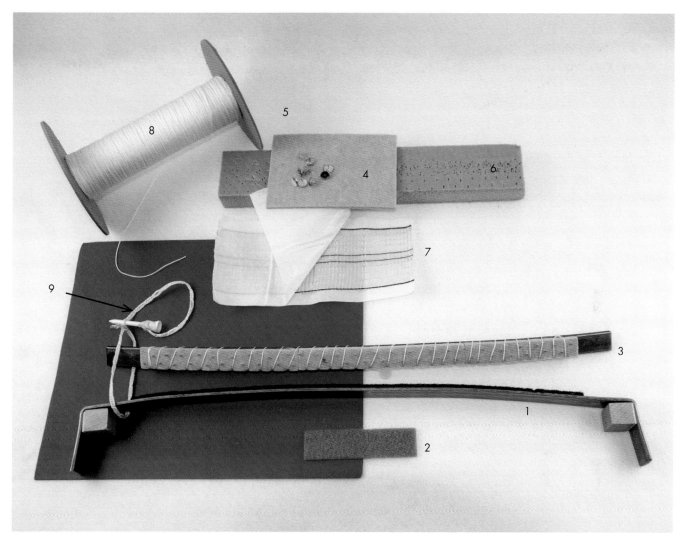

This narrow cloth trap was made for my Leclerc Dorothy table loom. The construction components are numbered in the order of their use during construction.

The construction of a cloth trap requires the following parts:

1. a steel bar of the needed length, ¾ inch wide, 9/32 inch thick

2. ¾-inch-wide, heavy-duty, self-sticking Velcro loop tape

3. a steel bar of the needed length, ½ inch wide, ⅛ inch thick

4. self-sticking furniture or floor protection material without a foam core

5. thumbtacks, with the longest pins available to you

6. a piece of dense foam board

7. double-sided, self-sticking, heavy-duty carpet tape

8. fine nylon cord

9. cinches, made from Texsolv cords, golf tees, and masking tape

The bottom steel bar (1) must be longer than the top bar in order to bend it at each end. These bends sit outside the cloth trap supports on your loom and prevent the cloth trap from sliding off. If you need to shorten either piece of metal, clamp it into a bench vice and saw it off with a hacksaw.

To bend the ends, insert one end of the bar into a well-secured bench vise and bend the other end down. The bend should be hammered as you go to make it bend sharply at an angle approaching a right angle. It's better for the angle to be a little larger than 90 degrees, since in the last step, the entire bar will be bent so that it bows slightly. Once the bar is bent, cover the top surface with the heavy-duty Velcro loop tape (2). This self-sticking tape can be found in the carpet section of your local hardware store.

Cut the self-sticking furniture or floor protection material (4) into strips ½ inch wide. You will need enough pieces to cover one side of the top of the cloth trap (3) except for an inch at each end. Note that there are several types of this material available in your hardware store. Do not purchase the type that includes a thin layer of white foam core, since it will be too thick for your thumbtacks.

Remove the paper protecting the sticky side of the floor protection material. Push the thumbtacks (5) into the sticky side of the floor protection material and into the dense foam board (6). The purpose of the dense foam board is to give you something to push against that also allows the tacks to be completely inserted into the floor protection material. The heads of the thumbtacks should be as close as possible without overlapping each other.

The floor protection material with the thumbtacks sticking out keeps your woven cloth from sliding out of the cloth trap. It must be attached to the underside of the top piece of the cloth trap, but the heads of the thumbtacks now cover most of the surface of the sticky backing. Cut ½-inch-wide strips of the double-sided, heavy-duty carpet tape (7) without removing either of the pieces of plastic-coated paper that protect it. This tape is so sticky that it will gum up your knife or scissors, so you will have to clean the residue off with lighter fluid when you are finished.

Apply the carpet tape pieces to the heads of the thumbtacks by removing one of the plastic-coated pieces of paper, using the other one to keep it from sticking to your fingers.

Once the sticky tape is attached to the thumbtack heads, you can peel the other piece of paper off and stick the whole piece to the top of the cloth trap. As you work, be careful not to let the thumbtacks stick your fingers. You can use a knife or fork to push on the material to ensure that it has good contact with the metal bar.

The sticky tape holding the thumbtacks and floor protection material onto the top of the cloth trap can slide off to the side as it provides tension on your woven cloth. To keep it in place, you must tightly wrap the top of the cloth trap with fine nylon cord (8). Wrap the cord around the entire length of the top of the cloth trap, making a loop every half inch or so. I usually wear leather gloves for this step to prevent the thumbtacks from poking my fingers.

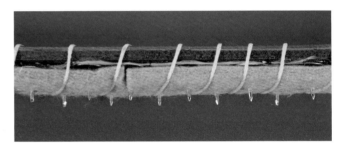

Detail: the top of the finished cloth trap

The final step is to slightly bend both the top and bottom pieces of the cloth trap. The bottom piece must bend in an upward arc, and the top piece must bend in a downward arc, so bend the two pieces of the cloth trap independently. To bend the metal, use the padded edge of a table or countertop and gently push on both ends of the cloth trap at once. The goal is a smooth curve, so don't use too much force.

If the pieces are not bent, the cloth will not be trapped. Straight pieces of metal cinched together at each end will bow in the middle, and the cloth will not be caught in the thumbtacks. If the metal bars are bent too much, the cloth trap will also open up in the middle as you cinch it shut. The bars are easy to bend, so start with just a little bend, cinch them together, notice how the cloth trap closes, and make adjustments as needed. Again, be careful of the tacks and wear leather gloves while bending the top of the cloth trap.

Straight bars bow when cinched

Bars bent just right

Bars bent too much open up in the middle

The cloth trap won't trap the cloth unless it's bent properly!

The cloth trap cinches (9) are described in chapter 3. You will need four cinches. One set is placed at each end of the cloth trap and tightened to close the trap. The second set keeps the cloth trap parallel to the breast beam. It's helpful to use long-enough pieces of Texsolv for the second set, so that the top of the cloth trap can be rolled off the cloth but left in the cinches while the bottom of the trap is being repositioned. Once the cinches are made, use a piece of tape to keep the golf tees from sliding out of the Texsolv.

The Leclerc Dorothy loom has side pieces that can support a cloth trap, since the beater is mounted inside the loom frame. However, those side pieces are too low to support the cloth trap at the right height. The solution is either to add pieces of wood to the side supports or add pieces of wood to the cloth trap itself, as shown in the first image. These pieces of wood must be held in place with screws. If you plan to add these wood spacers to your cloth trap, remember to take their thickness into account so that you have enough metal to bend over and extend beyond the spacers.

Properly mounted, the bends at both ends of the bottom of the cloth trap should be at about the same height as the woven cloth. The upward curve in the middle of the bottom piece of the cloth trap will straighten out once the top piece is cinched into place.

I have three different looms on which I do 3-D weaving: my Leclerc Dorothy, my Louët Magic Dobby, and my Macomber. Each loom is a different weaving width, so I've constructed a cloth trap specifically for each loom.

SUPPORT OPTIONS FOR YOUR CLOTH TRAP

When the loom beater is mounted outside the loom frame, the cloth trap must be supported by the breast beam. Here one cloth trap support is shown on my Macomber loom.

The cloth trap must be supported at each end, but when the loom beater is mounted outside the frame of the loom, side supports interfere with the operation of the beater. The solution is to let the breast beam support the cloth trap. These supports are mounted under the breast beam, must be adjustable so that the reed can approach the fell at various distances, must prevent the cloth trap from sliding off in a foreword direction, and cannot slide out of their attachment to the breast beam.

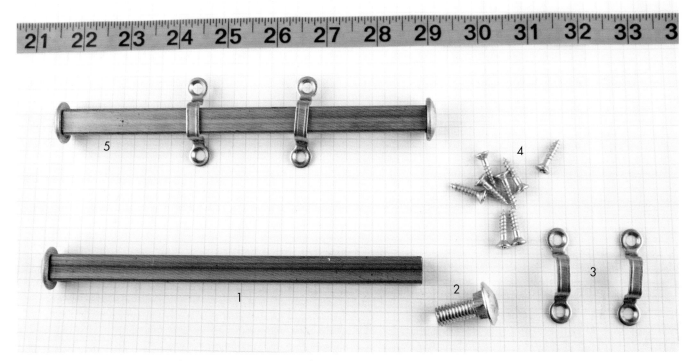

Cloth trap support components: these supports are required to allow the cloth trap to be supported by the breast beam, when side supports won't work.

The supports are made from the following:

1. two pieces of ½-inch-square steel tubing, cut to length

2. four short stove or carriage bolts, fitted to the end of the steel tubes

3. four ⁷⁄₁₆-by-1¾-inch eye straps

4. eight wood screws

The length of the square steel tubing will depend on the width of the breast beam. My Macomber beam is 2½ inches wide, so I used two pieces of steel tubing, 7 inches long each. The tubing can be cut to length with a hacksaw. To keep the cloth trap from sliding off the steel tubing and to keep the supports from coming out of their attachments, I pounded a short stove or carriage bolt (2) into both ends of each of the pieces of tubing. A carriage bolt has a square

piece of metal between the bolt head and the threads. The proper size of bolt fits perfectly, and tightly, into the end of the tube. Cut your metal tubes and take them to the hardware store to find the right-sized bolts.

Each square steel tube is attached to the bottom of the breast beam with a pair of eye straps (3), using wood screws (4). The supports, once finished (5), are installed under the breast beam at each end with the steel tubes, perpendicular to the breast beam. Build your cloth trap first so that you can determine exactly where to install the supports at each side. The steel tubes are able to slide in and out as needed, toward and away from the beater.

Since the supports are mounted under the breast beam, you will need to attach a piece of wood to each end of the bottom of the cloth trap to raise it up to the proper height. The cloth trap that was built for my Leclerc Dorothy table loom required these pieces of wood also, because the loom sides were too low to support it. The beater on the Dorothy loom was inside its frame, so I could have raised the sides instead.

MAKING RATCHET-AND-PAWL SETS FOR A ROD BEAM

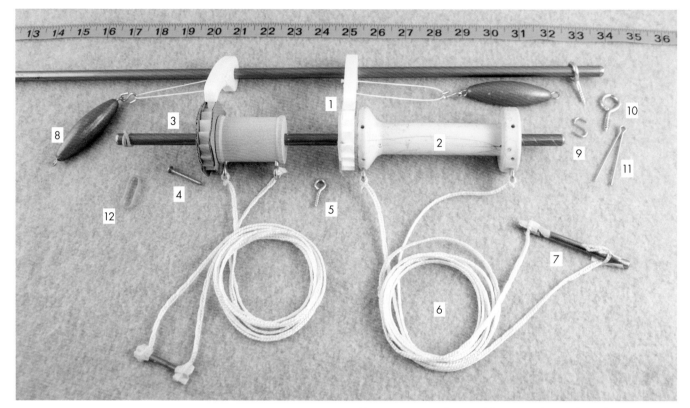

The components for a rod beam ratchet-and-pawl set

The ratchets and pawls that I use on my rod beams are 3-D printed. I had them designed to my specifications, and they can be ordered by anyone from Shapeways. See the "Sources" section of this appendix for details.

The components of a ratchet and pawl set are:

1. the Shapeways 3-D-printed ratchet and pawl

2. a spool or dowel for the warp beam

3. two cardboard or plastic stops, to keep the pawl on the ratchet

4. three screws to attach the ratchet to the spool or dowel

5. two eye screws to attach to the spool or dowel

6. Texsolv or other cord to attach to the spool or dowel warp beam

7. a rod or nail, attached to the cords with tape

8. a weight and cord to attach to the pawl

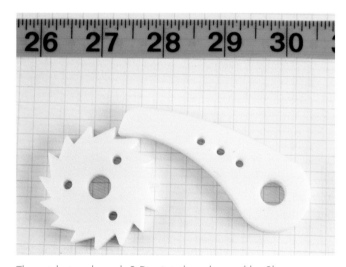

The ratchet and pawl, 3-D printed on demand by Shapeways

9. optional: S hook to make the weight removable

10. optional: eye screws to hang the rods

11. optional: cotter pins to keep the rods from sliding off

12. rubber bands to keep the rods from sliding off

The ratchet and pawl (1) were designed with a ⅜-inch hole in the middle for the metal rods. The three holes on the ratchet are used to attach them to a spool or a piece of wood that acts as a small warp beam. The pawls also have three holes that are used to hang a weight to keep the ratchet engaged with the pawl.

The rod beam itself consists of two ⅜-inch-diameter metal rods: one to hold the ratchets and one to hold the pawls. These rods are a bit longer than your loom width, including any support pieces. The rods are mounted approximately 2¾ inches apart for the best fit. The mounting supports are not shown since they will vary by loom. Test that the ratchet and pawl are able to rotate freely on the rods that you plan to use. If they don't, you can enlarge the hole slightly with a drill.

To assemble the pieces for a ratchet-and-pawl set, first determine what you will be using for the small warp beam (2). I like to use wooden spools, but any symmetrical piece of wood or material without sharp edges will work. Drill a hole through the center, if needed, large enough to hold the rod. Put this piece on one of the rods along with a ratchet in order to align the parts. The ratchet should have a piece of cardboard (3) or plastic on both sides of it as a stop. These stops prevent the pawl from sliding sideways off the ratchet.

Use three small screws (4) to attach the stops and the ratchet to the small warp beam, using the three small holes in the ratchet. Remove this assembly from the rod and attach two small eye screws (5) to each side of the small warp beam, as shown. Attach a piece of Texsolv or other cord (6) to each of the eye screws. The cords should be long enough to reach from the rod beam, when it's mounted on your loom, to the back of the loom shafts. Attach a short piece of metal rod or a small nail (7) to the ends of the cord, so that you can spread the warp out a little and wind it on flatly. You can use masking tape to keep the rod or nail from sliding out of the cord ends.

I use 6-ounce fishing weights (8) to hold the ratchet into the pawl, but any weight will do. Fishing weights come with a small metal loop at each end, which can be used to attach an S hook (9) so that the weight can be hung on a cord attached to the pawl. The fishing weight could be attached directly to the pawl, but I use S hooks to make the weights removable.

By varying the length of the material that you use for the small warp beam, you can create tension for any width of warp that you want, and you can string any number of these ratchet-and-pawl sets along your rod beam, limited only by how many of them will fit at once. Since the ratchets are attached to the small warp beam by three small screws, you can easily remove them and attach them to a larger warp beam as required by your project.

The view from under the loom at the back shows a ratchet-and-pawl set mounted on the rod beam.

Placement of the rod beam at the back of the loom, and a rod beam or just one rod for an anchor point at the front of the loom, was discussed earlier. As mentioned, these rods can be mounted onto your loom by using wood supports containing holes for the rods, mounted at each side of the loom. Or they can be mounted on the loom frame or the infinite-extension frame by using sets of eye screws (10). It's necessary to make sure that the metal rods don't slip out of their supports as you weave. This is especially likely if you mount them with eye screws, since the metal rods slip easily through the metal eyes. One way to prevent the rods from falling out is to drill a hole through the side of the rod at each end and insert cotter pins (11) into the holes. This is not an easy thing to do and requires a grinder and a drill press. An easier alternative is to wrap a rubber band (12) tightly around each end of both rods.

Like the metal rods used for lingos, the ⅜-inch-diameter metal rods used for a rod beam are covered with a layer of oil to prevent them from rusting. They must also be cleaned and polished with paste wax before they can be used on your loom.

The back of my Macomber loom, with the 3-D components added. The aluminum bars used to raise and lower the lingos are not shown.

I used the same 3-D-printed ratchet-and-pawl sets to add infinite-tension warp beams to two of my floor looms. When I added the infinite-tension warp beam to my Louët Magic Dobby, I used one ratchet-and-pawl set at one end of the warp beam. The Macomber loom is wider, so there is more stress on the ratchet and pawl. For that reason I used two ratchet-and-pawl sets, one at each end of the warp beam. I was careful to align the ratchets with each other so that both pawls engaged with the ratchets at the same time and in the same way.

The exact components required for your loom will be different. To add an infinite-tension warp beam to my Macomber loom, I used:

1. two extension arms and supports, plus wood screws to attach them

2. two ratchet-and-pawl sets, screws to attach them, and two fishing weights

3. a 2-inch-diameter wooden dowel for the warp beam

4. two lag bolts, attaching the warp beam and ratchet to the extension arms

5. two bolts and two nylon locking nuts to attach the pawls

6. washers to position the ratchets and pawls (not visible in the picture)

7. a warp beam rod (not shown), cords, and screws to attach the cords to the beam

8. four pieces of aluminum C channel and screws to space out the lingos

9. four aluminum lingo-lifting bars with Texsolv and golf tees (not shown)

The extension arms (1) and their supports create sturdy triangles. The ratchets (2) are attached to both ends of the warp beam (3) with screws. Each end of the warp beam is attached to the loom with a lag bolt (4) that goes through the extension arm, through the ratchet, and into the end of the dowel used for the warp beam. It's not necessary to use cardboard or plastic stops on either side of the ratchet, because the pawl is also attached to an extension arm with a bolt (5) that prevents it from moving side to side. Its exact alignment with the ratchet is accomplished by adding washers (6) to the bolt where needed. The bolt holding the pawl cannot be tightened so much that it prevents the pawl from operating. I use nylon locking nuts (5) to keep the bolt from unscrewing on its own, while still allowing enough slack for the pawl to operate.

One end of the infinite-tension warp beam, installed on my Macomber loom

The screws that attach the ratchet to the infinite-tension warp beam will rub on the extension arm as the ratchet rotates, creating friction and scratching the wood. Small washers (6) placed on the bolt between the ratchet and the extension arm keep the screws from rubbing and protect the wood.

Don't cut the warp beam to length until after you attach the first ratchet to one end. When you are drilling holes into the ends of the warp beam dowel for the lag bolts, start by drilling a small pilot hole; the small hole will be easier to center than a larger hole. Attach one ratchet and test mount it on one side of the loom extension, with the necessary washers. That will give you a good idea about how long to make the warp beam.

You must also attach cords (7) along the length of the warp beam so that you can attach a rod (under the beam but not shown) on which to wind your warp. These cords must be able to reach from the beam to the back of the shafts on your loom. I like to use the heavier weight of Texsolv for these cords because it's stronger and the holes in the cord are large enough to hold a ⅜-inch-diameter metal rod.

Warp length considerations: Remember, when you are weaving with infinite tension, the rod on the warp beam will be able to extend the warp only as far as the first C-channel spacing bar. Since the warp beam can serve as a second warp beam on your loom, it can also be used without infinite tensioning. In that case the rod will be able to extend the end of your warp up to the back of the first shaft. That is why I recommend using cords that are long enough to reach the shafts.

To place my cords (7), I drew a straight line down the side of the warp beam and measured and marked the location of each piece of cord. I drilled and countersunk the holes at the marked spots and attached each cord with a wood screw put through one of the holes in the heavyweight Texsolv.

Aluminum C-channel spacing bars (8) help space out the lingos. These spacing bars are attached to the extension arms with screws. The flat aluminum bars that are used to lift the lingos (9) are not shown. They are hung on the spacing bars with a loop of Texsolv and secured with golf tees, as explained in chapter 6.

The Shapeways ratchets and pawls that I use are made from a strong nylon material, and I've never had one break or chip. They are quite sufficient for use on the narrow warp beam sections used on a rod beam. If you also want to have a brake release mechanism on your infinite-tension warp beam to use when not weaving 3-D projects, or if you are nervous about using a nylon material on a full-loom-width warp beam, see the "Sources" section of this appendix for other options.

IDEAS FOR ADDING A SECOND BACK BEAM TO YOUR LOOM

Several chapters in this book discuss double weave. Whenever one section of a warp must travel on top of another and they will be advanced at different rates, they cannot be allowed to rub on each other as they go over the back beam. My Macomber already had a second back beam, but there are two easy methods for adding one to your loom, whether or not you use any of the techniques in this book.

One method is to attach a second wooden back beam to your loom. Beams with a rectangular profile are easier to mount than round beams. The new beam should be the same length as your existing back beam, should have rounded edges, and should be sanded smooth and finished with varnish or paste wax to prevent abrading your warp.

The new back beam will be located a small distance behind the existing one, but a half inch higher in order to raise the warp layer off the existing back beam. Drill holes completely through each end of the new back beam and through each end of your existing back beam. These four holes are all drilled in a parallel direction with respect to the floor but perpendicular to the beams, making sure that the holes in the old beam line up with the corresponding holes in the new back beam. Make sure that the holes are farther apart than the weaving width of your loom, and make sure that the holes in the new back beam will cause it to sit higher than the existing one.

Prepare two spacers to hold the two beams about an inch apart. You can use pieces of metal tubing, pieces of wood with holes, large nuts, or washers. Insert bolts of the needed length through one beam at each end, through the prepared spacers, and through the other beam. Secure both bolts tightly with locking nuts. You now have a second back beam.

The second method for adding a back beam is even easier. This back beam is created by using heavy metal rods and eye screws. You will need one or two rods, depending on the geometry of your loom. The rods must be large and strong enough not to bend under the tension of the warp. The eye screws must be large enough to hold the rods. The

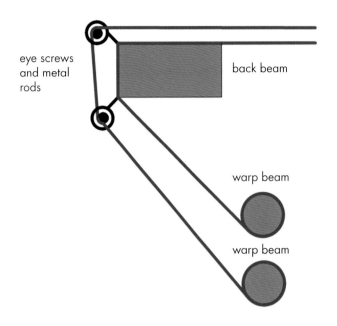

eye screws and metal rods

back beam

warp beam

warp beam

This back beam is made from eye screws and metal rods, and it's easy to add to any loom. The path of the warp is shown in blue for each warp beam.

path of the different warps will determine the placement of the eye screws. Once the eye screws are placed in pairs at each end of your back beam, insert the rods and secure them with rubber bands or cotter pins so that they don't slip out.

If you are adding a back beam to use with your infinite-tension beam, you will need only one set of screws and one rod on the top of the existing back beam, since the infinite-tension warp is parallel to the floor. If you are adding a back beam to use with a second warp beam on your loom, you will need two rods to guide the warp around the existing back beam, as shown in the diagram.

A side benefit of using rods and eye screws for a back beam is that the rods can easily be removed while the bottom warp layer is being put onto the loom, and then added again later. By buying long eye screws and positioning them correctly, you can raise the warp as much or as little as you need.

Appendix 2

Sewing and Finishing Tips

Weaving 3-D cloth that isn't a rectangle introduces some complications for the finishing work. This section assumes a basic knowledge either of hand or machine sewing.

FINISHING EXPANDED AREAS

Chapter 4 discusses weaving an expanded area with a double-weave layer underneath. This is done in order to prevent the fabric from bulging out due to the extra weft picks. If you are weaving expanded areas scattered at several places along the cloth width, you may want other methods to avoid the trouble of weaving double-weave layers.

If you are using the infinite-tension technique to weave expanded areas that migrate across the cloth, double weave requires a complicated double-weave layer under a large section of the warp. Sometimes it's fun not to do too much planning and just experiment with the placement of expanded areas, and the infinite-tension technique is perfect for that, but having to plan a double-weave layer takes away much of the fun.

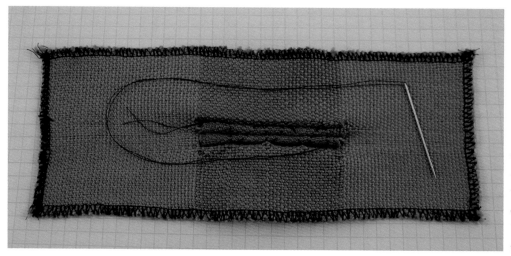

Using the sample expanded area from chapter 4, I hand stitched the pleats together on the back of the fabric. In this case I also stitched through the individual folds in the cloth, but that is optional.

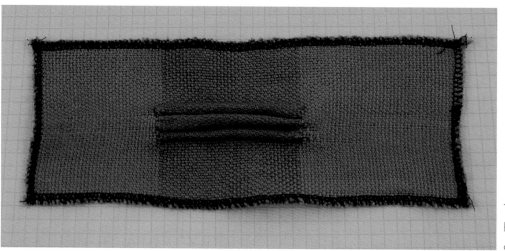

The effect of the stitching on the back is a little series of pleats on the front of the cloth.

There are two basic techniques for keeping your cloth edges straight despite the woven expanded areas. The first technique is to hand stitch the expanded-area sections together with a running stitch placed on the back of the fabric. I used a contrasting color of thread to make the photograph clearer, but you will want to use thread that is the same color as your weaving. I stitched through the multiple expanded-area sections, creating little pleats on the front of the fabric, but you may choose to stitch through only the beginning and ending of the expanded-area section.

If you think you might want to stitch through the individual sections, insert a piece of marker thread with a contrasting color into the shed wherever you might be stitching. Let the tails hang loose on the backside of the cloth. I didn't do that, and it made it more difficult to find exactly where to stitch the individual cloth folds. You will remove the marker threads later, whether or not you end up using them, but having them available is helpful.

The second technique involves stitching or fusing a piece of fabric to the back of the cloth. This piece of fabric acts like a double-weave layer without all the trouble of weaving one. I like to use a bit of fusible interface fabric because there are no stitches to show on the front.

Position the fabric you are going to use under your cloth. Pin one edge of the expanded area to the woven cloth. If you have access to a cardboard cutting board, or just a large piece of cardboard, you can help position the layers by pinning them to the cardboard before you pin the pieces together. Once one edge is pinned, continue pinning around the expanded area until the two pieces of cloth are attached all around. The goal is for the picks woven just before and just after the expanded area to be straight and parallel. I recommend doing this from the front of the woven fabric. The bulk of the expanded area makes it difficult to get two pieces of fabric to align correctly if you try to do it from the back.

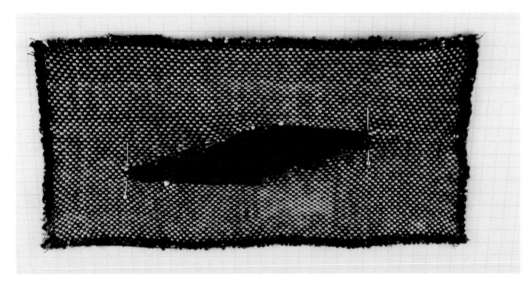

Here is an example of migrating expanded areas, woven with the infinite tension technique. The fabric edges are distorted by the extra picks in the expanded areas.

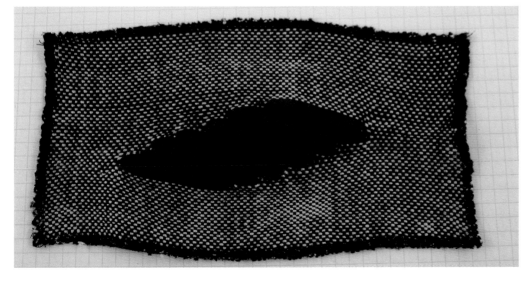

Use sewing pins to position the woven cloth over the backing before you fuse or sew the layers together.

If you are using fusible cloth for the back, fuse just the area that is outside the expanded areas. You can iron or steam the cloth while it's still on the piece of cardboard, if you used one. It's always good to be careful while ironing, but cardboard won't burn any faster than cotton cloth.

If you are sewing the woven cloth and the backing together instead of fusing them, hand stitch or machine stitch the two pieces together where the expanded area and the normal area of weaving meet. If you also want to position the different pleats within a larger expanded area, I recommend stitching them to the backing by hand.

The jabot neck ruffle was created by weaving expanded areas next to a narrow area of normal weaving at both ends of the warp. To finish this piece, fold the normal area of weaving toward the back and hand stitch it to the expanded area where they meet. The normally woven area, between the expanded areas at each end of the warp, is too wide to be comfortable going around the neck. Fold the cloth in thirds as shown and hand stitch them together. Finish the ends of the warp with a simple hand-stitched hem.

In chapter 9, I mentioned that I should have woven a little more fabric to create a loop to hold the two sides of the jabot together, but there are other options. You can wear a decorative pin to hold the two sides together, or you can use magnets. Rare-earth magnets are small but mighty, and you can find many sources for them online. I use them to hold fabric together temporarily.

They don't come with holes to attach them, so the easiest way to use them is to place each of them into a small pocket of fabric made from a thin piece of lining material or seam binding. The little pockets can be hand stitched onto the woven fabric wherever you need them. For this jabot, the magnet pockets could be stitched onto the fabric where the jabot ends cross each other when worn. The pockets can be stitched to the backside of one end of the jabot, and to either the front side or backside of the other end. Before you decide where to place the magnets, consider how you want your jabot to hang, and determine how many layers of fabric the magnets can hold.

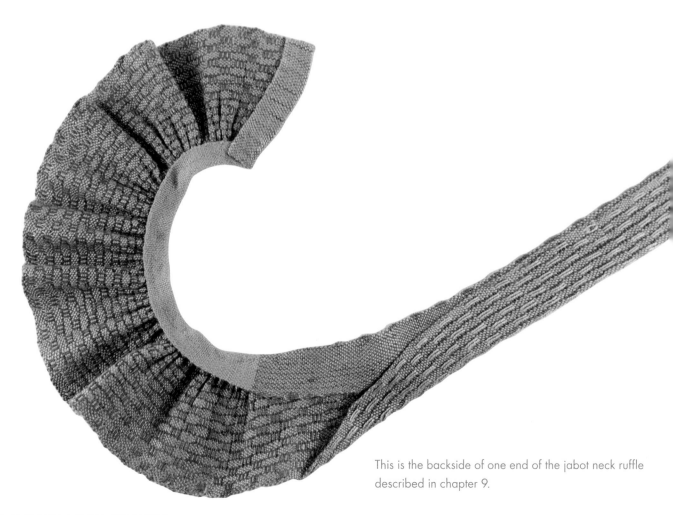

This is the backside of one end of the jabot neck ruffle described in chapter 9.

You could also use snaps to hold the sides of the jabot together, but the stitches holding the snaps are more likely to be visible.

Be careful! Rare-earth magnets come in different sizes, like buttons, although some of them are very small. Magnets can be dangerous to children and pets, so be careful. If a child or a pet swallows one magnet, it's not usually a problem because they are small with no sharp edges. But if they swallow two or more, the magnets can travel through their digestive system and cause two parts of their intestines to be pinned together. This can cause serious medical conditions, so please be careful when using or storing magnets.

A bit of seam binding or thin lining fabric can be used to make small pockets for magnets. These pockets can be stitched onto the woven fabric in hidden locations.

FINISHING DENSE AREAS

The two challenges presented by dense areas are dealing with the capture threads, and lining the fabric if desired. As explained in chapter 5, the capture threads are used when dense areas are woven at a selvage. These capture threads need to be hidden in the final fabric. Remember that capture threads are made of the same yarn, or the same color of yarn, as the weft, and they have a small knot at the end that was used to help tension the warp width during weaving. Now you will find out why I recommended that the knots in the capture threads not be tied close to the woven dense areas.

To hide the capture threads, work from the backside of the woven fabric. Insert a fine crochet hook through the dense-area section of warp threads, toward the selvage. Cut the knot off the capture thread for that dense area and pull the capture thread through with the crochet hook. If your dense areas are woven tightly, you can then cut the capture thread tails off at the edge of the dense area. If you are worried about them slipping through, tie a small knot in the capture thread to keep it in place.

The capture threads, together with the floating selvage, keep the weft picks from sliding out of the warp dense areas. Because of the way they are created, the capture threads can be loosened and replaced. The triangles vest shown in chapter 10 is an example. When finishing this piece, I loosened the three dense-area capture threads where the point of the triangle hit the selvage. Using a fine crochet hook, I inserted it into the loops of weft threads of all three dense areas. When the crochet hook was in place, I removed the three capture threads and pulled a single, thick bundle of capture threads through all three dense areas. Once those thread ends were pulled through their loop, I was able to braid the ends to make a buttonhole loop. To secure the other end of the braided threads, I hand stitched it to the wrong side of the three woven dense areas.

Replacing the capture threads in this way is easier if you use a contrasting color of yarn while you are weaving the dense areas. Note that the capture threads can be replaced with yarn of any length, opening up other possibilities. For example, if you replace the capture threads with very long pieces of yarn, they can be braided or used for macramé.

The capture threads are hidden on the back of the cloth by pulling them through the dense-area warp thread groups.

Capture threads from several dense areas can be replaced by a single capture thread group. These threads can be braided or twisted to make a button loop.

OTHER CONSIDERATIONS

The infinite-tension technique doesn't require any special finishing methods, but there are other considerations that are common to all the techniques. No matter how a shape is woven, lining your woven fabric can be challenging because the fabric is not rectangular or flat. If you are weaving cloth for clothing, these shapes can be difficult to iron after the fabric is washed.

I've used two approaches that work fairly well with regard to lining 3-D woven fabric. One approach is to lay the fabric out on a large piece of paper, trace around it, and cut the lining to match the shape the fabric will take while in use. This works if the shaped fabric will lie flat or almost flat. If the fabric is going to take on a different shape, the lining must take on that shape also, with the help of darts, pleats, or other common sewing techniques. For example, it would not work to line the bustier apron from chapter 9 with a flat piece of material.

A 3-D fabric created using the infinite-tension technique will be a series of flat pieces. Each piece will need its own lining cut to the shape of the piece. The woven fabric and the lining can be ironed together once they are sewn together.

The other approach is to create a lining that is partly independent from the woven cloth. Part of the lining can be attached with snaps or Velcro, which means that it can be detached from the handwoven fabric to iron. The whole lining does not need to be independent; only the lining under the 3-D woven fabric. The part of the lining that detaches may need to be lined itself. Otherwise, random loose threads from the cut edges of the lining can escape into view.

Bibliography

Dalgaard, Lotte. *Magical Materials to Weave: Blending Traditional & Innovative Yarns.* Translated by Ann Richards. North Pomfret, VT: Trafalgar Square Books, 2012.

Essen, Deb. *Easy Weaving with Supplemental Warps: Overshot, Velvet, Shibori, and More.* Fort Collins, CO: Interweave, 2016.

Field, Ann. *Collapse Weave: Creating Three-Dimensional Cloth.* London: A & C Black, 2008.

Goerner, Doris. *Woven Structure and Design: Part 1—Single Cloth Construction.* Leeds, UK: Wira Technology Group, 1986.

Goerner, Doris. *Woven Structure and Design: Part 2—Compound Structures.* Leeds, UK: British Textile Technology Group, 1989.

O'Connor, Paul R. *Loom-Controlled Double Weave: From the Notebook of a Double Weaver.* Saint Paul, MN: Dos Tejedoras Fiber Arts, 1992.

O'Connor, Paul R. *More Loom-Controlled Double Weave: From the Notebook of a Double Weaver.* Saint Paul, MN: Paul R. O'Connor, 1996.

Reeves, Martha. *Weave Leno: In-Depth Instructions for All Levels, with 7 Projects.* Atglen, PA: Schiffer, 2016.

Richards, Ann. *Weaving Textiles That Shape Themselves.* Ramsbury, UK: Crowood, 2012.

Sutton, Ann, and Diane Sheehan. *Ideas in Weaving.* Loveland, CO: Interweave, 1988.

Todd-Hooker, Kathe. *Shaped Tapestry.* Albany, OR: Fine Fiber Press, 2004.

Zielinski, Stanislaw A. *Encyclopedia of Hand-Weaving.* Toronto: Ryerson, 1959.

Index

Courtesy of Albert's Photo Studio, Waltham, Massachusetts

Sally Eyring has been working with fiber and cloth since childhood. She has been improving techniques and inventing tools for almost as long. Trained as a mathematics teacher, she later earned her MFA in fine arts from Leslie University in Cambridge, Massachusetts. She frequently teaches and lectures on various weaving, sewing, and loom construction topics and is a winner of the Complex Weavers Award for Excellence. Eyring does glass casting in addition to weaving and sewing and has been published in weaving and glass periodicals.